BLACK LIFE

in Old New Orleans

BLACK LIFE

in Old New Orleans

Keith Weldon Medley

PELICAN PUBLISHING
NEW ORLEANS 2020

First edition, September 2014
First paperback edition, November 2020

Library of Congress Cataloging-in-Publication Data

Medley, Keith Weldon.
Black life in old New Orleans / by Keith Weldon Medley.
pages cm
Includes bibliographical references and index.
ISBN 978-1-4556-2551-2 (pbk. : alk. paper) — ISBN 978-1-4556-1938-2 (ebook) 1. African Americans—Louisiana—New Orleans—History. 2. African Americans—Louisiana—New Orleans—Social life and customs. 3. New Orleans (La.)—History. 4. New Orleans (La.)—Civilization. 5. New Orleans (La.)—Social life and customs. I. Title.
F379.N59N44438 2014
305.896'073076335—dc23
2014010440

All photographs by the author

Printed in the United States of America
Published by Pelican Publishing
New Orleans, LA
www.pelicanpub.com

For my descendants:
Keith S.
Kwesi
Adam
Emily Rose
Quentin
Auden

If you have faith as small as a mustard seed, you can say to this mountain, "Move from here to there," and it will move.

Matthew 17:20

Contents

Acknowledgments 9

Introduction 11

Chapter 1 1790s: Inside Old Treme. 17

Chapter 2 1800s: Congo Square—African Seeds in American Soil .43

Chapter 3 1837: The Will of the Widow Couvent 63

Chapter 4 1912: The *Woods Directory*. 79

Chapter 5 1900s: Growing Up Satchmo 103

Chapter 6 1928: Educators for a New Society 121

Chapter 7 1929: Fannie C. Williams—a Pioneer in Public Education. 135

Chapter 8 1940s: Wright Speaks! 143

Chapter 9 1954: The Life and Times of Lincoln Beach 159

Chapter 10 1950s: A. P. Tureaud and the Martinet Society. 169

Chapter 11 1960: Two, Four, Six, Eight 177

Chapter 12 1961: Lighting Freedom's Torch. 187

Chapter 13 1960s: Mardi Gras through the Ages 201

Chapter 14 2000: Sire to Son, Chief to Chief 221

Chapter 15 New Orleans in the Decade of Change 233

Notes 253

Selected Bibliography 269

Index 273

Acknowledgments

I want to extend my deepest gratitude to all who have assisted and encouraged me in bringing this book to fruition. I am once again indebted to the Louisiana Endowment for the Humanities for supporting me in this endeavor. I also want to thank Gail C. Christopher of the W. K. Kellogg Foundation for all of her help on my previous book, *We as Freemen: Plessy v. Ferguson*.

I greatly appreciate the staff of the *Louisiana Weekly* newspaper for keeping its legacy intact. Without that stalwart institution, which began publishing in 1925, there would have been scant acknowledgment of historic black New Orleans and its culture and accomplishments. The *New Orleans Tribune* is another institution that supported my writing efforts since 1985. Dwight and Beverly McKenna have given many writers in New Orleans the opportunity to hone their skills and have their voices heard. I also am extremely grateful to Karen Yvette Clemons for her time, enthusiasm, steadfastness, and creativity in finalizing, formatting, and tightening this project. I also want to thank Girard Mouton III for the author photograph.

Many thanks to Louise Mouton Johnson for the artwork she has contributed to New Orleans over the years. She produced the art for my *Smithsonian* magazine article in 1994 and the cover for *We as Freemen*. Thank you, Louise, for the striking dust-jacket art for *Black Life in Old New Orleans* and its message: *Lift Me Out of Darkness—Set My Spirit Free*.

I give thanks to my good and trusted friend Bonnie Britt, who served as an editor for this book. I also want to thank my friend Barry M. Walton for all of his timely critiques and opinions throughout the years. Readers along the path included Dr. Kim Marie Vaz, Freddi Williams Evans, Denise Walter McConduit, Debra Campbell, Marcia Livingston, Jackie Knightshade, Marilyn Vandergriff, Tia Calvin, Marian Moore, and others.

I am also deeply indebted to my family for their love and guidance. My gratitude extends to Bernadette Green and our two sons, Keith S. Medley and Kwesi Medley.

I also thank my longtime friend Dr. Earl Picard for his assistance in my travels to Accra, Ghana. He introduced me to Mr. Kwaku Passain, who guided me as I retraced the footsteps of Louis Armstrong's 1956 meeting with Kwame Nkrumah. I am also thankful to Bernadette Diaz and her son Adam for smoothing the way. Dr. Priscilla Gibson, Dr. Debra Lewis, and Freddi Williams Evans provided me with information on traveling to Ghana. My friend Laura Buchwald offered me shelter in Manhattan.

I am also grateful for the comradeship of Keith M. Plessy, Phoebe Ferguson, Brenda Square, A. P. Tureaud, Jr., and other members of the Plessy and Ferguson Foundation. I would also like to thank Leslie Major for helping me stay organized.

Introduction

New Orleans is one of North America's most intriguing and beloved cities. From the air, you can see the winding Mississippi River, vast Lake Pontchartrain, and the bayous and marshlands that define this region's topography. Claimed by the French in 1718 as a strategic outpost near the mouth of the Mississippi River, this city has endured nearly three centuries of floods, plagues, fires, and hurricanes. Its old oak trees, nineteenth-century buildings, riverbanks, narrow streets, and sultry summers all have tales to tell. Neighborhood layouts have not changed appreciably since their earliest beginnings. Even now, you can often go to the exact addresses that housed the people and institutions that left their marks on city history. You can walk the same streets that New Orleanians have walked for nearly three centuries.

I grew up on Burgundy Street in Faubourg Marigny in the 1950s and 1960s, during the modern Civil Rights Movement. My father was a plasterer who was "raised to the trade," as they say in New Orleans. He and his fellow carpenters, lathers, bricklayers, laborers, roof slaters, and other old-line tradesmen provided the grit and muscle that were instrumental in the city's survival. Growing up, I walked past historic and architectural treasures every day. Many of these buildings constructed by people of color before the Civil War still stand as functional residences and businesses.

Those who study New Orleans without seeking its African and African-American influences invariably *miss* what it means to *know* New Orleans. Enslaved and free, people of African descent have been here since the city's earliest days. Between 1718 and 1722, boatloads of Africans from the Senegambia region of Western Africa and outcasts from French society arrived for forced toil in the Louisiana marshes. They hacked through and drained swamps, constructed buildings and levees, and dug canals. For the

French indentures, the term of their forced labor was three years. For most Africans, New Orleans represented a lifetime of bondage under the city's Black Codes.

New Orleans also contained a vibrant community of free people of color who possessed property rights but could not vote or establish organizations without permission. Still, the African-descent community contributed mightily to the growth and survival of *la ville de la Nouvelle-Orléans*. Their sweat was in its early architecture; their handcrafted ornaments adorned its oldest buildings; their rhythms moved its music; their creativity and flair spiced its cuisine. I have come to view New Orleans as an entwined collective of ancestral neighborhoods, history, and culture. Without the history and the neighborhoods, the culture has no context. Without the culture, the neighborhoods have no spirit.

Early on, I appreciated the unique aspects of my city. Mardi Gras clubs paraded on North Claiborne Avenue and Canal Street. I remember my parents coming home late at night with goodies from the Plantation Revelers' annual Carnival dance. I was captivated by the second-line parades that brought us uptown and back. On Saint Joseph's Night, Mardi Gras Indians chanted and danced their way through the ancestral neighborhoods. My neighbors across Burgundy Street were Mardi Gras Indians.

The more I delved into the history and culture of New Orleans, the more I discovered touchstones of my family history. While writing about the historic Valena C. Jones Elementary School in New Orleans' Seventh Ward, I came across a photograph of its proud teaching staff that included my mother, my godmother, and many of their teacher friends. My mother also appeared in a yearbook for McDonogh #35, which was the first black high school and teacher training school in the city. While studying the 1913 *Woods* business directory of African-American entrepreneurs, I saw advertisements for my grandfather's ice-cream factory and my cousin John Guillaume's business college, as well as photographs of my great-great-uncle Charles Medley, who managed the Boyer and Taylor Funeral Home in Faubourg Treme. I attended an elementary school around the corner from my house that had been educating children of African descent since 1848. There are so many stories left untold.

The purpose of *Black Life in Old New Orleans* is to explore different eras of black New Orleans by focusing on specific institutions, social movements, and individuals. Each chapter is self-contained. When read cover to cover, the book provides a timeline of black New Orleans. It explores neighborhoods such as Faubourg Treme, Faubourg Marigny, Central City, and Louis Armstrong's Black Storyville area. It continues with Armstrong on his historic trip to Africa in the midst of an independence movement in Ghana. It spotlights the sacrifices and heroism of activists such as Homer Plessy and the Citizens Committee, Ernest Wright and the People's Defense League, the four brave six-year-old girls who challenged white supremacy in 1960, and the lawyers who defended them. Other chapters of *Black Life in Old New Orleans* give a look into the times and accomplishments of activist-educators such as Fannie C. Williams and Lucien Alexis, who fought for decades to bring education to black children. This book seeks to highlight the history of black New Orleans and recognize those who survived and achieved in spite of social and racial obstacles. Thus, the book is inspirational as well as historically enlightening. The accounts in this volume are just a few of the many notable episodes in black life in old New Orleans.

BLACK LIFE

in Old New Orleans

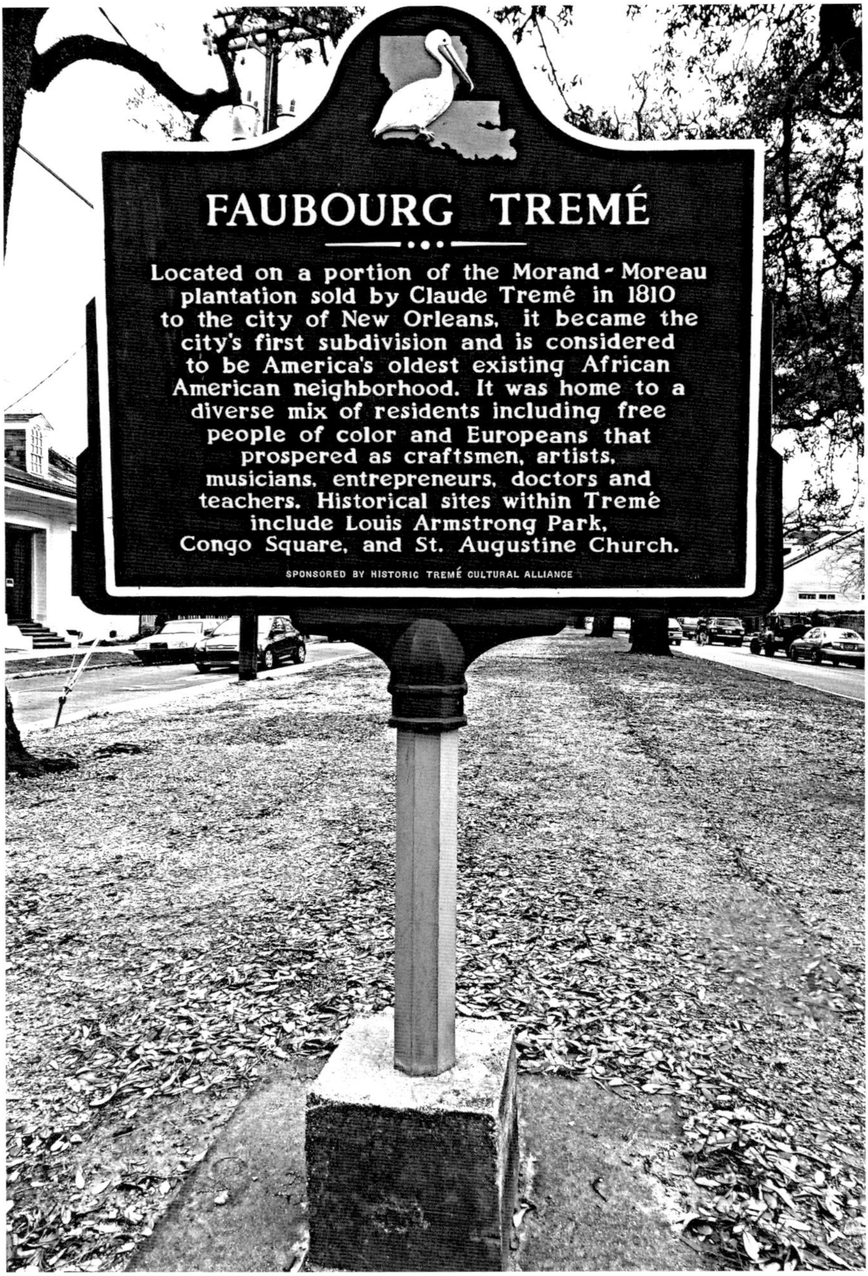
FAUBOURG TREMÉ
Located on a portion of the Morand - Moreau plantation sold by Claude Tremê in 1810 to the city of New Orleans, it became the city's first subdivision and is considered to be America's oldest existing African American neighborhood. It was home to a diverse mix of residents including free people of color and Europeans that prospered as craftsmen, artists, musicians, entrepreneurs, doctors and teachers. Historical sites within Tremê include Louis Armstrong Park, Congo Square, and St. Augustine Church.
SPONSORED BY HISTORIC TREMÉ CULTURAL ALLIANCE

Chapter 1

1790s: Inside Old Treme

Faubourg Treme has emerged as one of New Orleans' most storied enclaves. Its preserved nineteenth- and twentieth-century architecture pays homage to the carpenters, plasterers, bricklayers, lathers, and other specialty tradesmen whose expertise kept the weather-beaten city afloat. The architectural mélange that characterizes Treme includes ornate townhouses, Creole cottages, and stately center hall villas. Side-porch and shotgun houses, former slave quarters, and benevolent-society halls stand as lasting contributions to the culture and history of old New Orleans.

1123
1125

A stucco Creole cottage, 1123-25 Treme Street

In the 1790s, three free women of color, Rose Tissoneau, Gotton Meunier, and Agnes Mathieu, became the first purchasers of new lots on the *Chemin du Bayou* (Bayou Road, now Governor Nicholls Street) between Saint Claude Avenue and North Rampart Street. Of the thirty-seven original lots in Faubourg Treme, free people of color purchased thirteen parcels, initiating a lasting link of downtown Creole culture with the Treme neighborhood.[1]

Treme stands adjacent to the French Quarter at North Rampart and within walking distance to the Mississippi River, the Saint Louis cemeteries, and Canal Street. Its development pushed urban New Orleans northward toward Lake Pontchartrain. In *New Orleans Architecture Volume VI: Faubourg Tremé and the Bayou Road,* Roulhac B. Toledano and Mary Louise Christovich stated, "From the time of Faubourg Tremé's earliest settlement to its urbanization, free people of color played a predominant role within the entire geographical area. . . . Eighty percent of the lots between Dumaine and Saint Bernard, North Rampart and North Broad

Streets, were owned by people of mixed heritage one or more times since the Spanish Colonial period."[2]

Treme provided an inspirational ambiance for writers, artisans, musicians, and those who fought for freedom. Toledano and Christovich wrote, "A roster of the names and addresses of musicians who played in New Orleans dixieland, brass, and jazz bands between 1880 and 1915 indicates that well over half lived in the Creole suburbs, primarily Faubourg Treme."[3]

"Pickle Meat" on Claiborne Street

Treme's past and present remains personal to me. My father, who lost both of his parents at an early age, grew up in Treme, where he learned plastering from an uncle. He was "raised to the trade," as the old people would say. My mother's sister, Antonia Toca, "did hair" next door to the Claiborne Poultry Market.[4] My mother's teaching assignment brought her to Joseph A. Craig Elementary School in Treme. As a young boy with Saturday chores, I bicycled to Joe Dave's meat market on North Claiborne Avenue to buy "pickle meat" (pickled meat) for cooking red beans that day to eat on Monday. When Hurricane Betsy destroyed our parish church in 1965 (Holy Redeemer on Royal Street), my parents became members of Saint Augustine Catholic Church, where we attended Mass. As a teenager, I played basketball and football in Saint Augustine's churchyard and went to weekly dances and parties. I also spent time in Esther Barnum Green's shotgun double in the 1000 block of Treme Street. Miss Esther's stewed crabs and rich, lumpy eggnog were legendary in the neighborhood.

Early Treme

From its beginning, Faubourg Treme inhabited a unique corner in America's racial history. Carved from the plantation of Claude Tremé, the area that bears his name has been home to slave masters and enslaved Africans, free people of color, Native Americans, and immigrants from Europe and the Caribbean. Slave labor did the heavy lifting in the early development of Treme. Africans used their bare hands to drain the swamps. Author Henry C. Castellanos described the effort:

TREME ST

200
SAINT
AUGUSTINE
CHURCH
IN 1841, THIS PARISH WAS ESTABLISHED FOR THE INHABITANTS OF FAUBOURG TRÉMÉ. THE JOINT BENEFICENCE OF BISHOP ANTOINE BLANC AND THE URSULINE NUNS MADE POSSIBLE ACQUISITION OF PROPERTY AND ERECTION OF THE CHURCH. UNTIL 1925, THE BUILDINGS OF THE COLLÉGE D'ORLÉANS AND THE MOTHERHOUSE OF THE SISTERS OF MOUNT CARMEL STOOD IN THIS SQUARE. IN 1842, THE SISTERS OF THE HOLY FAMILY BEGAN THEIR APOSTOLATE FOR BLACKS WITHIN THIS PARISH UNDER THE GUIDANCE OF ABBÉ ÉTIENNE ROUSSELON, FOUNDING PASTOR. ALEXANDRE P. TUREAUD, ATTORNEY AND NOTED LOUISIANA CIVIL RIGHTS LEADER, WAS BAPTIZED HERE APRIL 2, 1899. IN 1963, PRIESTS OF THE SOCIETY OF THE DIVINE WORD BEGAN SERVING THE PARISH.

> Under the administration of Baron Carondelet, in 1794, the scheme of uniting New Orleans by means of a navigable canal with the Bayou St. John was first conceived and partially carried out. . . . Thus it was that, after the subsidence of the flood from the crevasse at Macarty's Point, in 1816, a number of African slaves were put to work in pumping out the water from one compartment into the other. . . . Never was a severer task or more astonishing work ever imposed. . . . They spoke nothing but their native language (Congo). . . .
>
> In the extreme heat of the summer solstice, with only their cotton trousers on, bared breasts and shoulders, protected from the sun by large straw hats or *tignons* merely, they would delve into the midst of our murky swamps, hewing out with picaxes enormous stumps, and spading and throwing up immense clods of dirt. . . .
>
> They had no machinery, no steam contrivance to assist them in their arduous labors. Even the driving of the piles had to be done by hand. The carpenters and educated mechanics were whites and mulattoes, and thus was this huge undertaking carried out toward the main branch of the Bayou St. John. It may be said to be the great initial step toward the drainage of the immense territory, known later as the Faubourg Tremé.[5]

As a port city, New Orleans has been home to diverse groups of people. Before Europeans arrived, the Houma Indians came to the area to celebrate corn harvests. The French and Spanish ruled New Orleans before it was sold to the United States in 1803 as part of the Louisiana Purchase. The city eventually housed Germans, Italians, Irish, West Indians, and other groups. Benjamin Henry Latrobe noted the wide range of people when he visited New Orleans in January of 1819. "Along the Levee, as far as the eye could reach to the West . . . ," he wrote, "White Men and women, and of all hues of brown, and of all Classes of faces, from round Yankees, to grisly and lean Spaniards, black Negroes and negresses, filthy Indians half-naked, Mulattoes, curly and straight haired, Quarteroons of all shades long haired and frizzled, the women dressed in the most flaring yellow, and scarlet gowns, the men caped and hatted."[6]

Treme's early years dovetailed with New Orleans' emergence as a major American city. In 1810, the city of New Orleans paid $40,000 for the Morand-Moreau plantation.[7] While the city contained private subdivisions such as Faubourgs Marigny and Saint Mary, Treme became its first public subdivision. Early Treme's street names included Saint Claude (now Henriette Delille), Treme, and Saint Julie (now Esplanade).

The *Rue de Marais* (Swamp Street) provided an apt description of the marshland that lay beyond. In 1796, except for the houses scattered along the Bayou Road, Fort Saint Ferdinand guarded the city as the only structure north of the French Quarter. Beyond the fort lay the Congo Plains, where enslaved Africans gathered for dance, song, and ancient rituals.

1842: Saint Augustine Catholic Church

One of Treme's most beloved institutions has been Saint Augustine Catholic Church, opened in 1841 at the corner of Governor Nicholls and Saint Claude, in the heart of old Treme. According to James B. Bennett in *Religion and the Rise of Jim Crow in New Orleans*, "Creoles of color supplied much of the funding to build the new St. Augustine Church. . . .

Saint Augustine Catholic Church

Free blacks rented half of the new church's pews, with many of the aisle seats reserved for slaves. Together, slaves and free blacks totaled nearly half of the congregation's membership, with free people of color playing an important role by their ongoing support of the church's budget."[8] In the 1850s, Henriette Delille, Juliette Gaudin, and Josephine Charles recited their vows there as the Sisters of the Holy Family. This order of black nuns ministered to the poor and enslaved.

Carved from the Saint Louis Cathedral parish, Saint Augustine's parish boundaries encompassed the area bounded by North Rampart and Saint Peter streets and North Claiborne and Elysian Fields avenues. The church and rectory were constructed in 1841-42 for $25,000 under Antoine Blanc, who became the first archbishop of New Orleans. Many ethnicities found spiritual comfort at Saint Augustine Church.[9]

Saint Augustine Church had particular significance to New Orleans' African-Americans because of their role in creating the parish. French architect Jacques de Pouilly designed the church building. Architectural historian Ann Masson commented in *Louisiana Cultural Vistas* that he combined "ideas and ornament and influences to create buildings that were completely out of his imagination, rather than following a trend."[10] Toledano and Christovich stated, "The church was designed in the Greek revival style by its French architect, yet it reflects a knowledge of Italian Renaissance buildings and has an international flavor not expressed in the architecture of other New Orleans churches."[11] In 1926, its exposed bricks were covered with cement.[12] For the 1941 centennial, DIVO AUGUSTINO ("Saint Augustine") was inscribed in bronze over the entrance to the church.[13]

Pre-Civil War New Orleans had a history of integrated churches. In 1819, attendees at Saint Louis Cathedral "consisted of at least 4/5 women, of which number one half at least were colored . . . ," Latrobe noted.

Saint Augustine's entrance

The sanctuary at Saint Augustine

The Good Men of the Parish, circa 1980s

There were half a dozen Candles stuck upon the steps by old colored women, who seemed exceedingly devout."[14] Thomas L. Nichols observed in 1845, "White children and Black with every shade between knelt side by side."[15] Author Charles Barthelemy Rousseve told of a lady who attested that in the 1860s, "colored singers" sat "side by side with whites in the choir of Saint Augustine's Church," and black parishioners knelt "at the altar rail indiscriminately with white first communicants."[16]

1846: Slavery in Treme

Many called slavery "the sum of all villainies." Still, it was an integral part of the Treme story. With slavery as an established component of New Orleans life, newspapers of the era thrived on advertisements of rewards for the capture of runaway slaves. New Orleans in the early 1800s contained nearly 15,000 slaves, along with 7,000 free people of color and 19,000 whites. Shamefully, advertisements in the city's newspapers helped slave owners purchase slaves and hunt down escapees who only sought freedom:

> $50 REWARD—Ran away from the subscriber, on Sunday the 26th, the slave boy EMERSON. Twenty dollars will [be] paid for his apprehension, or fifty dollars on conviction of the person or persons harboring or employing him. Said boy is about 5 feet seven inches high, slender make, a griff in color, with large eyes, and is fond of dress. Had on when he left a black coat and pantaloons, and a black glazed cap. Steamboats, vessels and all persons are forbid employing or harboring said boy, under penalty of the law. E. I. Tracey
>
> $20 REWARD—Ran away from the subscriber or decoyed off by some white person, and the undersigned thinks the latter quite the most probable—a mulatto girl named JANE . . . was arrested from my house last night, by some person, as she required a ladder to escape. She had in her possession a pass until Saturday next. The above reward will be paid for her, and if stolen, One Hundred Dollars for the thief. J. D. Currin
>
> $10 REWARD—Ran away from Mobile, about the 1st of April, 1846, the mulatto slave WILLIAM, belonging to Mrs. A. Sands. Said slave is about 5 feet 4 to five inches high, stout built, sometimes wears a beard on his chin and in walking carries his head down. . . . He will no doubt make his way to New Orleans, and endeavor to pass as a free man. Captains of vessels and steamboats are warned against harboring said slave.

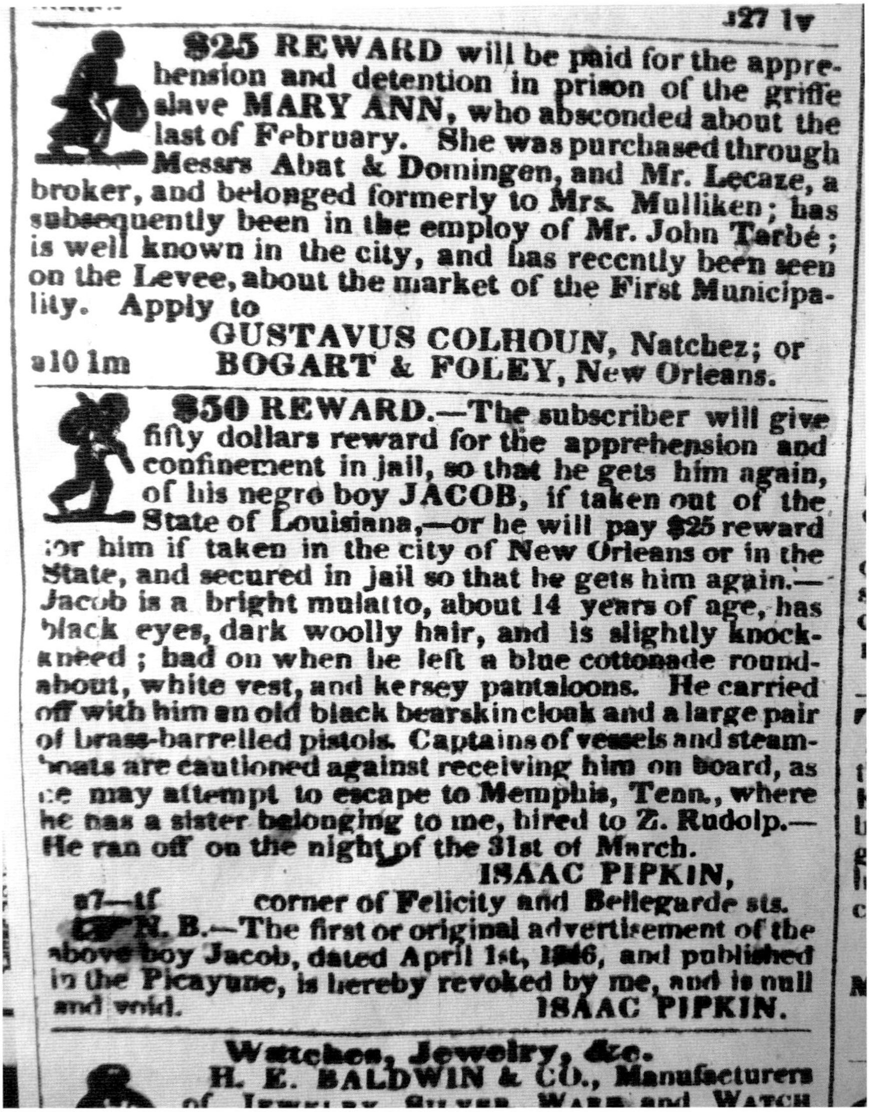

j27 1y

$25 REWARD will be paid for the apprehension and detention in prison of the griffe slave MARY ANN, who absconded about the last of February. She was purchased through Messrs Abat & Domingen, and Mr. Lecaze, a broker, and belonged formerly to Mrs. Mulliken; has subsequently been in the employ of Mr. John Tarbé; is well known in the city, and has recently been seen on the Levee, about the market of the First Municipality. Apply to

GUSTAVUS COLHOUN, Natchez; or
a10 1m BOGART & FOLEY, New Orleans.

$50 REWARD.—The subscriber will give fifty dollars reward for the apprehension and confinement in jail, so that he gets him again, of his negro boy JACOB, if taken out of the State of Louisiana,—or he will pay $25 reward for him if taken in the city of New Orleans or in the State, and secured in jail so that he gets him again.—Jacob is a bright mulatto, about 14 years of age, has black eyes, dark woolly hair, and is slightly knock-kneed; had on when he left a blue cottonade roundabout, white vest, and kersey pantaloons. He carried off with him an old black bearskin cloak and a large pair of brass-barrelled pistols. Captains of vessels and steamboats are cautioned against receiving him on board, as he may attempt to escape to Memphis, Tenn., where he has a sister belonging to me, hired to Z. Rudolp.—He ran off on the night of the 31st of March.

ISAAC PIPKIN,
a7—tf corner of Felicity and Bellegarde sts.

N. B.—The first or original advertisement of the above boy Jacob, dated April 1st, 1846, and published in the Picayune, is hereby revoked by me, and is null and void. ISAAC PIPKIN.

Watches, Jewelry, &c.
H. E. BALDWIN & CO., Manufacturers

Runaway slave notices from the 1840s

Stolen—On the 18th of March last, from O. K. Field, one mile below Natchez, a black boy, Bill, 14 years old, slight built and small of his age. He is supposed to have been kidnapped by several negroes and one or two white persons of suspicious character who were seen lurking in the vicinity of my place about the time the boy left. A liberal reward will be given for the delivery of the boy, or for his lodgement in any jail where I can get him. O. K. Field

$10 REWARD—Ran away from her mistress on the 11th, a negro girl slave named MARGARET COLLINS, aged about 17 years being acquired of Thomas Bonder about a month ago. The above reward will be paid for her apprehension and delivery at her mistress's residence, at No. 76 Royal Street.

$50 REWARD—For the Negress Martha or Matilda, absent since the 10th; blind in the right eye, and wears a headdress so as to cover the defect; aged 28 years, and slim. She was formerly owned by M. I. Pesigo in 1844; J. Allen in 1843; James Carter, of Algiers in 1842; and P. Hanson, Lafayette in 1841.

For Sale—A LIKELY NEGRO GIRL, about 15 years of age, fully guaranteed and sold for no fault. Apply to J. H. Morrison & Co. Front Levee.

$50 REWARD—The subscriber will give fifty dollars reward for the apprehension and confinement in jail, so that he gets him again, of his negro boy JACOB, if taken out of the State of Louisiana, or he will pay $25 reward for him if taken in the city of New Orleans or in the State, and secured in jail so that he gets him again. Jacob is a bright mulatto, about 14 years of age, has black eyes, dark woolly hair, and is slightly knock-kneed . . . he may attempt to escape to Memphis, Tenn., where he has a sister belonging to me, hired to Z. Rudolp. He ran off on the night of the 31st of March. Isaac Pipkin.[17]

It is hard to imagine that the savagery of slavery was tolerated in New Orleans in the shadow of houses of worship such as Saint Augustine Catholic Church. Slaves in the city were governed by the Black Codes of 1806. Across the street from the church lived a slave woman named Pauline. She was said to be the first woman subjected to public execution in New Orleans. Her story was well covered in newspaper articles in 1846. She had become a concubine of her owner, Rabbenack, who instructed her to handle the affairs of the house at 52 Bayou Road, between Rampart and Marais streets, across from Saint Augustine Church. His wife and children lived there as well. While the owner was away, a neighbor reported to police that a white woman was being held captive and confined to a closet. The court consisted entirely of slave owners. It was alleged that Pauline had struck Rabbenack's wife.

The Black Codes of that time mandated that "any slave who shall willfully and maliciously strike his master or mistress . . . or any white overseer appointed by his owner to superintend said owner's slave, so as to cause a contusion or shedding of blood, shall be punished with death; or imprisonment at hard labor for a term of not less than ten years."[18] Although a number of people petitioned the governor to commute Pauline's sentence, they were rebuffed, and the newspapers reported her fate. The end of her life graphically unfolded outside of Parish Prison in Faubourg Treme:

> The slave Pauline was executed yesterday at half past 12 o'clock, at the Parish Prison, in accordance with the sentence of the court, for cruelty to her mistress. . . .
>
> Shortly before 12 o'clock the sheriff waited upon the unfortunate culprit, who had been in company with Priest Louis in her cell, and announced that all was in readiness. She was then dressed in a long white robe, her arms bound with a black cord, the white cap was placed upon her head, and walked, accompanied by the priest, sheriff, keeper of the prison, and officers

The Tomb of the Unknown Slave

> of the Criminal Court, to the gallows, which was erected upon a platform between the two prisons, fronting on Orleans Street, screened by a double gate. She was perfectly firm, and apparently indifferent to her fate. After praying with the clergyman upon the gallows the crucifix was placed upon her neck, and a white pocket handkerchief in her left hand; the rope was adjusted upon her neck by one of the convicts, whose face was blackened, and she took her seat upon the bench erected upon the platform. The gates were then opened, and a loud murmur ran through the populace at the sight of the wretched woman. The party on the platform uncovered, the cap was pulled over the culprit's eyes, and the gallows was slid out so that it projected a few feet into the street. In a few seconds the drop platform fell, the seat upon which she sat gave way, and she dangled in the air. It was painful, terrible, to see the fearful struggles of the dying woman, for it was several minutes before all was over, as her neck was not broken by the fall, and she died from strangulation. At the expiration of about twenty minutes, she was taken in, and pronounced dead by the physician. As she was taken in and the gates were closed, a sort of ill-suppressed shout rose from a portion of the crowd, and gradually the whole assemblage broke up and went away.[18]

1863: Emancipation in Treme

During the Civil War, Treme residents played a vital role in calling for universal suffrage and equality. Lifelong Treme resident and philanthropist Thomy Lafon helped fund the Underground Railroad and donated to the American Anti-Slavery Society. Rodolphe Lucien Desdunes, of Marais Street, was a member of the Citizens Committee, along with Homer Plessy and many Treme residents who fought for equality. Lawyer, philanthropist, and Civil Rights leader Aristide Mary lived on Ursulines Avenue. Dr. Louis Charles Roudanez published two newspapers (*L'Union* and the *New Orleans Tribune*) in the midst of the Civil War.

In July 1863, Africans freed by the Emancipation Proclamation witnessed the funeral procession of black Civil War hero André Cailloux, in Congo Square. He was one of the first black officers in the Union Army to be killed in combat. In 1864, Arnold Bertoneau sent a petition to Abraham Lincoln that called for voting rights. In a speech he delivered that year in Massachusetts, Bertoneau declared, "As slavery is abolished, with it must vanish every vestige of oppression. The right to vote must be secured; the doors of our public schools must be opened, that our children, side by side, may study from the same books, and imbibe the same principles and precepts from the Book of Books, learn the great truth that God 'created of one blood all nations of men to dwell on all the face of the earth.'"[19]

In 1864, thousands of New Orleanians gathered in Congo Square to celebrate Louisiana's adoption of the Emancipation Proclamation. The city's church bells rang and a 100-gun salute was fired. The Fourth Colored United States Cavalry and Battle of New Orleans veterans, including the former drummer boy Jordan Noble, joined an array of social-aid societies, political clubs, and first-time students and their teachers in marching from Congo Square onto Rampart Street in a glorious parade through the city. "Is not emancipation a fixed fact?" queried the *Era* newspaper. This first "Grand Emancipation Programme" produced speeches, poetry, and a jubilant procession that marked the beginning of the end of American slavery:[20]

> Place d'Armes, formerly called Congo Square, and its surroundings were swarming with thousands of our colored population yesterday. At an early hour the different parts of the city where colored schools are located, or colored societies meet, became alive with them dressed in their holiday attire and ornamented with national flags and colors. About nine o'clock they began to move towards the place appointed for meeting—Congo Square—and at about half-past eleven o'clock they had all arrived, the majority of them accompanied by field-bands, and with banners and flags floating in the breeze.
>
> In the square a large platform, rising in the form of an amphitheater, had been erected, with a stand for the speakers. The platform was decorated with flags and evergreens, and seats were arranged on and in front of it. The speakers' stand was covered by a large awning, underneath which we found a number of ladies, teachers of the colored schools established by General Banks. Among those on the platform, we noticed old Jordan and some fifteen or sixteen of the colored veterans of 1815. Some of them appeared as strong and hearty as the day when they showed their devotion to the glorious stars and stripes.

The proceedings were opened with a prayer by Reverend Forrest:

> He called on all to thank Almighty God for the goodness which allowed them to come together on the eleventh day of June, 1864, to celebrate

> the breaking of the chains of slavery. Thousands of their brethren had looked in vain for relief, but they were the ones privileged to enjoy liberty. He prayed that God would give the Union armies strong arms to help in breaking down this rebellion, and the chains of slavery. . . .
>
> A song in honor of emancipation was sung by the children under the direction of the Rev. C. A. Conway. After which the following address was delivered by the Rev. S. W. Rogers, the orator of the day. Mr. Rogers, although a colored man, spoke of the war, the existence and downfall of slavery, and other prominent topics before the country in a manner that showed his thorough knowledge of the subjects.

One of the speakers at the emancipation celebration was Joseph A. Craig, who now has a school named after him in Faubourg Treme. Addressing the First District Emancipation Club, he stated:

> We have assembled here this evening to court public opinion and to weigh them in the scales of justice, civil rights, and religious liberty. Public opinion says, in language as loud as heaven's artillery, with the deep mutterings of an indignant people, that the slave is a free man all over the United States of America. The *vox populi* is the *vox Dei:* the voice of the people is the voice of God.[21]

1865: Lincoln's Assassination

The following "Notice to the Colored People of the City of New Orleans" appeared in the *New Orleans Tribune* on April 20, 1865:

> Fellow Citizens,
>
> In order to give our fellow citizens at large an opportunity to express in a public manner their grief and sorrow by the untimely death, by assassination, of His Excellency Abraham Lincoln, President of the United States:
>
> Be it therefore Resolved, That all of the Pastors of colored churches throughout the City and State are respectfully requested to have their respective places of worship opened on Saturday, April 22, 1865, and to have in their respective churches Divine Worship appropriate to the occasion.
>
> Be it further Resolved, That all the Benevolent Societies and other associations composed of colored persons are requested to meet at their respective places of meeting, and proceed to the Place d'Armes (CONGO

SQUARE) at 8 o'clock A. M., Saturday and participate in the exercises there.

On the appointed day, New Orleanians came to Treme to mourn Lincoln. The *New Orleans Tribune* commented:

> We mourn a man who more than any other of his time, was a representative of the people of America. By the nobility of his nature, not less than by the value of his services, he won his way to the hearts of his fellow-countrymen. They loved and greatly respected him while living. Their tears flow for him now.[22]

The newspaper went on to describe the observance:

> MASS MEETING ON CONGO SQUARE
>
> Over ten thousand of our race assembled on Congo Square to pay their [spirit] of regret to the memory of the [departed] Abraham Lincoln—the immortal patriot shot by an infamous assassin, at the very time that he was about to restore the Union upon the basis of freedom and [liberty].
>
> At ten o'clock Mr. Oscar J. Dunn called the meeting to order. The names, Vice-President and Secretaries in the call of the National Equal Rights League were unanimously ratified. The Rev. Wm. A. Dove then offered a [prayer]. . . .
>
> The procession was then formed, under the guidance of a picket of the 20th New York colored regiment. The march was taken through Rampart Street, down Canal, up St. Charles, down Poydras, and up Camp to Lafayette Square.[23]

"Go on any plantation," spoke the Reverend George W. Levere, chaplain of the Twentieth Regiment of the United States Colored Troops, "and you will see every man of African descent with tears in his eyes, saying his prayers to God, and lamenting this national calamity and affliction. Let the name of Abraham Lincoln be blessed forever."[24] Out of respect for President Lincoln, mourning badges were worn for the next thirty days.

Community Activity

In the 1890s, literature, music, commerce, and protest coalesced in

Treme. One group on North Claiborne named the Ida Club advanced "music, literature, and the drama."[25] The *Crusader* newspaper printed poems, fiction, and nonfiction in French and English. People came out in Treme for "grand dancing festivals" given by benevolent and social organizations, with proceeds going to widows, funds for libraries, and other community causes. For an admission price of fifteen cents, Prof. Joseph Moret's String Band, the Tio and Doublet Orchestra, and Professor Coustaut's String Band held sway on Saturday nights at the various benevolent halls in Treme.[26]

In his 1911 book *Nos Hommes et Notre Histoire* (*Our People and Our History*), Treme resident Rodolphe Desdunes wrote of the sculptors, writers, philanthropists, builders, and others who populated the area. Michel Saint Pierre, a poet who lived on Ursulines, contributed to *Les Cenelles*, noted as the first poetry anthology by people of color in the United States.[27] Free man of color Basil Crockere, who once owned the lot at the corner of Rampart and Ursulines, taught fencing at his *Salle d'Armes*, in a city where dueling under oak trees settled questions of honor.

By the 1890s, Treme encompassed a goodly mixture of industrial, residential, service, and religious sites. Commercial concerns settled in between the houses. A lumber yard, stables, and corner grocery stores

flanked the cobblestones on Ursulines. The sprawling Pelican Brewery arose on North Villere Street between Esplanade and Hospital (now Governor Nicholls). On North Claiborne, every four minutes, mule-drawn yellow streetcars of the Canal and Claiborne line clopped toward the vegetable markets at Saint Bernard Circle.[28]

In the 1940s, North Claiborne Avenue served as a linear business district, with hat manufacturers, a coffee mill, the Claiborne Candy Company, and the black-owned People's Industrial Life Insurance Company. A National Bank of Commerce branch awaited depositors at the corner of North Claiborne and Saint Ann. The National Youth Administration, the Negro branch of the New Deal program, offered services at 831 North Claiborne. Barbers Chattard and Santiago cut hair down the street from the Black and Tan Lounge.

Society halls provided insurance and death benefits to their members. Republican activists protested for constitutional rights at the Globe Hall, located at the corner of Saint Peter and North Rampart. The Globe Hall was also the scene of the formation of the American Equal Rights Association in the 1890s. The Friends of Hope Benevolent Hall, at 922 North Liberty, hosted a large protest accompanied by a pamphlet entitled *Violation of a Constitutional Right.*[29] Homer Plessy lived at 1108 North Claiborne, next to Congregation Hall.

A Visit with Miss Esther of 1027 Treme

In 2007, I visited Miss Esther Barnum Green, who had lived in the 1000 block of Treme Street since the 1930s. I attended Holy Redeemer School with her children and was good friends with her son Bobby. Every Mardi Gras, Miss Esther would open her home to anyone seeking respite and sustenance during their Mardi Gras trek. In the back room of their shotgun double, her daughters Kathy, Sheila, Dale, Yolanda, and Myra

Miss Esther's shotgun double

peeled potatoes and onions, served hot dogs with chili, and provided sweet red punch to the parched revelers. It is in homes such as Miss Esther's that the spirit and soul of old Treme can be found.

Born in Pascagoula, Mississippi, Miss Esther was six years old when she came to New Orleans. She lived at 1802 Saint Philip Street and subsequently moved to 1027 Treme. During that time, horse-drawn wagons passed and sold fruits and vegetables. She lived around the corner from Mr. Schiro, who was the father of New Orleans mayor Victor Schiro. "He used to sell coal in the wintertime and in the summer he sold ice cream," she stated. "Everybody used to buy coal for their fireplace and he had the shop. He used to have snoballs and sherbet and he used to make it and sell it. He would sell the li'l two-cents cone, five-cents cones, and then as much as you want. There was another man who used to pass with the horse and wagon. He sold the taffy candy."[30]

Miss Esther recalled that Carnival Day was marked by the annual arrival of the bawdy "Baby Dolls." "We used to go to the parade. We still have open house every Carnival." Mardi Gras Indians passed in front her house on lively Treme Street on Carnival Day and Saint Joseph's Night.

"I raised six children in the house at 1027 Treme," Miss Esther told me. "It was a mixed neighborhood, with black and white living there. I didn't go to Saint Augustine Church until my later years. Before that it was a white church. Black people could go, but they had to sit to one side. The last ten seats on one side was where black people had to sit. You could go in the church but that was their church."

Her great-aunt was principal of Joseph A. Craig Elementary School in Treme. "She was principal at Craig when they first built it. Then, Miss Dedeaux came," Miss Esther said. Her brother Herman was in the band and her sister "Bebee" was a majorette. Her other brother, Willie, also went to Craig. Miss Esther attended Craig and also Saint Mary's Academy, which was then on Orleans Street in the French Quarter. "I went to Saint Mary's three years," she continued. "My mother died when I was five years old. 'Sister' was taking care of us. Norman Barnum was my father. My grandmother was Clara Durand. I had nine brothers and sisters.

"We went to the lakefront, to the park on North Claiborne and Lafitte. One side of Claiborne was for white people, the other side of Claiborne was for black people. I used to go to the Dew Drop on La Salle. They had breakfast places up that way. I didn't go there when I was young because it was too adult.

"Quite a few musicians lived in my neighborhood. The parades had brass bands. The neighborhood had clubs. Caledonia used to be around the corner. I lived on Treme Street for seventy years. Long time ago, we used to play ball in the street."

Treme Today

In 2002, the New Orleans African American Museum commissioned a group of artists to express the accomplishments of the people of Treme. Their efforts produced "Restore the Oaks," an enlightening public-art

The New Orleans African American Museum

project that stretches for a mile on eleven blocks of North Claiborne Avenue between Saint Bernard Avenue and Saint Peter Street under Interstate 10. Using the pillars of the interstate as a canvas, numerous artists depicted the history of Treme with renderings of Chef Leah Chase, the old Treme market, slave revolts, Civil Rights activities, Africans drumming in Congo Square, the Rebirth Brass Band leading a second-line parade, and other representations of the area's traditions. The outermost pillars were painted with tree limbs and leaves as an homage to North Claiborne's days as a promenade.

Paintings, sculpture, and poetry are evocative representations of historic Treme. But the area itself is the historic treasure. Homer Plessy, Aristide Mary, Louis Armstrong, and others walked these same streets and passed the same houses that exist today. What is the future of Treme? It has been over two hundred years since it became a developed suburb of New Orleans. As the sun once again set on this Sixth Ward neighborhood, I spotted a girl sitting outside on a stoop on Treme Street, braiding another

Art under the Claiborne Avenue Overpass

Street banners celebrating musician "Uncle Lionel" and Treme's 200th anniversary

girl's hair. Next door, a boy strummed an acoustic guitar. In that narrow snapshot, all seemed normal.

I met Rick Mathieu on Treme Street, restoring a house two blocks from Miss Esther's. He is a third-generation construction worker raised to the trade by his father, Emanuel Mathieu. His house in the Seventh Ward took on eight feet of water during Hurricane Katrina. Mathieu and a rescue group dubbed the "Soul Patrol" spent eleven days picking up stranded residents with a pontoon boat and bringing them to safety.

"The challenge is redoing something that's beautiful," Mathieu told me. "Why take something beautiful and replace it with something that's not going to last? If that house stood up 200 years, that's telling you something right there."[31] He pointed across the street to an empty lot where a recently built pre-storm house fell to the winds of Katrina, the only house on the block to do so. "It was a brand-new house that wasn't five months old. It blew down," Mathieu stated. "They didn't know the old way and the [old way] is what counts."

Chapter 2

1800s: Congo Square—African Seeds in American Soil

> An old man set astride of a Cylindrical drum about a foot in diameter, and beat it with incredible quickness with the edge of his hand and fingers. The other drum was an open staved thing held between the knees and beaten in the same manner.
>
> Benjamin Henry Latrobe, New Orleans City Engineer, 1819[1]

There is no better place to start the journey to New Orleans' African roots than Congo Square. Walk down Orleans Street from the back of Saint Louis Cathedral, and continue past the Creole cottages and shotgun-style homes that mark this oldest part of New Orleans. Cross North Rampart and enter Louis Armstrong Park. On this hallowed ground over two hundred years ago, a community of Africans pounded ancient rhythms on handcrafted instruments and performed ritual dances such as the *calinda* and *bamboula.* They sang ballads with themes that embraced religion, history, rebellion, survival, love, and lost love. Congo Square's name and character evoke the memory of thousands of Africans who journeyed to this place on weekends in old New Orleans.

To meander back in time to its origins proves as intriguing as an archeological dig. Each layer of history offers a peek into the nooks and crannies of New Orleans' cultural legacy. I found faded newspaper reports,

Louis Armstrong Park
HOURS 9:00 A.M.– 10:00 P.M.
Congo Square
HOURS 9:00 A. M. – DUSK
Louis Armstrong Statue
Municipal Auditorium

letters, and other documents detailing the frequent African rituals, sometimes accompanied by drawings or descriptions of an instrument or dance. Benjamin Henry Latrobe and traveler Christian Schultz recorded their observations of Congo Square with astonished curiosity at this unique expression of Africa in the American South. Through their studies of similar forms in Africa and the Caribbean, contemporary musicologists Laura Boulton, J. H. Kwabena Nketia, and Katherine Dunham provided an even broader template for examining the social and religious significance of Congo Square events.

Paving stones cover this once dusty expanse. The branches of oak trees reach toward the center of the Square, giving respite from the noonday sun. Nearby, where Africans once sounded melodies from wooden horns and danced with square pieces of cloth called *madras* held above their heads, a life-size sculpture of Louis "Satchmo" Armstrong grasping his trumpet and trademark handkerchief faces Congo Square. To Satchmo's right, lights from chandeliers in the Mahalia Jackson Theater for the Performing Arts glitter over areas where West African women chanted Voodoo incantations. In the 1990s, New Orleanians came to Congo Square to witness the inauguration of the city's mayors and for gospel concerts, family days, African drum lessons, and any number of events that filled Sunday afternoons.

Congo Square drumming

For New Orleans' earliest African communities, Congo Square preserved and expressed centuries-old traditions of homelands they would never see again. Tracing the origins of *Place Congo*, we learn that the city's unique rhythms reach back in time to old New Orleans and also across rivers, oceans, and centuries to the West African cultures that gave the city much of its legacy and verve.

From West Africa to New Orleans

According to historian Gwendolyn Midlo Hall, more than half of the 5,000 Africans who arrived in Louisiana during the early French period came from the Bambara kingdoms of the Greater Senegambia region in coastal West Africa. This area encompassed the Gambia and Senegal rivers and included all or part of today's Senegal, Mali, Guinea, Mauritania, Guinea Bissau, and Guinea Conakry. The Bambara people trace their ancestry to the Mali empire of the thirteenth century. As people with strong oral traditions, they initially resisted the spread of Islam and kept their indigenous culture intact, even as the Bambara people spread across

West Africa. Hall wrote, "The collective wisdom of the Bambara is passed on by the frequent reciting of proverbs in ordinary conversation."[2]

In the fertile Senegal valley, Africans grew rice, corn, tobacco, indigo, and cotton. They worked as blacksmiths, horseshoe makers, and coppersmiths. The first Africans arriving in Louisiana in the 1720s cleared and drained swamps, constructed levees and buildings, dug canals, hacked down trees, and assisted in public-works projects. Rations consisted of one-and-a-half pounds of corn and a half-pound of lard per day.[3] In addition to the Bambara, other Africans came from as far south as Angola and included Mandinkas, Yorubans, and Fanti. West Africans left a lasting imprint on the fabric of New Orleans.

From Congo Plains to Congo Square

Congo Square lies outside and to the north of the original city plan. While the *Place des Armes* (now Jackson Square) served as the city's official promenade, Congo Square evolved as the outback of the city proper. Originally called the "Congo Plains," its setting of barren land melting into mossy cypress swamps allowed room to roam. The Houma Indians celebrated their corn feasts there and viewed the land as holy ground. In the eighteenth and nineteenth centuries, this public area was the scene of bullfights, footraces, and hot-air balloon demonstrations. It also hosted rousing and sometimes dangerous games of *raquette*, a wide-open sport played by as many as 160 poor whites, blacks, and Choctaws. Summer months in Congo Square marked the arrival of the traveling circus of Monsieur Cayetanne from Havana.

Maps, documents, and newspapers variously called Congo Square *Congo Plains*, *Place des Nègres*, *Place des Armes*, *Place du Cirque*, *Circus Place*, and *Circus Square*. German immigrants who held festivals there wanted to name it "Humboldt Square," after the German naturalist, artist, and mapmaker Alexander von Humboldt. In the 1740s, Africans and Choctaws used it as a marketplace. In 1762, France erected Fort Saint Ferdinand on a portion of Congo Plains as one of five military structures protecting the city's perimeter. Also in 1762 after Spain acquired Louisiana, Spanish administrators visualized a grander plan for New Orleans than as a military outpost. During the forty-year Spanish reign, the number of Africans in the city quintupled, adding to the diversity of Congo Square's history.

Dance and drum rituals at Congo Square provoked an array of reactions. Some officials feared a breeding ground for slave conspiracies, while others saw a harmless way for slaves to release tension. Neighbors complained of noise, while others appreciated the Sunday-evening diversions. Some took umbrage at such practices occurring on the Sabbath. In 1786, a Roman Catholic bishop called the dances "hideous" imports brought from Africa by the "Yolofs, Foulahs, Bambaras, and Mandingoes."[4] Despite the reverend's indignation, early Congo Square rituals reflected deep religious faiths called *Udun* in Dahomey and *Voodoo* in Louisiana. Voodoo adherents practicing in Nigeria, Ivory Coast, Gold Coast, Senegal, and Angola believed in a Supreme Being called *Damballah* whom they beseeched through intermediate deities called *loas*. A practicing Roman Catholic, Voodoo priestess Marie Laveau lived less than a block from Congo Square.

In 1803, the United States acquired Louisiana. The Americans also gave in to the inevitability of the dances. An 1806 law mandated that "slaves must be free to enjoy Sunday, or be paid fifty cents a day if they worked."[5] In 1808, North American traveler Christian Schultz happened upon Congo Square and noted "the sight of twenty different dancing groups . . . collected together to perform their worship after the manner of their country." He continued, "They have their own national music, consisting for the most part of a long kind of narrow drum of various sizes. The amusements continue until sunset."[6]

Visitors noticed markings on the skins of some of the dancers and drummers. These scarifications denoted class, nationality, and family in West African societies. For example, according to studies by German clergyman Christian Oldendorp in Dutch Guiana (now Suriname in South America), the Bambara men had knife-like gashes from their temples to their necks, Loango women had spots all over their bodies, the Ibo people displayed straight vertical cuts on their temples, and the Amina showed horizontal cuts. The Mocco decorated their bodies from the middle of the breast with a laurel design. The scarification procedure involved sharp knives for incising straight lines or needles for poking dots.[7]

In the 1810s, the last remnants of Fort Saint Ferdinand tumbled as the surrounding area developed into Faubourg Treme. By 1817, African dancing in Congo Square was continuing past midnight on Sundays and had spread to vacant lots. As a regulatory measure, the mayor refurbished the Square, constructed a fence around it, and declared it the only legal place for slave dancing. City law ordered that the dances occur only on Sunday evenings and end at nine o'clock.[8]

Congo Square in the 1820s

Imagine yourself on a journey to Congo Square on a summer Sunday evening in the 1820s. Walk along the wood-planked *Rue d'Orléans* (Orleans Street), the main street through the French Quarter, past the Orleans Theater, the three-story Orleans Ballroom, and the homes of midwives, harness makers, charcoal merchants, and coffeehouse workers. Church services have ended, and the bells of the town clock at the Church of Saint Louis (Saint Louis Cathedral today) rang at five o'clock.[9]

Cross *Rue des Remparts* (Rampart Street). Along the sidewalk, or *banquette*, entrepreneurial women of African descent, their heads covered by distinctively wrapped headscarves called *tignons*, set up tables with cotton awnings to shield foodstuffs from the sun. They sell roasted peanuts, pralines, pies, ginger cakes called *estomac de mullatres* (mulatto's belly), and *calas* (rice cakes). For the thirsty, vendors serve lemonade and *bièrre du pays*, a refreshing drink made from fermented apples and gingerroot. Female vendors, called *marchandes*, walk along the sidewalk with trays of treats hanging from their necks. A waist-high iron gate encloses Congo Square, with city police officers monitoring each entrance.[10]

In the center of Congo Square, shirtless musicians gather in a semicircle, straddling drums constructed from hollowed logs ranging from two to eight feet in length. Wire keeps sheep or goatskin fastened tautly over one end of each log. Some drummers carry an instrument made of a block of new wood with a deep slit down the center. Others sit crosslegged, holding smaller drums fast between their thighs. During the week, the drummers are called darkies and slaves. In Congo Square, they are *candios*, or chiefs.[11]

A musician beats two large beef bones against an empty barrel, the *bamboula* drum, to announce the evening. The drummers, astride their larger instruments as if on horseback, lean over and use their hands to send a long, slow dirge reverberating across the city. Callused fists and fingers pound the smaller drums to add another layer of beats to the crescendo.

Latrobe likened the sound to "horses trampling on a wooden floor."[12] In Congo Square, as in Africa, the drum reigns supreme. The drum is "the pulse beat of Africa," Boulton observed. "To the African it gives life its continuity. He is born to it, dies to it, works to it, worships to it, and dances to it for days and nights on end. It brings dignity to the coronation of kings and terror to the witch-smelling ceremony. Whether the rhythms are gay or somber, pompous or sinister, they are always insistent and never to be forgotten."[13]

The drums set the stage and mood for the dance. Dancers form a semicircle directly in front of the drummers. Women rattle cornucopia-shaped gourds filled with grain or pebbles. Others hit two sticks against dried calabash studded with brass nails. Triangular cymbals join the onrush of percussion, as do thumb pianos, tambourines struck against open palms, cane pipes, and fiddles or banjos with necks carved into elaborate human figures. Participants pass keys rhythmically across the teeth in the jawbones of mules or oxen. Others blow cow-horn-shaped wooden trumpets. As the evening progresses, the sound vibrates through the ground and echoes off the plaster and brick buildings of old New Orleans.[14]

African Seeds

There are remarkable similarities to West Africa and the Caribbean in Congo Square. The wooden slit drum in a Latrobe illustration appears in African societies as the "talking drum," so called because of its ability to create tonal sounds. Nketia found it in Guinea, Sierra Leone, Liberia, eastern Nigeria, and Cameroon.[15] Dunham (the choreographer, author, songwriter, and anthropologist who has been called the "Matriarch and Queen Mother of Black Dance") described the *bamboula* drum in Trinidad as one made from a "very thick bamboo that has been scooped out."[16]

George Washington Cable recounted the events of Congo Square based on others' reminiscences. He wrote of women holding gourds partly filled with pebbles that "flourished violently at the end of a stout staff with one hand and [were] beaten upon the palm of the other."[17] Similarly, Dunham noted the use of "calabashes filled with pebbles." Nketia classified these as primary, rattle-type instruments and described secondary rattles as those attached to the wrists of a performer or an instrument, conforming to Cable's mention of "a belt of little bells" on the *bamboula* dancer.

In 1819, Latrobe wrote, "The most curious instrument however was a stringed instrument which no doubt was imported from Africa. On the

Bamboula dancer depicted by E. W. Kemble in 1885, based on Cable's description of earlier dances

top of the finger board was the rude figure of a Man in a sitting posture and two pegs behind him to which the strings were fastened. The body was a Calabash. It was played upon by a very little old man, apparently 80 or 90 Years old. . . . A Man sung an uncouth song to the dancing which I suppose was in some African language, for it was not french, and the Women screamed a detestable burthen on a single note."[18]

The women in Congo Square whose sorrowful wailing Latrobe called a "detestable burthen" echoed the women in Africa whose "function [is] to wail, with or without words, in choral laments as well as dirges sung individually."[19] The combination of form and function as seen in the figurines adorning instruments in Congo Square also spoke of African traditions. Bow harps from Zaire featured carved human faces as the necks of the instruments. The thumb piano presented another African transposition. Called an *mbira* by Nketia, a *marimba brett* by Cable, and a *zeze* by the Ashanti of West Africa, this instrument consisted of reeds stretched across a board with a hole in its middle. Musicians created music by plucking the reeds with their fingers. In Africa, the thumb pianos ranged in size from five to twenty keys.[20]

"Soleil Couche"

Each Sunday evening, reality set in at nine o'clock for slaves in antebellum New Orleans. At that hour, police officers rolled the curfew cannon from Jackson Square to Congo Square, where its explosion abruptly ended what one writer called a "half-day of half-freedom." As the last trace of sunlight dissipated beyond the mossy cypress swamps, Africans went out into the New Orleans night and back to slavery. "*Bonsoir, danse,*" they chanted as they walked through the narrow city streets. "*Soleil couche.*" ("Goodbye, dance. The sun has gone to bed.")[21]

Proverbs of Wisdom

Beyond drumming and dancing in Congo Square, Louisiana's Africans rendered proverbs and songs of events, feelings, legends, and wisdom. Lafcadio Hearn translated them from Louisiana Creole, which is a mixture of European and African dialects. The proverbs could be satirical or ominous, but mainly, they offered lessons for day-to-day living. Some counseled patience, such as "*Piti a piti, zozo fait son nid.*" ("Little by little, the bird builds its nest.") Other proverbs offered relationship advice: "*Di mon qui vous lamein, ma qui vous qui vous ye.*" ("Tell me who you love, and I'll tell you who you are.") Another adage warned of the consequences of sloth: "*Bon-temps fait crapaud manque bounda.*" ("Idleness leaves the frog without buttocks.") Others preached against ostentation: "*Bel tignon pas fait bel negresse.*" ("A fine headdress does not make a fine Negress.") Another applied to the law that required twenty-five lashes for Africans who did not leave Congo Square when the cannon sounded: "*Apres ye tire canon, negue sans passe c'est negue-marron.*" ("After the cannon fires, a Negro without a pass is a wild Negro.")[22]

Creole Slave Songs

The Creole slave songs addressed sanctuary, love, work, adventure, and survival. Mark Twain protégé George Washington Cable collected and transcribed songs from the memories of others. One ballad told the story of Jean Saint Malo, an African who established camps for runaway slaves.

These *maroons* dwelled below New Orleans in unsettled Saint Bernard Parish in the late 1700s. Protected in whereabouts accessible only through dense swamps, Saint Malo's followers survived on a diet of sweet potatoes, seafood, and wildlife. They clandestinely obtained weapons through contacts with free people of color and enslaved Africans on plantations. In 1784, the colonial government, which ruled from the Cabildo, called Saint Malo "audacious, daring, and active" and dispatched contingents to crush the camps. In response, Saint Malo thrust an ax into a tree at the entrance to his settlement and declared, "Woe to the white who would pass this boundary."[23]

After a number of skirmishes, Saint Malo was captured. On June 19, 1784, he was hanged in what is now Jackson Square, despite protests from the Capuchin pastors of the Church of Saint Louis.[24] Jean Saint Malo died on the gallows, but "The Ballad of Saint Malo" kept his story alive:

> Alas! Young men, come make lament/For poor Saint Malo in distress!/They chased, they hunted him with dogs./They fired at him with a gun./They hauled him from the cypress swamp./His arms they tied behind his back./They tied his hands in front of him./They tied him to a horse's tail./They dragged him up into the town/Before those grand Cabildo men./They charged that he had made a plot/To cut the throats of all the whites./They asked him who his comrades were./Poor Saint Malo said not a word./The judge his sentence read to him/And then they raised the gallows-tree./They drew the horse—the cart moved off/And left Saint Malo hanging there./The sun was up an hour high/When on the levee he was hung./They left his body swinging there/For carrion crows to feed upon.[25]

Another song spoke with the voice of those maroons who disappeared into the swamp, chanting a taunt at the general as they escaped: "They got one schooner out at sea/O General Florido!/Indeed for true they can't catch me!/O General Florido!"[26] For those who rowed pirogues (dugout boats) on long swamp excursions, singing of love for Zoë (the feminine ideal) interrupted the monotony:

> Sing, fellows, for our own true love/My lottery prize! Zoë, my belle!/She's like a wild young doe; she knows/The way to jump and dance so well./Black diamonds are her bright, black eyes./Her teeth and lilies are alike./Sing, fellows, for my true love, and/The water with the long oar strike.[27]

Other songs brooded. Love, betrayal, and envy marked the tale of "Poor

Miss Zizi," who after losing her lover to the stately Callalou lamented: "When love's chains upon thee lie/Bid all happiness good-bye."[28]

The events in Congo Square and the recorded expressions of Africans in Louisiana defied the myths of slavery. For the open-minded, it would be very difficult to view Africans as subhuman after witnessing their dance and musical organization, their constructing of instruments, their fiddle and banjo concerts, the words they spoke, and the songs they sang. Many dared to fight and die for freedom. Louisiana's slave rebellions ranged from the Bambara Conspiracy of 1731 to an 1811 slave revolt that ended with the heads of captured slaves displayed on posts leading to New Orleans. The Calaboose, the jail near Congo Square for blacks, imprisoned hundreds of runaways. Other slaves sought legal remedies, pursuing the painstaking task of working for their personal freedom, purchasing relatives, and then filing the legal petitions for emancipation.

Bras Coupé

One Congo Square drummer dared to free himself. A man named Squier escaped to become Bras Coupé (Cut Arm), the Robin Hood of the swamps. He was said to be "the highest-jumping" *bamboula* dancer in Congo Square and a formidable *raquette* player. He used his physical deftness to escape to freedom in the marshland beyond Congo Square, where he organized a ragtag band of runaways and poor whites into nighttime raiding parties. He received the name Bras Coupé after his arm was amputated—the result of being shot by a patrol of captors determined to return him to a life of slavery.[29]

Sometime during the 1830s, perhaps as a reaction to the Nat Turner insurrection, officials halted dancing in Congo Square. In 1845, a group of residents petitioned for its revival. With the ending of the international slave trade forty years earlier, the number of locals who had been born in Africa was dwindling. Their descendants had taken their musical skills to parties and underground venues. One, Massa Quamba, charged three dollars at nighttime parties to play the violin, while William Martin made money strumming his banjo. The dancing was revived until the Civil War.

Louisiana seceded from the United States in 1861. In 1862, the Union army captured New Orleans and silenced the nine-o'clock cannon. For enslaved Africans, Congo Square changed from a place of "half-freedom" into a forum for freedom of speech and freedom of assembly. As freed people, the former slaves pursued the interests of education, family, and citizenship. One minister noticed this phenomenon in Louisiana shortly after the Civil War. He met former slaves calling, "Books! Books! and 'when does school begin?'"[30] They reconstructed families and participated in politics. By 1880, males headed 80 percent of black households in New Orleans, and blacks voted in large numbers. Their future in America became the focus for many, and the dances at Congo Square seemed to be a remnant of the past. In 1871, the police commissioner closed Congo Square and the city auctioned its iron railing. In 1893, the name changed to Beauregard Square.

Historic Recognition

With the advent of the Jim Crow era, which lasted until the late 1960s, the Congo Square story largely disappeared from the public consciousness. In the New South of the 1960s and 1970s, interest in Congo Square reemerged. The late New Orleans jazz scholar and author Tom Dent formed the Congo Square Writer's Workshop to reacquaint his generation with the city's cultural roots. The first musical and cultural expositions of the now-established New Orleans Jazz and Heritage Festival took place there in 1970. A Congo Square stage remains one of the festival's popular attractions. In 1975, Congo Square became part of the Louis Armstrong Park complex. The 1980s ushered in an African dance troupe called Kumbuka Drum and Dance Collective and with it a series of Congo Square remembrances.

In the 1990s, New Orleans bandleader Luther Gray spearheaded a drive to bring greater attention to the history of the Square. In 1993, Congo Square joined other New Orleans landmarks on the National Register of Historic Places.

On April 28, 2010, new sculptures of Mardi Gras Indian Chief Big Chief Allison "Tootie" Montana, gospel great Mahalia Jackson, and jazz pioneer Charles "Buddy" Bolden were unveiled in further recognition of the Square's musical legacy. In 2011, the New Orleans City Council officially renamed Beauregard Square as Congo Square.

Master drummer Luther Gray at the Congo Square International Festival 2013

A work in the Roots of Music Cultural Sculpture Garden

Big Chief Allison "Tootie" Montana sculpture

Mahalia Jackson sculpture

Buddy Bolden sculpture

Sidney Bechet sculpture

Brass band sculpture

While the spirit of Congo Square remained alive in New Orleans music, writing, and legends, the historic designation ensured the survival of the physical site as well. One hundred years from now, people will still be able to go to the Congo Plains, pass their hands over this piece of ground, and feel the "pulse beat of Africa" in the ancient rhythms of New Orleans' earliest musicians.

Chapter 3

1837: The Will of the Widow Couvent

My name is Marie Justine Cirnaire. I was born in Guinea. When I was perhaps seven years of age I was carried to St. Domingue [Haiti]. I am as a result not aware of the name of my father or my mother, nor do I know my age. I was married to Bernard Couvent, free Negro, whose widow I now am. We have had no children.

I bequeath and order that my land at the corner of Grand Hommes and Union streets [Dauphine and Touro] be dedicated and used in perpetuity for the establishment of a free school for the colored orphans of the district of Marigny. . . . Also, I declare that said lands and buildings shall never be sold under any pretext whatsoever.

From the 1837 last will and testament of Marie C. Couvent, native of West Africa[1]

The compelling life story of Marie C. Couvent represents a fascinating chapter in the education history of New Orleans. Taken from Africa as a young girl in the 1760s, she left a legacy touching four centuries. Parentless as a child, childless as a woman, and lacking a formal education, Couvent became a patron for orphans and literacy. In her will, she established a school on her land at what is now the corner of Dauphine and Touro. That land was to be forever dedicated to the education of the orphaned children of color in the Faubourg Marigny, a suburb of the French Quarter. The school that she envisioned in her will still stands on the site. As the oldest extant school site for children of color in the city, Couvent's legacy survived financial turmoil, fires, and hurricanes and brought the gift of learning to thousands of eager students.

Those searching for tangible evidence of her legacy can visit the center aisle of Saint Louis Cemetery #2, Square 2, where she and her husband, Bernard, are buried. Affixed to the side of this tomb is a plaque that was installed by the Friends of New Orleans Cemeteries on February 27, 1999. Madame Couvent's educational legacy can be appreciated at the corner of Touro and Dauphine streets. This was the site of the schools that she bequeathed. The current edifice was built in 1956, when the school was popularly known as Holy Redeemer. The building contains a historic marker from that year and an older plaque that recounts the school's earlier legacy. Her last will and testament is stored in the Louisiana Division of the New Orleans Public Library.

The Journey to New Orleans

Couvent's journey from West Africa to New Orleans tells a story of slavery, caste, freedom, and legacy. Born in West Africa in the 1700s, Marie was taken from her home during the height of the Atlantic slave trade. She was captive at approximately seven years old, before she was old enough to remember her family name. She was first brought to Haiti, then known as Saint Domingue. The details of her arrival in New Orleans remain sketchy, but she subsequently married Bernard Couvent, a free man of color listed by Roulhac Toledano, Sally Evans, and Mary

Couvent plaque in Saint Louis Cemetery #2

Louise Christovich in *New Orleans Architecture Volume IV: The Creole Faubourgs* among the better known "early builders" of "some of the more interesting houses."[2] The couple lived on Barracks Street at the lower end of the French Quarter, a stone's throw from the raised earthen levee that shielded the city from the Mississippi River.

The Couvent Schools in the Faubourg Marigny

Although the Couvents lived in the French Quarter, the Couvent schools stood on property she owned in the Faubourg Marigny (established in 1805). Located just across Esplanade Avenue from the French Quarter, this now lively neighborhood of curved streets, pentagonal and triangular blocks, and a colorfully preserved nineteenth-century housing stock has withstood centuries of storms. At the corner of Dauphine and Touro streets, a restaurant serves stuffed peppers, pork chops, and po'-boy sandwiches to eclectic passels of Orleanians until late at night. Take a seat by the window facing Dauphine Street and you can view a nondescript, three-story brick building with a silvery cross affixed to the top floor. Since 1848, children have been educated on that land at schools of various names: the Catholic Indigent Orphan Institute, the Couvent School, Saint Louis School of Holy Redeemer Parish, Holy Redeemer School, Bishop Perry Middle School, and Saint Gerard Majella Alternative School.

History remains omnipresent in the Faubourg Marigny. Many of the homes that exist today date to the time of Marie Couvent. The magnificent Dolliole Creole cottage still hugs the curve as Bourbon Street turns into Pauger. Jean-Louis Dolliole, a free man of color, built this structure in 1820 as one of the earliest Creole cottages in the city.[3] Within walking distance of Couvent's school site and the Dolliole cottage, a free woman of color named Rosette Rochon owned numerous properties, including 1515-17 Pauger Street, which date back to the early 1800s.[4] The buildings near her land included Creole cottages with sloping roofs, shotgun houses, and villas with stately center halls.

Free People of Color in New Orleans

The Couvents belonged to a caste of free people of color that populated

New Orleans since its earliest days. Free status could be obtained through purchase by a relative or oneself, through manumission, or through migration from countries such as Martinique or Haiti that countenanced free black populations. A large number of free people of color migrated to Louisiana following the Haitian revolution. Others came from Cuba in 1809. They generally settled in the French Quarter or its Creole faubourgs of Marigny, Treme, and New Marigny.

During the period when the South based its economy on slavery, a number of free people of color, including the Couvents, held title to slaves. It was easier in New Orleans for people of color to purchase their enslaved relatives and loved ones than to go through the arduous process of emancipation. According to the Black Codes of the slavery era, a slave owner could not free a slave without a judicial declaration, a public posting of the emancipation request, and a final determination by the Superior Council. Thus the Emancipation Petitions located in the New Orleans Public Library portray free people of color applying for freedom for enslaved relatives.[5]

Though it is not clear what their relationship was to a woman called Pauline (not to be confused with the slave Pauline who was executed in 1846), Bernard and Marie Couvent filed emancipation petitions for her in 1821. Then in 1829, Bernard petitioned the Orleans Parish Police Jury for permission to emancipate two other women. He asked that they not be compelled to leave the state after their emancipation as Louisiana law required.[6] Before their freedom became final, Bernard, seventy-one, died on May 22.[7]

Two years later, in 1831, Marie Couvent re-filed the petition to free the two women, Seraphine, forty, and Fillette, forty-five, whom she stated had "faithfully served her for a great number of years past, [and] nursed her in grievous sickness at various times."[8] Unable to read or write, she put her mark, X, on the document as her signature. The Parish Court granted her request.

1837—The Last Rites of Marie Couvent

In her seventies, the widow Couvent told Fr. Constantine Maenhaut, a priest at Saint Louis Cathedral, of her desire to use the lot and building she owned at the corner of Grand Hommes and Union streets (now Dauphine and Touro) in the Faubourg Marigny to educate orphans. She instructed that rental income from her other properties be earmarked for the school's upkeep. She appointed Father Maenhaut and his successors at Saint Louis Cathedral to supervise the aims of her will. Henry Fletcher, a friend of her late husband, was designated to execute them.

Marie Couvent received the last rites of the Catholic Church. On June 28, 1837, a rainy Wednesday evening, the approximately eighty-year-old widow died at her Barracks Street home. After a funeral at Saint Louis Cathedral, she was buried in Saint Louis Cemetery #2, which was an ocean away from her birthplace in West Africa. The inscription on the Couvent tomb reads: *Ici repose* M. *BERNARD COUVENT natif d'Afrique*. ("Here lies Mr. Bernard Couvent native of Africa.")

The Catholic Indigent Orphan Institute

In the mid-1840s, a free person of color named François Lacroix organized ten other men to form the *Société Catholique pour l'Instruction des Orphelins dans l'Indigence*. They pledged to uphold Couvent's will by establishing "one or more schools for the instruction of indigent orphan children" and providing for their "discipline, education, health and religious instruction."[9] On April 20, 1847, they received a state charter, and in the following year, the school that Madame Couvent dreamed of accepted its first students. The *Louisiana Historical Quarterly* called her school "the first free school for colored in the United States."[10] In 1866, *Harper's New Monthly Magazine* called it the "largest colored Creole school in New Orleans."[11]

The First Classes

Many of the students were the progeny of white fathers.[12] Others had been orphaned by yearly outbreaks of yellow fever that began in 1793 and lasted into the 1900s. The need for the school became most acute in 1853, when hundreds of people a day died in the city from yellow fever. Sometimes entire families succumbed, leaving no one to make funeral arrangements or even place the bodies outside for the daily death buggies whose drivers made their rounds calling, "Bring out your dead."[13]

At the Catholic Indigent Orphan Institute, full orphans received free schooling. Children with one surviving parent ("half-orphans") paid twenty-five cents, and children with both parents paid fifty cents. The school provided students with paper, pencils, and books. The board of directors soon replaced the original small buildings with a new school. A sign in the school said *Sinite parvulus venire ad me Dame veuve Bernard Couvent Donatrice de Cette Ecole, fondee le 23 Aout, 1847* ("Let the little children come to the school founded by the widow of Bernard Couvent, established on August 23, 1847").[14] Felicie Cailloux became the first principal.

Students were taught by an enlightened corps of teachers of African descent, many of whom had received their education in France or Haiti. The faculty included poets and writers Paul Trevigne and Joanni Questy, mathematicians E. J. Edmunds and Basil Crockere, and dramatist Adolphe Duhart. Trevigne, who taught at the school for forty years, edited the *L'Union* newspaper after the Civil War, while Duhart's play *Lelia* was showcased at the Théâtre d'Orléans in the French Quarter. The second principal, Armand Lanusse, added to the school's literary flavor. A poet and writer, he published *Les Cenelles* in 1845, the first anthology of poetry by people of color in the United States. At the school's commencement exercises, a demonstrative Lanusse often crowned high-performing students with a laurel wreath, such as Victoria Lecene for her "elocution and creative poetry." With student assistance, he organized an annual Mass and religious presentation in memory of Marie Couvent. Each year on November 1, the school celebrated All Saints Day, and students walked in procession to her gravesite. Rodolphe Desdunes wrote in 1911:

> It is of interest to note that every year on the feast of All Saints the directors held a school funds drive. They did this by placing at the gate of the cemetery two trays to receive offerings. The trays were supervised by orphans chosen by the director. . . . Also, it was a custom each year to have a Mass said for the repose of the soul of the good widow, Madame Couvent. The upkeep of her tomb, located in the last cemetery on Claiborne Avenue [Saint Louis Cemetery #2] was paid for by the board of directors. In the latter years, the board placed a commemorative plaque in the school to honor the foundress of the institute. We believe it is the duty of the Creole people of color to erect a larger monument to the memory of this noble woman. . . . It is an undeniable fact that she was the first among us to give the example of enlightened charity, and for a long time she was the only one who held this distinction.[15]

Descriptions of Couvent called her pious, generous, chaste, and a "Black African woman."[16] By 1866, 260 pupils attended the school. It provided Catholic instruction but accommodated other religious denominations. Students were taught in French and English. Boys and girls studied on separate floors. Until 1900, report cards contained individual progress evaluations rather than grades. The school community raised money through solicitations, festivals, fireworks displays, Carnival balls, and raffles of lacework, umbrellas, and holy pictures. Perhaps influenced by teacher and swordsman Basil Crockere, the school even put on fencing exhibits to raise funds. People paid two dollars and forty cents to be on the board of directors.[17]

In 1866, a writer for *Harper's New Monthly Magazine* visited the school and reported:

> The method of instruction is good. Some of the pupils have mastered the principle rules in Arithmetic, and progressed as far as the square and cubed root. The specimens of writing . . . are very neat and correct. . . . Their general conduct is quiet and orderly. They are neat in their person and tidily dressed.

The writer also found that students were reading aloud in both French and English with great fluency and modulation.[18]

A Brush with History

In the 1890s, the Couvent School, as it was popularly called, was drawn into American Civil Rights history when its president, sail maker Arthur Esteves, presided over a citizens' committee that initiated a bold civil-disobedience campaign and legal challenge to racial segregation in the South. Four members of that historic *Comité des Citoyens* also served on the school's board of directors. Their actions led to the famous Supreme Court case of *Plessy v. Ferguson*, one of the three pivotal Supreme Court decisions in Civil Rights history. The school's legal advisor, Louis A. Martinet, notarized Homer Plessy's affidavit after Plessy refused to relinquish his seat on an East Louisiana railroad car. Plessy's act of civil disobedience portended the strategy and tactics of the Civil Rights movements of the 1900s.

In the spirit of the legacy of Marie Couvent, Republican icon Aristide Mary left money in his will to help finance construction of a new Couvent school building. With another significant bequest by philanthropist Thomy Lafon in 1894, the board of directors opened a new school amid much fanfare, with a large hall, basement, and classrooms. Archbishop Francis Janssens gave a sermon commending Marie Couvent as a philanthropist. Board member Rodolphe Desdunes would echo that sentiment in his 1911 book, *Nos Hommes and Notre Histoire*. He wrote, "There were schools in our city but poor people were unable to attend them. We are happy to see that numerous writers, poets, artists, who displayed exemplary conduct and superior intellects, went forth from the doors of the institute for indigent orphans."[19]

Throughout its existence, the school symbolized resilience and tenacity, faith and hope. It withstood challenges as it navigated the days of slavery, emancipation, Reconstruction, and the Jim Crow era. For the remainder of the nineteenth century, the school educated students, pursued revenue sources, and saved itself from extinction. At one point, a federal official tried to convert the private school into a public school, but Father Maenhaut vetoed the plan. Another group unsuccessfully attempted to convert the school to a convent. In the 1880s, public schools siphoned its student body, but a new board of directors rallied to save the Couvent legacy.[20]

Rising from the Ruins

The twentieth century also tested school's mettle. The hurricane of 1915 destroyed entire swaths of New Orleans and leveled the school. A fundraising drive elicited donations from New Orleans' network of social-aid and pleasure clubs, such as the *Société des Jeunes Amis*, a black Creole fraternity, and the Ladies of Morality. The school's board of directors raised $1,250.[21] Mother Katherine Drexel, of the Sisters of the Blessed Sacrament, accepted an invitation to tour the school and donated $2,000 to complete construction. However, she required that the school be renamed Louis, in memory of her brother. There were other conditions for her financial assistance. According to James B. Bennett, "To receive Drexel's gift, the school that had been run entirely by black educators since before the Civil War, had to turn over its administration to the white Sisters of the Blessed Sacrament, who would also provide the

HISTORY

OF THE

Catholic Indigent Orphan Institute

Dauphine and Touro Streets

DESTROYED BY THE HURRICANE

SEPTEMBER 1915

REBUILT IN 1916

PUBLISHED BY THE

BOARD OF DIRECTORS

This history would be published by the board of directors in the early 1900s teachers for the school. The new school was placed under the supervision of a priest who was white."[22] This school was renamed Saint Louis School.

On August 26, 1917, a fourth building replaced the school destroyed by the storm of 1915. The *Times-Picayune* described the school as "rising from the ruins." A large gathering assembled at the Sunday-afternoon dedication to hear the speeches of L. J. Joubert, the Very Reverend J. M. Jeanmard, Walter L. Cohen, construction supervisor Louis Charbonnet, and a Father Vautier, who spoke to the crowd in French. Former students Lizadie Diaz and Raymond Narcisse stood as the school's honorary godmother and godfather. The cornerstone carved by Italian sculptor Romeo Celli read:

> Destroyed by the storm, September 29, 1915. In the year A. D. 1916, started rebuilding from individuals, benevolent, social and other organizations. August 26, 1917, completed due to the magnificent contribution of a benefactress. Named in gratitude, "Saint Louis School."

Social turmoil, acts of nature, and lack of finances perpetually threatened

The 1915 hurricane destroyed the school.

The Catholic Indigent Orphan Institute rebuilt as Saint Louis School.

the school's existence. It stood firm under protest by segregationists and adjusted its mission after demographics and changing times depleted its student population. Its treasury once sank to twelve dollars, and teachers went unpaid. But those who appreciated and loved the institution always mustered the grit to move forward, even as circumstances and the end of yellow-fever plagues moved the school away from its original mission of educating orphans. Once the only Catholic school for blacks in New Orleans, by 1925 it was one of nine. Every other Catholic school in the diocese attached itself to a church parish, but the school for orphans existed as something of an orphan itself, cared for by a secular board of directors and the Archdiocese of New Orleans.

Saint Louis School of Holy Redeemer Parish

In 1919, the Josephite priests opened Holy Redeemer Church a few blocks from the school. They assumed spiritual and eventually administrative oversight of the school, which became popularly known as Holy Redeemer. Processions and religious celebrations continued to be a school hallmark. In 1945, the Catholic Indigent Orphan Institute dissolved. This officially transferred the school to Holy Redeemer Church, ending a relationship that began in antebellum New Orleans.

In February 1956, the city condemned the site. The quest to rebuild was met with opposition from segregationists in the Faubourg Marigny, but the school prevailed. In the interim, students attended classes in converted French Quarter barrooms, dry-goods stores, and the church's basement. My brother Alfred Medley remembered attending seventh-grade classes in Benny's Jolly Time Bar on Decatur Street. My sister Marilyn Medley wrote an article that recounted her experiences as a sixth-grade student:

> During the time they were building the new school, we were forced to use temporary quarters for our classes. Some classes were in the church, some in the hall, some in the back of the choir loft, and the rest in rented buildings. . . . The sixth grade held classes in a former barroom. . . . At last moving day came. On November 26, 1956, we began classes in our new school. . . . My school is more than just a school. It is a monument to the dream of a wonderful woman, Marie Couvent. I know that she must be just as proud of my school as I am.[23]

A plaque from the 1956 dedication of Saint Louis School of Holy Redeemer Parish

A Fight for Survival

Decreases in attendance closed Holy Redeemer School. As its principal, Sr. Bernadette McNamara left the school for the last time in 1995, in tears. There seemed little hope for the Couvent legacy. In a crude parallel, her grave in Saint Louis Cemetery #2 shamefully deteriorated. Her headstone dislodged from its moorings, and a tomb once so fastidiously tended became a lump of brick and plaster.

But as so often in the school's history, in the back of someone's mind, the widow Couvent 's words resounded across the ages: "I bequeath and order that my land . . . be . . . used in perpetuity for the establishment of a free school." In 1995, three months after Holy Redeemer closed, Fr. David Cray of the Society of Saint Edmund arrived in New Orleans, searching for a location to place a school for talented at-risk kids. By that September, they opened Bishop Perry Middle School on the site willed by Marie C. Couvent.

Though not acutely aware of the school's earlier mission, the Bishop Perry Middle School moved closer to Madame Couvent's original intentions. It offered free tuition and small classes to promising students, along with a culture of long hours, discipline, literary appreciation, and academic achievement. After Hurricane Katrina in 2005, out-of-state benefactors no longer supported the school and it closed to be replaced by the Saint Gerard Majella Alternative School.

A Voice from a New Orleans Cemetery

Marie C. Couvent has been the common thread connecting Catholic Indigent Orphan Institute students with those of the Couvent School, Saint Louis School, Holy Redeemer, Bishop Perry, and Saint Gerard Majella Alternative School. At the same time that Bishop Perry began an outreach program to Holy Redeemer graduates, a group called the Friends of New Orleans Cemeteries planned for the restoration of Marie Couvent's tomb. In the waning months of 1998, workers at Saint Louis Cemetery #2 busily shored and rebuilt the tomb. A plaque would later be unveiled, quoting Couvent's will.

In the more than 170 years since the widow Couvent 's interment in her humble, stepped-top tomb in the main aisle of Saint Louis

Murals at Bishop Perry Middle School

Cemetery #2, the burial ground had become the final resting place for influential persons of African descent.

But the widow Couvent preceded them all. In 1998, Bishop Perry students Jason Watson and Dannon Dutton stood at her gravesite and read a quote from Rodolphe Desdunes that spoke to remembering her legacy: "May the future generations not reproach us for our neglect in this matter especially when the spirit of the times exhorts us to glorify the good deeds accomplished by her gifts."[24] Thanks to the Friends of New Orleans Cemeteries, the widow Couvent's tomb is now restored. Thanks to the students and staff of Bishop Perry Middle School, her dream lived on as well.

Chapter 4
1912: The Woods Directory

> New Orleans is now passing through the most interesting period of its history. Great heads are at work devising ways and means to meet the vast trade which must of necessity come with the opening of the Panama Canal. Ideas are being formed to work out the new problems and conditions which confront us. Antiquated methods must go. In this great movement, the colored people must play a part.
>
> Allen T. Woods, 1914[1]

As the publisher of the *Woods Directory*, stenographer Allen T. Woods presented a fascinating picture of the workaday world of New Orleans' black citizenry in the early 1900s. For as little as twenty-five cents, he published the business cards of the city's black tradesmen and tradeswomen, musicians, modistes, market vendors, hairstylists, and caterers. Larger concerns such as construction companies and funeral homes purchased full-page ads, which Woods accentuated with illustrations and crisp photographs. The *Woods Directory* documented the spirit of enterprise that our ancestors possessed a century ago.

For Allen T. Woods, the *Woods Directory* provided added income, a vehicle for his advertisers to promote their products, and a roadmap to black-oriented businesses for the early-twentieth-century consumer. In the absence of black newspapers in New Orleans during that period, the directory gave a vibrant snapshot of the people who made New Orleans work. After soliciting advertisements from across the city, Woods organized, printed, and distributed 5,000 free copies of his directory. Surviving copies of his work reside in the collections of Tulane University, the New Orleans Public Library, and the University of New Orleans.

The directory's outlook and production garnered praise from prominent people nationwide. Booker T. Washington wrote, "Such a publication as this is bound to accomplish great good, and I congratulate you upon the enterprise of your Colored business men which makes . . . such a publication as this possible."[2] The secretary of the New Orleans Board of Trade wrote to say that he was "agreeably surprised to see the large number of your people engaged in different business enterprises." The National Association for the Advancement of Colored People's *Crisis* magazine observed that the "Woods Directory shows the remarkable organization of the Colored population of New Orleans."[3]

Allen T. Woods

Allen T. Woods was born circa 1884 to Dennis Woods and Florence Johnson Woods. Allen's father was a laborer, while his mother kept house. They lived at 2606 South Rampart Street in New Orleans' Central City area. Dennis Woods was a native of Mississippi, while Louisiana was home to Florence. Allen came of age during the Progressive Era in American history. During that period, emerging social movements called for safe working conditions, regulation of capitalism, more citizen participation, and access to citizens' rights. The National Association for the Advancement of Colored People (NAACP) and the Urban League formed during this time. By 1920, women protested and obtained the right to vote. A new age of discovery began when the Wright Brothers proved the sky was no limit. In an era of expansion, New Orleans reigned as the South's Queen City. According to the book *United States History from 1865*, "The period 1900-20 was a social era that had a flavor all its own, an all-pervading confidence in the future of the nation that came with the new century."[4]

Allen T. Woods was a visionary who intended to be a part of that future. His comments throughout the directory depicted a person with a distinctive viewpoint and a sense of the new opportunities. In 1905, at twenty-one, Woods landed a job as a clerk at the Customs House on Canal and Decatur. Imagine the ambitious young man of color walking through its lavish, fifty-four-foot-high Marble Hall. It held the reputation of being the "finest business room in the world."[5]

The Customs House was home to the U.S. Circuit Court of Appeals, district attorney's office, and post office. A number of African-Americans, including Republican leader Walter L. Cohen and writer Rodolphe Desdunes, worked there as appointees. Allen T. Woods worked for the appraiser of merchandise.[6]

On December 5, 1906, Woods, twenty-two, married Marita Newton, twenty.[7] New Orleans was a thriving city, with numerous businesses owned by people of color. Even in the era of Jim Crow, there were undeniable accomplishments and milestones. As a young man, Woods saw initiative and progress all around him.

In the Heart of Central City

In addition to his job in the appraisers' office, the energetic Woods sidelined as an advertising writer. He operated a stenography business, which copied and addressed the envelopes for mass mailings. The 1910s were a busy time for the Woodses, who lived at 823 Seventh Street with their young daughter, Alva. In 1912, Woods published his first edition of

1912 Woods Directory

the *Woods Directory*. Describing his work as "Being a Colored Business, Professional and Trade Directory of New Orleans, Louisiana," in the front of each edition he listed the churches, parks, schools, hospitals, and theaters that were open to African-Americans.

Woods' office at 2125 Dryades placed him in the heart of the Central City neighborhood and within close proximity to many of his advertisers and clients. Created in 1806 from the Delroy-Sarpy plantations, this area reflected the architecture, culture, and history of uptown New Orleans. Many of New Orleans' first jazz musicians lived in Central City, including Buddy Bolden (2311 First Street), Kid Ory (2135 Jackson Avenue), and Jelly Roll Morton (2621 Fourth Street, demolished). Jordan Noble, the famous black drummer boy of the 1815 Battle of New Orleans, once resided at the corner of Dryades and Clio streets. As Central City's main thoroughfare, Dryades attracted bold entrepreneurs of different religions, races, and classes. Jews, Russians, Italians, and other ethnicities found their livelihoods along the strip of shops, insurance companies, clothing stores, churches, and photography studios. The *Woods Directory* highlighted Dryades in the 1910s as an avenue with an eclectic mix of

dressmakers, caterers, barbershops, and dentists. As the directory illustrated, you could purchase a fashionable all-wool suit for fifteen dollars at Porter's Tailoring Company, 1010 Dryades; shop for matching shoes at Dejoie's Hub Shoe Store, 1224 Dryades; then dine at Victor Dubois' Great Southern Hotel and Restaurant, 1012 Dryades.

The *Woods Directory* reconstructed Dryades Street from a black perspective and helped characterize Central City in the early 1910s. Near Jackson Avenue, George Floyd's photography studio captured the smiles of New Orleanians, with some of the photographs appearing in the directory. On hot summer days at 1832 Dryades, Dejoie's Cut-Rate Pharmacy beckoned with its ceiling fan and its ice-cream parlor featuring pure-fruit sundaes, soda water, and assorted candies. Katie Robinson and William Morris at the Orleans Ice Cream Works at 2217 Dryades delivered ice cream, ices, biscuits, and charlotte russe, a dessert of sponge cake or ladyfingers with a whipped-cream or gelatin filling. The Dryades Pocket Billiard Hall billed itself as the "FINEST COLORED BILLIARD HALL IN TOWN" and one that ensured "strict decorum maintained at all times." The pool hall for men advertised the venue as "clean, sociable and respectable" and encouraged patrons to "come around with your friends and enjoy yourselves."[8]

One block from Woods' office, the Young Men's Christian Association (YMCA) for blacks, at 2220 Dryades, offered gymnastics, inspirational speeches on Sunday afternoons, and an employment agency for black laborers. Founded in 1905, the YMCA quickly became a source of education, employment, recreation, and inspiration for generations of New Orleanians. Prof. F. P. Ricard, who also served as an agent for the NAACP, instructed boys and men three times a week in the fundamentals and skills needed for gainful employment.

The Pythian Temple

The tenants of the Pythian Temple provided a steady clientele for Woods' directory. Just as the Customs House symbolized commerce in New Orleans, the Pythian Temple, at 234 Loyola Avenue (then Saratoga Street), was a crowning achievement for Woods' new-century generation of black Americans. Constructed at a cost of over two hundred thousand dollars, the Pythian Temple was fireproof, majestic, and built and operated

For a Beautiful Complexion, Use PRESTO FACE CREAM.

DEJOIE'S

Cut-Rate Pharmacy

1832 DRYADES ST. PHONE JACKSON 502

SPECIAL DELIVERY.

Our Prescription Department is Complete

ALWAYS A FINE LINE OF FRESH CANDIES, CIGARS AND TOILET ARTICLES. TRY OUR DELICIOUS ICE CREAM, SODA WATER AND ICE CREAM SUNDAE—ALL PURE FRUIT FLAVORS USED. :: :: :: :: ::

LET THIS BE YOUR FAMILY DRUG STORE.

Orleans Ice Cream Works

MRS. KATIE ROBINSON and WILLIAM MORRIS,
Proprietors.

ICE CREAM, ICES, CHARLOTTE RUSSE, AND BISCUIT FURNISHED FOR ALL OCCASIONS.

We deliver to all parts of the city. Country orders Solicited

2217 DRYADES STREET, Phone Jackson 842.

NEW ORLEANS, LA.

La Branche's Drug Store, 818-820 N. Claiborne Avenue. Phone Hemlock 1170.

by people of African descent. The *Times-Picayune* called it "the biggest business enterprise ever attempted by the colored race in the United States."[9] The *Indianapolis Freeman* newspaper described the achievement of constructing the first black-owned skyscraper in the history of New Orleans as a "monument to what the Negro can accomplish."[10] *Architectural Art and Its Allies* featured the proposed building in its March 1908 edition. The Pythian Temple's six stories contained multiple floor plans with office suites, meeting rooms, a banquet hall, and a second-floor balcony. The ground-floor entrances featured arched windows with hinged transoms and doors with brass kick plates at the bottom. A cement parapet wrapped around the top of the building. Following the dedication on August 18, 1909, the *Times-Picayune* declared in a headline, "New Orleans Negroes Lead Their Race in Enterprise."[11] The ceremony featured music by the Saint James AME Choir and the Glee Club of the Dryades Street YMCA. Black lawyer J. Madison Vance, who would become a 1912 delegate to the Republican National Convention, received frequent applause as he spoke of the "Power of Organization and Its Effects upon Civilization."[12]

For Allen T. Woods, the building provided a reservoir of potential clients as he put together his first directory. The Pythian Temple became the site of many New Orleans institutions. It housed a bank on the ground floor and a combination theater and auditorium on the second floor. The historic "theatorium" provided the venue that led to the formation of the Zulu Parading Club in 1909. The Temple Theater hosted local and visiting theatrical troupes, such as the Williams and Stevens Stock Company from Chicago.[13] A roof garden became a primary venue for orchestra concerts, parties, and balls, with performances by Louis Armstrong, Manuel Perez, Manuel Manetta, and others.

Education

No public high school existed for black Americans in New Orleans during the time of the *Woods Directory*, so Woods listed the available avenues for private education. His college listings indicated that New Orleans University offered college preparatory courses, music, domestic, oratory, and other studies in a total of ten departments. Other colleges of the time included Southern University, Flint Medical College, and Sarah Goodridge nurse training school on Canal Street. Guillaume College

Pythian Temple as it appeared in the Woods Directory

operated from the Pythian Temple and offered business and secretarial courses at night, as well as preparatory classes for taking government tests. In a section of the directory called "Location of Prominent Places," Woods listed nine public elementary schools. Also listed were three public parks for blacks: Oleander Park on Carrollton, Dixie Park on Bienville, and Lincoln Park.

Building the City

Many of the trades that were prominent in New Orleans during the 1800s persisted into the early twentieth century. Many black men worked in the building trades to keep the weatherbeaten city intact. The *Woods Directory* documented the carpenters, roofers, tinsmiths, plasterers, bricklayers, landscape artists, and slate layers whose skills predated the Civil War. Woods listed eleven black real-estate agencies and twenty-six building contractors. Louis Charbonnet, a millwright supervisor and construction engineer, advertised his ten-ramp conveyors—a banana and coal conveyor in the city and three banana conveyors in Mobile—along with rice-mixing plants and mills. Another contractor, M. R. Hite, built Trinity M E Church at Valence and Chestnut streets and Mills Preserving Plant on Tchoupitoulas Street. The directory also highlighted New Orleans' large black-owned insurance companies.

Nine black shoemakers advertised in the *Woods Directory*. In the French Quarter, practical horseshoers A. J. Cobette and Poche gave special attention to trotters and pacers. In addition to the traditional crafts, electrician D. W. McKay represented the twentieth century's new technologies: "The necessities of life we must have, the luxuries we can do without. Use electricity and get both at one price."[14]

An example of advertising by Allen T. Woods himself follows:

> Letters that count are the kind that carry with them vim and the personality of a qualified salesman. They must possess acumen and reflect integrity and business ability. Woods Directory maintains a Service Department having facilities for doing all kinds of typewriting. We form and typewrite circular letters, personal letters, notices, contracts, specifications, etc. Envelopes addressed. Our rates are low. Let us conduct your correspondence.[15]

Women in Business

Black women played a key role in the commercial life of New Orleans. Woods highlighted embroiderers, trained nurses, midwives, caterers, and

SPECIAL ATTENTION GIVEN TO TROTTERS AND PACERS.

Cobette & Poche

Successors to Thos. J. McTague.

Practical Horseshoers

Horses sent for in all parts of the city and returned. All work done with neatness and dispatch.

A. J. COBETTE.

JUNCTION OF PETERS AND DECATUR STREETS, BETWEEN CONTI AND ST. LOUIS.

HARNESS REPAIRED WHILE YOU WAIT AT RASCH BROS., PHONE MAIN 2416.

A. E. JOHNSON

House, Sign and Decorative

PAINTER

PAPER HANGER AND INTERIOR DECORATOR

OFFICE: 112 PYTHIAN TEMPLE.

SHOP: 2620 BANKS STREET.

ESTIMATES AND DESIGNS FURNISHED.

Read THE CRISIS. (See Ad. on Back Cover.)

HAIR GOODS

Mrs. Grace D. Brooks
Special Agent Madame C. J. Walker's Preparations
2418 S. Liberty Street
Phone Jackson 276

H. Caldwell
Wigmaker and Hair Manufacturer
2013-2015 Dryades Street

Mrs. C. J. Sylvester
Agent, Brownatone Ideal Hair Preparation
2623 Banks Street

HATS CLEANED AND BLOCKED

Roscoe Williams
Hats Cleaned and Blocked
3419 Saratoga Street

HORSE CLIPPING

Logical Point Horse Clipping Shop
H. J. Moore, Prop.
S. Rampart, cor. Washington Ave.

HORSE SHOERS

W. P. Brown
Practical Horseshoer
730 Louisiana Avenue

Cobette & Poche
Practical Horseshoers
411 N. Peters St. Phone Main 2416

L. P. Dupre and D. Dupre
Horseshoers
Stock called for and delivered
2009 Valence Street
Phone Uptown 2518

George U. Maury
The Famous Horse Shoer
1611 N. Claibore Avenue
Phone Hemlock 907

C. Wilson
Practical Horse Shoer
Corner Short and Hickory

HOTELS
(See also Restaurants.)

Astoria Hotel and Restaurant
H. E. Braden, Prop.
235-237 S. Rampart Street
Phone Main 1588 and Main 2308

Chicago Hotel and Restaurant
A. O. Smith, Proprietor
204-206 S. Rampart. Phone Main 2194

BEAUTY DEVELOPED ALONG LINES of distinctive simplicity—details of luxury that appeal to the desire to possess—enduring quality that assures the most economical service—are characteristics of the new

"LA CORALIE" CORSETS

THE CORSET IDEAL FOR DISCRIMINATING WOMEN.

Manufactured for and sold exclusively by

MRS. CORA VIGNES-WILSON

Designed, cut, and made to fit your individual figure by one of New York's biggest Corsetieres.

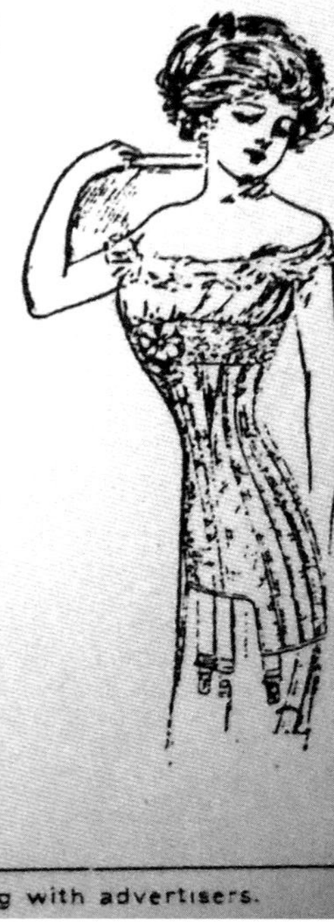

CORSETS FITTED AT YOUR HOME LET US CALL ON YOU WITH SAMPLES OF THE NEW MODELS.

Address

MRS. CORA VIGNES-WILSON

"LA CORALIE" CORSETS

927 Bienville Street. New Orleans, La.

CORSETS MADE TO ORDER.

Also sole representative of

MME. MABLE BECK'S SCHOOL OF DESIGN.

West Fifty-third St., New York City.

stenographers. The ad for Geddes Funeral Home proudly claimed the only "lady embalmer" in the South. Other women involved themselves in the city's fashion and style industry. M. J. Spotts operated the Crescent Hairdressing College at 2013-15 Dryades, with a curriculum of manicuring, massage, scalp treatment, and hair making. Mrs. Spotts' enterprise billed itself as the largest such facility operated by a black entrepreneur in the country. Cora Vignes-Wilson marketed corsets from her shop at 927 Bienville Street and also fitted customers for her "La Coralie" corset in

Mrs. W. A. Jackson,

MODISTE,

DESIGNER AND ARTISTIC CUTTER AND FITTER

ROBES TROUSSEAUX DRESSES

NEATLY AND STYLISHLY MADE.

927 VALENCE STREET, NEW ORLEANS, LA.

their homes. C. Dubuclet sold perfume from a stall in the Treme Market, while modiste W. A. Jackson designed and cut robes, trousseaux, and dresses from her shop at 927 Valence Street.

Food, Beverage, Lodging

Like present-day residents, New Orleanians in the 1910s had a love affair with their food. Caterer Laura Brown specialized in wedding cakes and fruitcakes from 2823 Dryades. Eliza Woods kept her Select Restaurant at 2632 South Rampart Street open all night as she dished up oysters, fish, and game. Other vendors operated stalls in the city's open-air marketplaces. The *Woods Directory* placed butcher John Ferrouilet in the Treme Market, while Joseph Touchard hawked fish, shrimp, and crabs at the French

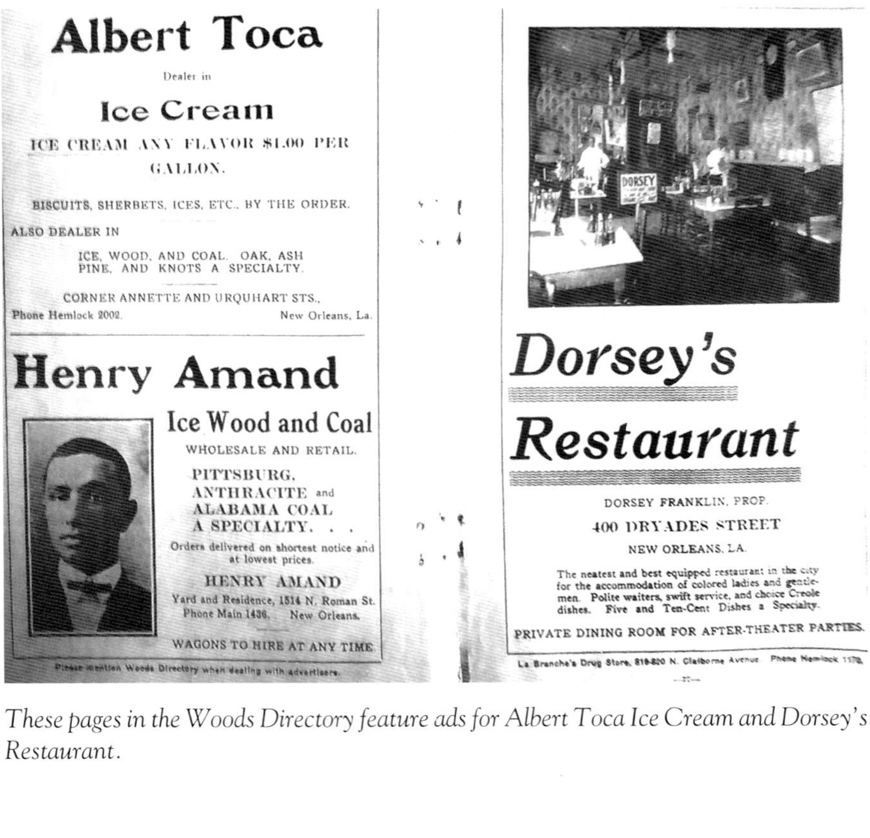

These pages in the Woods Directory feature ads for Albert Toca Ice Cream and Dorsey's Restaurant.

Market. At the market on Saint Bernard Circle at Claiborne, R. Van Cresson sold beef, pork, mutton, and all kinds of sausages. Dorsey Franklin's restaurant at 400 Dryades Street promised "polite waiters, swift service, and choice Creole dishes . . . neatest and best equipped restaurant for the accommodation of colored ladies and gentlemen."[16] Downtown, my grandfather Albert "Poppa" Toca manufactured and sold ice cream, ices, and his patented custard from his factory and parlor at the corner of Annette and Urquhart streets.

A number of saloons provided residents with a nightcap or two in pre-Prohibition days. In addition to the beverages at the Little Ruby Saloon at South Franklin and Gasquet streets, the High Art Café and Restaurant at the corner of Melpomene and Saratoga offered ice-cold beer, liquor, fine wines, and cigars. T. A. Simms, proprietor, and J. S. Ross, manager, operated a venture that sold cigars and F. W. Cook's beer on tap.

The directory carried a full-page advertisement for the Chicago Hotel. Mustached Alfred O. Smith's establishment at 204-6 South Rampart promised a quiet and homelike atmosphere for families visiting the city. His three-story brick building was open day and night, offering a barbershop, soda fountain, hot-water baths, and electric lights. His guests included the All-Cuba baseball team and the Williams and Stevens Stock Company theater troupe.[17]

Other pages of the directory featured people who had wagons to hire, coal to burn, and hands to let. O. T. Bocage and his sons built boats at 530 Powder Street in Algiers. Twine the Taylor was open for business at 523 South Rampart.

Emancipation Parade

Nineteen thirteen was a benchmark year. Abolitionist and Civil Rights pioneer Harriet Tubman died in 1913, and Rosa Parks, who took the struggle for Civil Rights one step further, was born. Separate but equal went national that year when Pres. Woodrow Wilson ordered the segregation of all federal workers in Washington, D.C. The 1913 edition of the *Woods Directory* contained more than one hundred pages listing about one thousand entries.

The fiftieth anniversary of the Emancipation Proclamation came on New Year's Day in 1913. A brass band led a parade through the city streets.

"We face the Future," one banner declared. Other banners pronounced, "Labor is Honorable" and "For us, Virtue not Vice." Descendants of the city's enslaved Africans, veterans of the Grand Army of the Republic, schoolchildren, and members of societies and lodges marched past the mayor's reviewing stand at Gallier Hall on Saint Charles.[18] After returning to Elk Place near the Pythian Temple, the crowd sang the national anthem, disbanded, and made their way to a soirée at the Fair Grounds. The ceremonies were a time to reflect on the past while walking into the future. Speaking of the freed slaves, the Reverend Alfred Lawless declared:

> Fifty years ago, which marks his period of existence as a man, he was a thing and instrument. The emancipation proclamation and the constitutional amendments, designed to give complete and permanent force to its provisions, were enabling acts, granting to the freedmen legal rights to enter upon the activities and duties of free men. No legal act could transform the slave into a truly free man, the instrument into a personality prepared to think and act independently. It could only prepare the way for training and development.[19]

Societies and Music

Imagine the breadth of social connections Allen T. Woods gained in compiling the directory. More than three hundred societies and Masonic organizations gathered regularly at twenty-four meeting halls throughout the city. For a dollar per listing, Woods published the meeting times and places of New Orleans' vast network of religious, Masonic, social, charitable, and benevolent societies. He also detailed their monthly meetings and listed the names of the officers.[20]

The Ladies of Equal Justice and the Seventh Ward Educational League engaged in civic undertakings. Morality societies such as the Ladies of Providence, the Ladies of Mercy, and the Ladies of Silence practiced virtue. Some of the societies that appeared in the directory, such as the Francs Amis and the Jeunes Amis, traced their roots to the French-Creole influences in New Orleans and provided health and burial benefits. Labor clubs such as the Longshoremen Protective Union attended to the needs related to specific occupations.

Music filled the streets, concert halls, living rooms, and watering holes

of Allen Woods' New Orleans. The Excelsior Brass Band and Orchestra, led by George Moret, listed its location as 1804 Saint Anthony Street in New Marigny. Joe Clement managed the Louisiana Orchestra, while J. P. Robichaux led the Robichaux Orchestra and Brass Band. Concert pianist Margaret Maurice taught at 1419 Burdette Street. Joseph Montegut tuned pianos. J. M. Jones was a special representative of the Davis Piano Company and sold them at 131 Dauphine. The Tulane Music Publishing Co., operated by George Jeanmarie, P. W. Beaulieu, and Roma J. Raymond, offered to set customers' lyrics to music.

The Nickerson School of Music, at 120 North Galvez Street, advertised full vocal and instrumental instruction at affordable rates. During World War I, W. J. Nickerson wrote a song called "The Colored Soldier Boys of Uncle Sam", which included these lyrics: "There'll be no stop till we're over the top. We're the colored boys of Uncle Sam!"[21]

News, Photography, Healthcare, and Burial

> Every colored business and professional person should be listed in the 1914 Directory, the charge for listing is only 25 cents. See that your Society is listed in it. Advertisers desiring to reach the entire colored population of New Orleans can find no better medium than the directory. No fake or otherwise objectionable advertising will be accepted. . . . To those who may not receive a copy we desire to state that the directory may be found at practically every Colored business place in New Orleans.
>
> Allen T. Woods, 1913[22]

The directory listed the *Daily Spokesman* as a local newspaper that published from the Pythian Temple. Although only a few years old at the time, the NAACP's *Crisis* magazine circulated in New Orleans. Resident agent F. P. Ricard advertised in the *Woods Directory* that the organization advocated "Manhood and self-assertion among Colored Americans; Freedom, Justice, and Human Brotherhood; [and] acts as a mirror for the Negro to see his progress."

The *Southwestern Christian Advocate* expressed pride in its forty-two years of publishing in New Orleans. One of the city's premier photographers, Arthur P. Bedou, offered sepia-tinted photographic enlargements. Henry W. Smith, at 336 Bourbon Street, artistically framed pictures and repaired cameras.

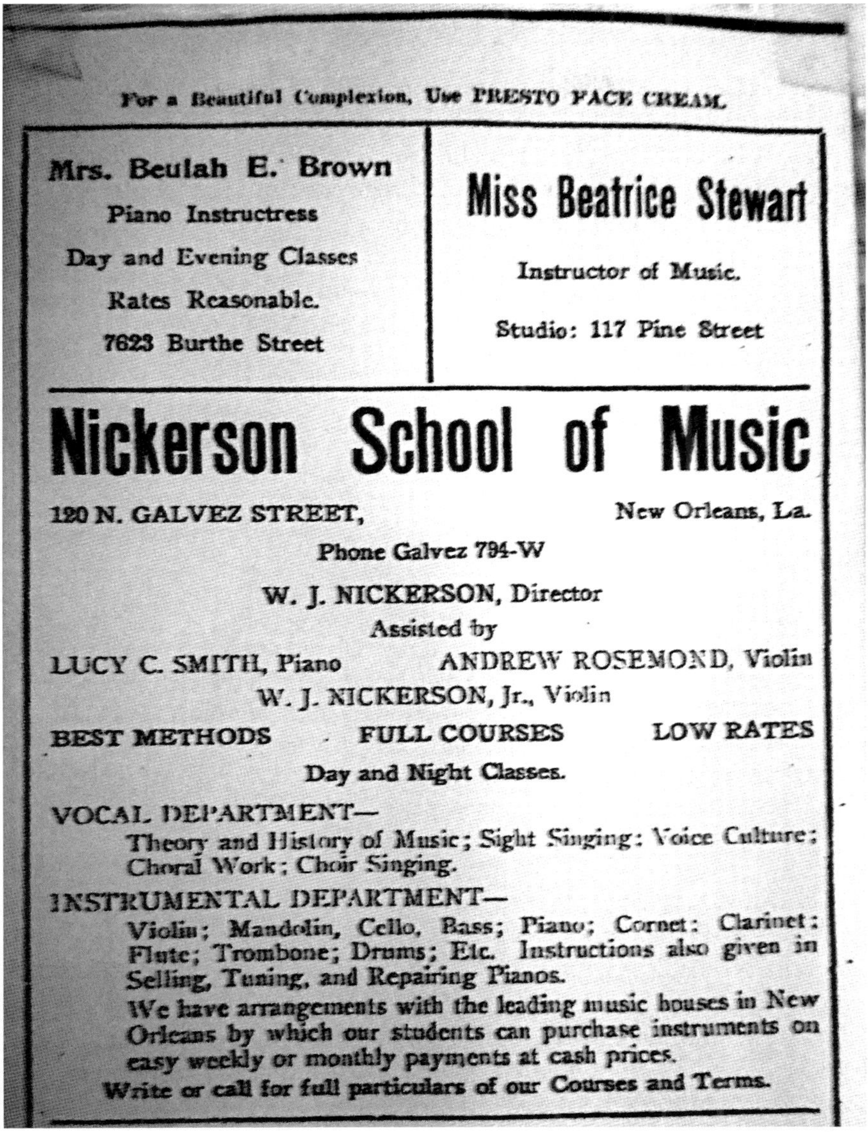

Dentists, pharmacists, doctors, nurses, and midwives represented the healthcare professions in the directory. Dr. Rivers Frederick operated his medical practice from Baumann's Drugstore uptown and Labranche's Drugstore on North Claiborne. Dennis J. S. Carter promised first-class

Boyer & Taylor Co., Ltd.

Funeral Directors,

Shippers and Embalmers.

Thos. A. Carr, Pres.

Raoul L. Llopis, Sec'ty & Treas.

A chartered corporation with a reputation for honesty and fair-dealing since its organization more than 30 years ago.

Note Carefully—It matters not what undertaker comes to your house to report to you the death of a relative or dear one who has died at the Charity Hospital or any other place, you are not compelled to give that undertaker the funeral. Just say, "I thank you, but I shall make my own arrangements."

Then ring up Boyer & Taylor Co., Ltd., the obliging Undertakers and Embalmers, Hemlock 46, or call at the office, 1309 St. Philip Street. No order too large or too small for us. No hour too late or too early. No weather too bad.

All orders promptly attended to.

Boyer & Taylor Company, Ltd.

FUNERAL DIRECTORS, SHIPPERS AND EMBALMERS.

1309 St. Philip St., New Orleans
Office Phone, Hemlock 46
Residence Phone, Uptown 307

Mrs. Ella P. Taylor, Vice-Prest.

Chas. Medley, Manager

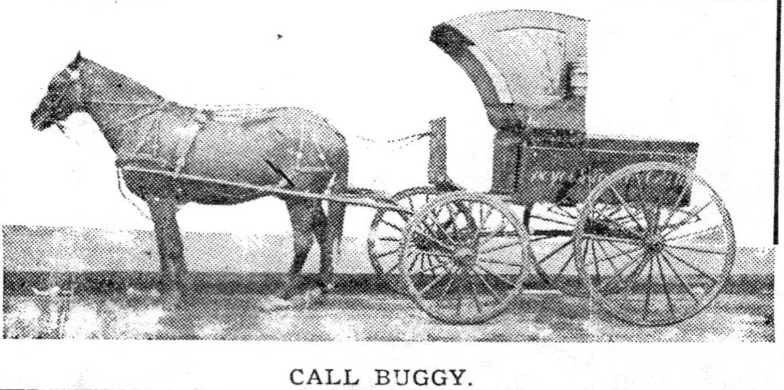

CALL BUGGY.

dental work. Imperial Dental Parlor offered painless extractions for fifty cents and a set of dentures for as low as six dollars.

The city's funeral businesses bought full-page advertisements that featured their mule-drawn death buggies. George Geddes pledged in his, "If you come to me when you have money, I will know you when you haven't money." He also touted the availability of his carriages for balls, parties, and theater outings. The ads by Clem Geddes and Arnold Moss declared, "We Prepare and Ship Bodies to All Parts of the Country. No Order Too Large, None Too Small."

Boyer and Taylor Company's advertisement indicated competitiveness among the undertaking concerns:

> It matters not what undertaker comes to your house to report to you the death of a relative or dear one who has died at the Charity Hospital or any other place, you are not compelled to give that undertaker the funeral. Just say, "I thank you, but I shall make my own arrangements."
>
> Then ring up Boyer & Taylor Co. , Ltd., the obliging Undertakers and Embalmers, Hemlock 46, or call at the office, 1309 St. Phillip Street. No order too large or too small for us. No hour too late or too early. No weather too bad. All orders promptly attended to.

In the 1914 edition of the *Woods Directory*, Allen T. Woods predicted that the 1915 edition would be better than ever, but for unclear reasons, it would never appear. He moved to New York, where he lived until his death on June 11, 1926. Still, Woods' efforts in New Orleans provided a snapshot of African-American entrepreneurship in the early twentieth century. His directory was a gift twice given, as we in the twenty-first century become inspired by the accomplishments of a people who dared to dream.

Chapter 5

1900s: Growing Up Satchmo

Louis Armstrong personified the spirit and genius of the street culture of New Orleans. In a 1950 edition of *Downbeat* magazine, Dave Garroway called him "an ordinary-sized man who takes a piece of metal weighing a couple of pounds and just by blowing air through it makes a sound that has influenced just about everybody who listens to or plays music today."[1]

During his lifetime, Armstrong defied all odds to bring New Orleans jazz to a worldwide audience. In his journey to West Africa in 1956, the city's most famous son came face to face with his ancestral homeland, the seeds of his music, and the possibilities of social and political progress.

His final resting place in Flushing Cemetery in Queens, New York, sits a long way from the hardscrabble neighborhoods of his youth. A cement bench facing the headstones of Louis and his wife, Lucille, offers a contemplative space. In this quiet, well-tended cemetery, one can ponder this child of a New Orleans neighborhood known as Black Storyville, setting the world on fire with music created and honed in the streets of old New Orleans. Louis Armstrong's life paralleled the twentieth century, with all of its prejudice and promise. Through it all, he maintained a deep and abiding love of New Orleans in a Louisiana that did not always love him back.

Born to Willie and Mary Ann Albert Armstrong, Louis Daniel Armstrong arrived in 1900. His mother's family lived in Boutte, Louisiana, a small town in Saint Charles Parish upriver from New Orleans. He called his mother Mayann. According to Louis, her family descended from former slaves who only knew poverty. His father worked at a New Orleans turpentine factory. Louis spent his first years on Jane Alley, in the area occupied a century later by the city's municipal court complex. After his parents separated, his mother moved into a house closer to the river. Louis remained on Jane Alley with his grandmother, Josephine Albert. It was

The Louis Armstrong statue in Armstrong Park

there, amid his grandmother's church congregation, that Louis developed a love of singing and music. When his parents briefly reconciled, Louis's mother gave birth to a daughter, Beatrice, whom the family called "Mama Lucy."

As a young boy, Louis went to live with his ill mother on Perdido near South Franklin Street. At age five, he took his first streetcar ride. It would be his first taste of the "Jim Crow" social order as well. When he walked to the front of the streetcar, the woman accompanying him dragged him to the back and indicated the For Colored Passengers Only signs. "What do those signs say?" Louis asked. "Don't ask so many questions!" she responded. "Shut your mouth, you little fool."[2]

On to Liberty

"As we got off the car," he wrote, "I looked straight down Liberty Street. Crowds of people were moving up and down as far as my eyes could see."[3] The four-block Black Storyville served as the poor man's version of the famed Storyville red-light district.[4] Black Storyville did not offer the glitz, glamour, and top-shelf champagne of its more renowned neighbor across Canal Street. The environs of the area roughly included Tulane, Gravier, Perdido, North and South Poydras, and Lafayette, which paralleled Canal Street. The cross streets from the river toward the lake were Dryades, South Rampart, Saratoga, South Franklin, South Liberty, Howard, and Freret.

In 1910, Louis lived at 1303 Perdido Street, near the corner of South Franklin (across the street from present-day City Hall). The apartment building where he lived housed six other families, with Louis as the only young boy. He and his mother shared the apartment with Thomas Lee, listed in the 1910 United States census as head of household and

companion to Louis's mother. Lee worked as a laborer on a schooner.[5]

On the periphery of the New Orleans Central Business District, Black Storyville stood within walking distance of the French Quarter and Central City. Alecia Long wrote of Storyville proper and Black Storyville: "Although both sections were heavily populated by brothels and other vice establishments, significant numbers of working-class families, black, white, and recent immigrants, continued to live in and on the margins of these two areas. There is substantial evidence that only the area below Canal Street was considered Storyville proper, but there's also no question that the area above Canal Street also functioned as a prostitution district frequented and inhabited by people of all races, classes, and colors."[6]

Inside Black Storyville

Despite the poverty of the neighborhood, the census painted a workaday picture of its residents. Mayann Armstrong and nine other local women labored as laundresses. Calvin Morris was employed at the Sewer Works, while Mose Smith made his money on a steamboat. Other neighbors worked the coal yards, sugar plants, sawmills, and blacksmith shops.[7]

Black Storyville contained a number of institutions that offered educational, social, musical, and religious sustenance. Louis wrote appreciatively of the Fisk Colored School on South Franklin, at the corner of Perdido directly across the street from where he lived, for teaching him to read and write. He and his mother attended the nearby Mount Zion Baptist Church. His block on Perdido housed the United Sons of Honor Hall, established February 12, 1868, to assist the sick, bury the dead, and "attend to the distressed widows and succor the orphans of its members."[8] This hall later became the site of the legendary Funky Butt, where Buddy Bolden played. The neighborhood pulled in two directions. While characterized as a slum, many positive influences existed. In Louis's rough-and-tumble childhood, pastimes included playing street games such as coon-can and craps. He grew up around characters nicknamed Cocaine Buddy, Sister Pop, One-eyed Bud, Black Benny, Nicodemus, and Steel Armed Johnny. Louis roamed nearby South Rampart Street, a high-energy entertainment strip that hosted the early jazz musicians.

For many of the people in the neighborhood, securing food during hard times required creativity and hustle. Restaurants in the area fed Louis's fascination with culinary New Orleans. He loved his mother's red beans and rice and relished the "poor boy" sandwiches sold on Liberty Street. He shared an anecdote of running away from home to work in the sugarcane fields, but on the way, he recalled the smell of the spaghetti and meatballs that had been cooking that morning and returned home before his mother even knew he was gone! He also talked about one of his "step daddies," as he called them, bringing home treats from the Desoto Hotel.[9]

Louis spent his days barefoot, as shoes were a luxury. New clothes consisted of men's pants rolled up over his knees to simulate knickerbockers. Without fifty cents or a dollar to pay a doctor, his mother went to the swamps to collect pepper grass, which she boiled and applied to scrapes and wounds. To keep them healthy, Mayann administered a "physic" as a laxative to oust germs. This could be Pluto water (a laxative) or pepper grass, which was high in fiber. During one illness, instead of signing his letters with his traditional "red beans and ricely yours," Louis signed them, "Am Pluto Waterly Yours."[10]

Louis reflected the work ethic of his neighborhood. He delivered coal to Mahogany Hall and other Basin Street Storyville haunts. Through his pre-adult years, he worked as a dishwasher at Canal and Rampart and whitewashed fences in the Irish Channel. He unloaded banana boats and earned money on the side singing with a street quartet for tips on South Rampart Street. He also sold the *New Orleans Item* newspaper.[11]

Louis was surrounded by a musical culture and honored rituals that persist a century later. His neighborhood's brick and cobblestone streets reverberated with the rambunctious sounds of brass bands and social-aid and pleasure clubs. Louis marched with Tammany's Social and Pleasure Club as well as the Bulls, Hobgoblins, and Zulu Club. The costumed Million Dollar Baby Dolls sported for cash, and the Mardi Gras Indians settled scores on what they called the "Battlefield." Even though he had strained relations with his father, Louis relished seeing him march as grand marshal of the Odd Fellows Parade.

Louis Armstrong could have been a character in the Ray Charles song "Born to Lose." Men rotated in and out of his life and some of them physically abused his mother. Although his working-class neighborhood attracted unsavory characters, he found salvation in the musical culture around him. He watched Buddy Bolden's band at the Eagle Saloon and listened in as Bunk Johnson played at the Funky Butt and Joe Oliver jazzed Pete Lala's Cabaret.

A City of Parades

Armstrong went to the jazz funerals and society parades as far back as he could remember. Black parading in New Orleans has a rich history. In the 1800s, city engineer Benjamin Henry Latrobe observed what he considered the peculiar funeral processions of black New Orleans. Though he made his comments in 1820, they depicted how entrenched the death and burial traditions are in the city:

> The parade of funerals is still a thing which is peculiar to New Orleans alone, among all the American cities. I have twice met, accidentally, a funeral. They were both of colored people; for the coffin was carried by Men of that race, and none but negroes and Quadroons followed it. First marched a Man in a military uniform with a drawn Sword. Then came three boys in [surplices], with pointed caps, two carrying staves with [candelabra] in the form of urns on the top and the third in the Center a large Silver Cross. . . .
>
> At some distance further came the coffin. It was carried by four well

A second-line parade

> dressed black men, and to it were attached 6 White ribbands about 2 Yards in length the ends of which were held by 6 colored Girls very well dressed in white, with long veils. A crowd of colored people followed confusedly, filling the street across, many of whom carried Candles lighted. I stood upon a step till the whole had passed, and counted 69 candles.[12]

In the 1900s, music and second-line parades had been appended to funeral processions. Louis Armstrong stated, "Once the band starts, everybody starts swaying from one side of the street to the other, especially those who drop in and follow the ones who have been to the funeral. These people are known as the 'the second-line' and they may be anyone passing along the street who wants to hear the music."[13]

1913: Louis at Twelve

On January 1, 1913, New Orleans celebrated the fiftieth anniversary of the Emancipation Proclamation. For the black community, it served as a time to rejoice in freedom from slavery and take stock of America's progress. A committee met for months to organize the events. The brass bands, lodges, and other parading entities geared up for the festivities, but on the appointed day, young Louis sat in jail awaiting transport to the Colored Waif's Home, near City Park. The night before, on New Year's Eve, he had taken one of his step-daddy's guns and joined in celebratory shooting of guns and other fireworks. He was arrested at the corner of South Rampart and Gravier, four blocks from home.[14]

Louis's first appearance in a New Orleans newspaper was not for his musical abilities:

> Very few arrests of minors were made Tuesday, and the bookings in the Juvenile Court were not more than the average. Six white boys were arrested in Canal Street for disturbing the peace, and one for being drunk. The most serious case was that of Louis Armstrong, a twelve-year-old negro, who discharged a revolver at Rampart and Perdido streets. Being an old offender he was sent to the negro Waif's Home. The other boys were paroled.[15]

Music in His Soul

Though he missed the grand emancipation parade, Louis's stay at the

Colored Waif's Home brought him stability and discipline. Capt. Joseph Jones and his wife, Manuela, had raised money to convert the House of Refuge at 301 City Park Avenue into a home for 25 boys. The couple worked without pay, living on income from a printing business. By 1913, it became the Colored Waif's Home, with 200 boys. Joseph Jones stated in a 1950s interview, "In those days, there were a great many homeless youngsters in the city, children from broken homes, some who had never known their parents. Some of them were supposed to be 'bad,' but it seemed to me that they were just kids who never had a chance."[16]

Louis's first trumpet came as a gift from Joseph Jones. "I gave Louis his first lesson in how to blow the trumpet," Jones said. "I wasn't any outstanding musician myself, but I knew enough to teach him. And the boy had such fine lungs and so much talent he could have learned from anybody."[17] Jones saw the potential in Louis and allowed him a chance to grow into it. "When Louis came to the home, I could tell that he had music in his soul, so I taught him how to play my old bugle," Jones stated. "We used to blow police whistles to signal the boys to go to meals and work and classes. But I figured they'd had enough of police whistles. I thought it would be nice for them to do everything to bugle calls like in the Army. That's the way Louis Armstrong became our first bugler."[18]

Initially resistant to the Waif's Home, Louis wrote that he went without eating for a few days, but on day four, he arrived first at the supper table. He wondered why his music teacher, Peter Davis, did not like him. Davis stated later that shooting guns in the air "was the custom then, except that Louis was only 12 years old at the time and he didn't have a permit for the gun."[19] Davis finally allowed him into the band—but not as a horn player. For his first song with the Colored Waif's Home Band, Louis played "At the Animals' Ball" on the tambourine.[20] After learning to play the drum, bugle, and cornet, he became bandleader. Even though he had been in a nickel-and-dime singing quartet, the Waif's Home gave structure to his music. He obtained the nickname "Satchel Mouth" because of his wide grin. Davis recalled Armstrong as a boy who "used to walk funny with his feet pointing out and at the first note of music he'd break into comedy dances."[21] The next year the Colored Waif's Home Band paraded through Black Storyville and the Third Ward neighborhood that had nurtured Louis. Residents cheered him and filled the band members' hats with money to buy new uniforms and instruments for the coming year.

For Louis and many others before and after him, the streets and traditions of New Orleans provided a cultural safety net. Even though political and social reality often lined up against working-class kids like Louis, the city's culture provided self-esteem and purpose beyond what prevailed in mainstream society. During the week, one could be a shoeshine boy or bricklayer. On Sundays, shoeshine boys and bricklayers became grand marshals, Big Chiefs, and beloved musicians. In many ways, this reflected the olden days of Congo Square, where enslaved Africans gathered on Sundays to play their drums and honor their traditions. These cultural practices still exist today in the traditions of the brass bands, social-aid and pleasure clubs, and Mardi Gras Indians. These traditions offered the children of New Orleans a sense of purpose and hope.

1931: A Visit Home

As Louis traveled, he brought New Orleans' street sounds with him. After becoming nationally famous in the 1920s, he returned home in 1931 to an enthusiastic welcome. The newspapers covered his arrival. The *New Orleans Morning Tribune* reported that Louis Armstrong, who "[has] driven 'em crazy in New York, Chicago and Hollywood, is back in town with his band to play at a local night club."[22]

The *Louisiana Weekly* stated that Armstrong's visit created a sensation as thousands battled for a glimpse of their "homeboy," the world's greatest cornetist:

> It was one July morning back in 1922 that a young man packed a cornet, along with the rest of his belongings into a trunk and joined the exodus to the north, where he believed he would receive the full credit due him for his unusual skill with his musical instrument. In leaving New Orleans, the city in which he had spent his entire life, he left countless friends upon whom he could rely if the occasion should arise. Leaving it for a place of which he knew little and which knew less of him.
>
> Friday night, nine years later, Louis Armstrong returned to the town of his youth. But long before Friday New Orleans and its half million people knew he was coming. News, like wildfire, had raced around the town that Armstrong, "the World's Greatest Cornetist," was going to pay a four weeks' visit and on his arrival thousands of people, old friends and adoring admirers, were at the depot to welcome him.

> Few renowned persons have received the ovation that was tendered the nationally acclaimed musician. Five bands of music, the train of automobiles and the milling thousands of enthusiastic worshippers held up traffic on Canal Street, the busiest street in New Orleans for more than 30 minutes. . . . Everybody was there to see Louis Armstrong, the local boy whose striking, original expultation [*sic*] of jazz electrified the country. . . .
>
> The parade disbanded at the Astoria Hotel, where Armstrong and his party of ten were feted.[23]

1949: King of the Zulu Parade

In 1947, on a special trip to New Orleans, Armstrong announced that he would fulfill his lifelong ambition to be king of the Zulu parade. At the crack of dawn on Fat Tuesday of 1949, Louis Daniel Armstrong, king of the Zulus, arrived on a barge at Carrollton Avenue by the New Basin Canal to lead his parade of six floats through the Mardi Gras revelry.

Louis ruled in traditional blackface with white circles around his eyes while clad in a red velvet tunic and golden crown. He waved his scepter over his screaming subjects throughout Mardi Gras Day. As the sun set on Carnival 1949, his float collapsed at the corner of North Prieur Street and Orleans Avenue, leaving its contents prey to souvenir seekers.[24] In a 1952 writing, Armstrong reflected on that Mardi Gras Day when he was King Zulu: "You can tell everybody that Ole Satchmo . . . wouldn't miss this fine opportunity to write and let you all know how thrilled I was to be the King of the Zulus . . . and I'd gladly [live it] over again, if I had the chance."[25]

The barefoot boy from Jane Alley became the world's most renowned jazz performer. He met with kings, queens and presidents. John Lester, who presided over the National Jazz Foundation, described Louis's musicianship as "all heart . . . he gets notes out of the trumpet that just aren't there."[26] Louis described his nagging genius:

> You get an idea in your mind that bothers you. It makes you curse all the time to yourself. Nights you wake up cursing with it. But you got to get that idea on the horn. That's the doing of it. . . . I'm just the kinky-haired boy selling the papers. I don't know how this all happened, and I made so much money.[27]

Joseph Jones retired in 1951 after forty-three years of working with the youth of Milne Boys Home (formerly the Colored Waif's Home). The people of Milne described Jones as "probably the greatest Negro leader New Orleans ever had."[28] He still had the cornet Louis Armstrong first blew. "I keep it, as an example to other Negro boys to show them that someone who started in the slums of New Orleans has become one of the world's greatest musical artists."[29]

Louis in Accra

> We are indeed extremely happy to be visited by such an eminent character as Satchmo; and on this occasion we hope that he and his band and Mrs. Armstrong will do their level best to remember for the rest of their lives what they have seen today in the Gold Coast. We felt that it would have been wrong to have allowed them to come here to merely play and then go away without taking anything back with them.
>
> We are taking advantage of this occasion to extend a handshake to them; a cultural handshake to the United States of America; to the colored people there whom we look upon as our own. We look to them because we feel that deep down in their own hearts they must realize that they came from this part of the world.[30]

One of the pivotal moments in the life of Louis Armstrong was his visit to Ghana during the African Liberation movements in the 1950s. Those were tense but momentous times in the Gold Coast, as the Civil Rights Movement in America was coalescing. Less than a week before Louis arrived, Prime Minister Kwame Nkrumah, considered the father of African independence, announced that the legislative groundwork had been laid to form the Sovereign State of Ghana. On the day he arrived, Dr. Nkrumah called for a national referendum on independence and proposed to change the region's name from the Gold Coast to Ghana, after an ancient kingdom.[31] Ghana came to independence amidst a maelstrom of colonial-era geopolitics and a Cold War atmosphere as Louis flew into Accra, the capital city. And as the trip was hastily arranged, no one could predict the reception that would follow.

Louis's plane touched down at 10:00 a.m. on May 23, 1956, in 100-degree heat, with the people of Accra singing "All for You." Here, Louis would come face to face with his ancestral and cultural ties to the African continent. In his fifty-four-hour whirlwind sojourn through the Gold Coast, the street kid from New Orleans walked through a land and culture as old as the soul of the music he played. For Louis, the visit was an epiphany. He came to realize that his ancestors came from here and he had African blood in him.

Armstrong's visit included a concert at the Old Polo Grounds in Accra and lunch with Nkrumah. He met with the prime minister in his cabinet room. How did it feel for Louis, a son of segregated New Orleans, to converse with a man slated to be the father of Pan-Africanism and the leader of a free, powerful African nation? That evening at the Opera Cinema Theater, Louis played a concert for Nkrumah. One thousand tickets were distributed for the performance, and the guests witnessed their first jazz concert. Despite the enormity of the moment, Louis was

THOUSANDS CHEER LOUIS ON ARRIVAL

THE crowd (above) roared with joy when they saw Louis step out from the plane. "You are welcome", they shouted as the great trumpeter waved a white handkerchief at them. Right — Louis Armstrong making a short speech to the crowd. On the left stands Trummy Young his trombonist.

'All for you' greets him

Ghana's Daily Graphic chronicled Armstrong's visit.

Louis. "We'd like to lay this next one on the prime minister," Louis stated in the colloquial New Orleans style he used with queens, prime ministers, or people on the street. Nkrumah had attended school at Lincoln University in Pennsylvania and was familiar with Armstrong. Armstrong's selection of "Black and Blue" pondered race and exclusion:

> How would it end?
> Ain't got a friend.
> My only sin is in my skin.
> What did I do to be so black and blue?

On May 24, Armstrong visited the Accra Government Boys Middle School and handed out instruments, just as he did on his stops at Milne Boys Home on his trips to New Orleans. He also arranged for a trumpet to be donated to the school.

That afternoon, Louis's band traveled to the Achimota School, where 200 elders, chiefs, musicians, and dancers from nine of the Gold Coast's

Armstrong and Prime Minister Kwame Nkrumah appeared on the front page of the Daily Graphic

tribal regions greeted him with their traditional music. In this place, Louis came face to face with the music and rhythms that left West Africa centuries ago to take root in New Orleans. He sensed the commonality as he watched the tribal dancers and drummers perform. The chiefs were resplendent in robes with decorated umbrellas. Dancers from the Northern Territories wore hats studded with rectangular mirrors that dazzled as they moved.

This scene in 1956 was similar to the African rituals witnessed in New Orleans' Congo Square in the early 1800s. "This is the most colorful reception we've ever had anywhere," Louis said. "It sure makes me proud to think my forefathers came from this great continent." On May 25, at four in the afternoon, his entourage boarded the plane for home. The Raker's Dance Band of Accra struck up "All for You" in honor of Louis, as

In 2007, fifty years after Ghanaian independence, I went to Accra to retrace Louis's footsteps on his groundbreaking trip. I was able to locate the Old Polo Grounds where he held his concert (which is now the Kwame Nkrumah Memorial Mausoleum and Park, shown here), the opera theater where he performed for Nkrumah, and the school where the tribal elders drummed to greet him.

Educating Ghanaian children at the Kwame Nkrumah Mausoleum in Accra, Ghana

Chapel at the Achimota School in Accra, Ghana

Statues of Ghanaian musicians

A *Ghanaian lady*

My guide in Ghana, Mr. Kwaku Passain

he walked along a picket fence shaking hands and waving at the Africans of the Gold Coast who came to see him off. He wrote to the "folks" of Accra, "Here's saying so long for now, but since I saw one of the women dancing in one of the tribes yesterday who looked just like my mother Mary Ann, who died in 1927, I'll just have to return to my homeland to blow for the cats at least once a year—yeah, Love Louis Satchmo Armstrong."

"Before coming to Africa," Louis noted before he boarded the plane, "I never knew the folks down here would like that music the way we would play it way down yonder in New Orleans." Moses Danquah wrote in the *Daily Graphic*, "Satchmo is indeed the quintessence of all the yearnings for a better, brighter tomorrow of a people ruthlessly uprooted from their native soil in Africa and transplanted in the cotton fields of America and the sugar-cane plantations of the West Indies."[32]

Chapter 6

1928: Educators for a New Society

From a yellowing page in the 1928 McDonogh #35 yearbook, the eyes of twenty-six young women looked earnestly toward the future. Throughout the 1900s, the women who appeared in that photograph emerged as educators, community leaders, and voices of hope and promise. They were the first graduates of the McDonogh #35 teacher-training Normal School, and their many efforts on behalf of the city's knowledge-hungry youth proved remarkable. Equally compelling was the sisterhood they maintained through busy lives and long careers of community service. Beginning in 1930, the members of the Class of 1928 held annual reunions to preserve the bond forged by their pioneering efforts in educating the city's youth. In 1994, I attended one of these events at Dooky Chase Restaurant, on Orleans Avenue in Faubourg Treme. Despite the springtime challenge of a fierce New Orleans thunderstorm, Selina Butler Tinson and seven former classmates arrived. With jazz music playing in the background, the women supped on Leah Chase's gumbo, stuffed bell peppers, and fish. They still looked toward the future. But on that rainy night in New Orleans, their eyes glistened with the satisfaction, wisdom, and joy gained from imparting the ABCs of life to generations of the city's children.

Only One Public High School for Black Students

McDonogh #35 opened in 1917 and was the only black public high school in New Orleans until 1942. In the wake of the 1896 *Plessy v. Ferguson* Supreme Court decision, the establishment of any black public school required a major effort by community leaders and their allies. In 1900, the school board halted all public education for black children after fifth grade, "to fit him and her for that sphere of labor and social position and occupation to which they are best suited and seem ordained by the proper fitness of things."[1] Finally, in 1913, the board established a seventh grade for black students. Four years later, after a great deal of prodding, the board agreed to transform a formerly white elementary school into the first black high school within the segregated public school system. Eighty-two students enrolled at McDonogh #35 in the fall of 1917. In 1924, to serve the growing number of black students in New Orleans, a two-year Normal School program was added to its four-year college-preparatory curriculum. As its mission, the Normal School sought to prepare promising students for a lifetime of service through teaching. School administrators selected the best students according to their grade averages.

Principal Lucien Victor Alexis

Lucien Victor Alexis, thirty-one, became the second principal at McDonogh #35 in 1926, the same year that Selina Butler (Tinson) and her classmates began their teacher training. Born in 1887, by 1900 Alexis lived with twelve relatives in the New Orleans Seventh Ward at 1143 Columbus Street.[2] Scholarly and ambitious, he graduated cum laude from Harvard in 1918. During World War I, he became a member of the Seventeenth Provisional Training Regiment, commissioned as first lieutenant in the United States Army and assigned to Camp Upton in New York.[3] He saw combat in France and later served as the ranking black officer in the South.[4] While stateside, Alexis compiled data for the Chicago Commission on Race Relations and involved himself with the War Camp Community Service, a group that supported soldiers and their families. At McDonogh #35, he wrote at least six treatises that explored magnetic fields, relativity, and gravity. Alexis was described as a "stern, military-minded principal" who went into the neighborhoods and marched recalcitrant truants back to school.[5]

"We Learned How to Be Citizens"

Alexis's youthful vigor induced a surge in student activities. Under his administration, students witnessed the beginning of the *Hi Smile*, the school's first newspaper, which billed itself as "The Very Newsy Paper."[6]

Principal Lucien Alexis as he appeared in the 1928 yearbook

THE RONEAGLE

Fair Thirty-five

Fair Thirty-five, ever fair—even fairer!
Brave Thirty-five, ever brave—even braver!
Thirty-five, ever high!
Thirty-five, ever high!
High Thirty-five! Ever high—even higher!

1928

A 1928 yearbook photograph of McDonogh #35 High and Normal School

THE BOYS IN THE GLEE CLUB

Victor Augustine
Joseph Ball
Ferdinand Bechet
Herman Bush
Alexander Brumfield
Percy Golson
Alexander Gordon
Edward Goodman
James Haulsey
Julius Haulsey
Reuben Hughes
Willie Landry
Joseph Lewis
Robert McKinney
Oscar Robertson
Elwood Scott
Joseph Smith
George Stevens
Charles Span
Varry Turner
James William
Frederick Washington
Charles Young

Music

THE GLEE CLUB

BY MERCEDES BARRE

The Glee Club was organized in order that the boys from a tender age might begin to understand and to appreciate high class singing. Mr. O. Blanchet, who has marked talent for training voices for solo and chorus work, has spared no effort in preparing vocally the members of the Glee Club. The boys—tenors, baritones, and bases—number twenty-three. They have a varied repertoire of Jubilee, popular, and classic songs; and they are always ready when called upon to grace a program with appropriate music, whether the event is observed under the auspices of Thirty-five or some other local institution. Wherever they have appeared, they have added new glory to the good name of Thirty-five.

The boys in the 1928 Glee Club

The senior Normal class of 1928 on its yearbook page

The Senior Normal Room (Miss O. M. Baranco, teacher), which was awarded second prize in the Room Cleanliness Contest

1928

The senior Normal class of 1928

Elocution and debating contests; glee clubs; dramatics; football, baseball, and basketball teams; and a fifteen-piece orchestra produced a well-rounded atmosphere. Normal School seniors Jeanne Bagneris, Dorothy Gardner, Beatrice Jefferson, and Hazel Owens lent their voices to the choral club. The twenty-eight member football team lost the only two games it played that season to Xavier High and McKinley of Baton Rouge. Still, the senior Normal girls hosted an entertainment event in honor of the athletes.[7]

"Lucien Alexis was a dynamic principal," Annabel Nash Egana recalled in 1994.[8] She appreciated her time at the school where "students were well disciplined and friendly, the teachers were good, and everybody was interested in school and learning." Mrs. Egana observed, "We learned how to be citizens."[9] Her classmate, Lucille Mouton Hunter, remembered McDonogh #35 as one of the most positive influences in her life.

Alexis selected Annabel Nash and several other senior Normal classmates for his Office Force. A picture in the 1928 yearbook depicted the humble school office, with its candlestick telephone with a then-modern dial, an inkbottle, simple desks and chairs, a checkerboard-tiled floor, and a potbelly stove with a coffeepot on top. The Office Force

STUDENTS ON THE OFFICE FORCE

Dorothy Gardner
Dilcy Garrett
Gladys Johnson
Naomi Johnson
Josephine Lavizzo
Frances Lawless
Louise Metoyer
Annabel Nash
Ernestine Richardson
George Stevens
Myrtle Watts

The Office Force

BY MIRIAM CARTER

The Office Force is one of the many signs of progress at McDonogh Thirty-five. Several girls and boys of the school have grasped the opportunity to learn office work. Our principal, who is very capable and experienced in this line, offers the best of training to those who desire to do their part by working in the office. They are especially proud of the bouquets that have been coming their way lately, but it is acknowledged by the members of the Office Force that part of the praise must be given to the principal for his most encouraging suggestions and advice. Mr. Alexis, in turn, is very much pleased with the good service that has been rendered by the force. It is said to be very efficient.

Industry, affability, and accuracy are the chief qualities that must be possessed by an individual in order that he may become a part of the Office Force. It might be said that every one of the workers of the present group truly possesses these qualities. This is the opinion of nearly all who come in contact with them. Although they are envied by other students not as fortunate as they, neverthless all are proud of the Office Force. The members are exact, courteous, and industrious in performing their various duties.

The principal duties are answering the telephone, communicating important messages to the teachers, compiling statistics, and meeting visitors in the principal's absence. By taking the work seriously, the members of the force are learning rapidly the principles involved in office work. Such a training will prove most valuable to them in the near future if they choose to make use of it when they leave school life to enter life's school.

The Office Force

learned firsthand the process of school administration, as they answered the telephone, greeted visitors, and compiled statistics. "I very much enjoyed coming into contact with all the teachers and learning from them," Mrs. Egana recollected.[10]

Yearning to Learn

The establishment of McDonogh #35 addressed the yearning for more and better educational opportunities among Americans of African descent. As grandchildren of the slavery era, the Class of 1928 retained their forbearers' deep and abiding appreciation for the value of education. Before the Civil War, blacks faced scant educational opportunities particularly in the slaveholding states in the South. Many states outlawed slave instruction, fearing that formal knowledge fostered interest in insurrection. Still, some slaveowners taught blacks to read and write. Famed abolitionist Frederick Douglass acquired literacy under the tutelage of his owner's wife. In other instances, primarily in the North, religious orders such as the Puritans, Quakers, and Presbyterians established instructional institutions for free blacks as a means of propagating Christianity and promoting abolition. In 1865, the *New Orleans Black Republican* newspaper wrote, "Freedom and school books and newspapers go hand in hand. Let us secure the freedom we have received by the intelligence that can maintain it."[11]

The Normal School students had already graduated from the regular high school. As teaching students, they took courses in primary methods, school management, and general methods in reading. The Normal School senior students provided leadership and set standards of conduct for younger students. Senior Normal students Myrtle Watts, Ernestine Richardson, and Mercedes Mayfield headed the Girls' Decorum Club. Other students organized a cleanliness brigade to promote courtesy and neatness. When disciplinary violations did occur, detention consisted of carrying an armload of books on numerous walks around the school. In student pictures, boys wore coats and ties. Girls sat modestly with knees touching and ankles crossed.

In the Heart of South Rampart Street

Located along the South Rampart Street commercial and entertainment district, McDonogh #35 was a three-story structure with tall, arched windows, palm trees in the side yard, a high iron fence that wrapped around the property, and an American flag that flapped in the air. The school housed a library, physics and chemistry laboratories, sewing room, and cooking room. The seventeen-person faculty taught college-preparatory classes in Latin, psychology, and algebra along with practical applications such as gardening and domestic science. Historian Charles Barthelemy Rousseve, author of *The Negro in Louisiana*, taught English and economics. George Longe taught geometry, school management, and methods in arithmetic. Male and female students typeset and printed the *Hi Smile* newspaper in the school's print shop under the supervision of faculty member Vance Henry.

Miles for Education

Students walked miles for their education. The girls in the 1928 Normal School class came from the city's older neighborhoods. Annabel Nash lived on Dumaine Street near North Galvez in the Sixth Ward, while Elvina Armstrong trekked from Pauger Street in the Seventh Ward. Uptown residents Selina Butler and Lucille Mouton hiked to #35 from Danneel near Louisiana Avenue. Selina Butler Tinson recalled that parents provided carfare to catch a streetcar, but only to be used if it rained. Walking in neighborhood groups along South Rampart Street, the girls passed the commercial strip's shoe stores, tailors, jewelry shops, candy shops, drugstores, piano vendors, and the black-owned Unity Industrial Insurance Company. Across the street from the school, the aroma of fried fish and oyster sandwiches wafted from the stoves of Woods Famous Creole Kitchen.

The New Orleans Herald

One block away from McDonogh #35 on South Rampart Street stood the offices of the *New Orleans Herald* newspaper. This publication provided information in a city that largely ignored the contributions and concerns of its black citizenry. In September of 1925, the *Herald* set up shop in Room 103 of the Pythian Temple building. For a yearly two-dollar subscription, it gave the community the opportunity to read positive portrayals of their families, teachers, and citizens. An article in the premier issue highlighted McDonogh #35 teacher Alberta V. Dunn's appointment as principal of the McCarty School, in the Lower Ninth Ward.[12] Of equal importance, the black-owned *Herald* continued the spirit of activist newspapers during Reconstruction and beyond. For those interested in the daily lives of black citizens in Louisiana, it often provided the sole source of information.

Published by Constant C. Dejoie, Sr., the paper stood as an education watchdog for the black community. It criticized the school board for not promptly filling vacancies in the black schools and exposed inequality in educational opportunities. A headline in the newspaper's second issue stated: "Negro Schools Not to Receive New Books for New Course."[13] Another article examined the platoon system at black schools, under the headline "Public Schools Crowded Above Their Capacity."[14] The paper further reported that children in one neighborhood were "forced to walk as many as twenty and thirty blocks to attend public schools and over streets void of sidewalks and very muddy."[15]

Despite these challenges, the *New Orleans Herald* brought positive news about black Americans to New Orleans and the students of McDonogh #35. It covered the cultural doings of the Negro Literary Renaissance, which became the Harlem Renaissance. The *Herald* celebrated the poetry, dance, art, and literature of Jessie Fauset, Walter White, Jean Toomer, Countee Cullen, and Langston Hughes. Reports on concerts by contralto Marian Anderson and the Victor Talking Machine Company recording of Paul Robeson singing Negro spirituals shone a light on the unique musical offerings of black America.[16] After the first two issues, the paper was renamed the *Louisiana Weekly*.

The Legend of the Roneagle

With growing exposure to the world outside of New Orleans, McDonogh #35 opened imaginations and encouraged student expression. Former Normal School student Dorothy Gardner Clark remembered Principal Alexis promoting the written and spoken word with surprise visits to classrooms for impromptu student readings. He also encouraged students to look to their "Roneagle" mascot as a source of strength. Myrtle Watts scribed in a mythical writing style in the 1928 yearbook, "As the centuries, one after another, glide by, revelations more and more marvelous are brought to the ken of men. Perhaps the most extraordinary discovery of modern times is that of the Roneagle."[17] According to student-developed legends in yearbooks from 1928 to 1932, a Roneagle was a winged entity whose body was composed entirely of iron. His bitter foe was the dragon Ignoramis, who held the uneducated citizens captive in a dank swamp called the Vale of Gloom. It was the Roneagle's mission to slay Ignoramis, rescue the hostages, and lead them over mountains and valleys to a city of achievement and bliss.[18]

Myrtle Watts represented the senior Normal class on the staff of the *Roneagle* yearbook as the first assistant editor. She later married the yearbook's business manager, George Stevens. The *Roneagle*'s advertising section showcased the activities in 1920s New Orleans. Popular local photographer Willard Paddio promoted his studio at 1428 Dumaine Street. Classic New Orleans advertisers included Dejan's Orchestra, Kirschman's Department Store, Werlein's Music, Xavier University, the Orpheum Theater, the Bunch Club, and Labranche's Drugstore.[19] The Normal School's senior-class writings in the *Roneagle* exuded healthy doses of self-esteem. Mercedes Mayfield, Ernestine Richardson, and Myrtle Watts wrote in 1928, "Our prestige in the school was undeniable. Even the Junior Normal Class looked up to us with awe and admiration, as we, in our undaunted spirit of perseverance, soared far above the heights, athletically as well as intellectually."[20]

No Time for "Devilment"

At the end of the school day, senior Normal School students sometimes stopped at Woolworth's Five & Dime on Canal Street for bags of "brokers." These were cookie and cake pieces that the store bagged and sold for a nickel. Dorothy Gardner Clark also remembered spending time sitting along the train tracks that paralleled the Basin Canal near Lafitte Street. Train workers sent greetings by tossing complimentary samples of produce from the lumbering freight trains.[21]

McDonogh #35 hosted Monday-evening entertainment events with music by A. J. Piron's orchestra for twenty-five cents' admission. Selina Butler Tinson remembered the waltz, slow drag, and two-step as being the popular dances. "No jazz," she emphasized, which back then many considered lowdown music.[22]

A strong work ethic dominated the lives of the twenty-six Normal School students. Many came from modest backgrounds. Chores and jobs left little room for "devilment," Mrs. Tinson explained. Some worked during their lunch periods selling cakes, soft drinks, and milk in the school cafeteria, with a meal and soft drink as their only pay. "We helped our parents," Dorothy Gardner Clark recalled. "I worked in a house, taking care of a child and washing diapers for eighty-five cents a week." Pounding bricks into a gritty abrasive used for scrubbing the city's wooden porches also helped pay the bills. "Seventy-five cents a bucket," Dorothy asserted. "I would take the money, buy two and a half yards of material at ten cents a yard, and my sister would make the dresses that we wore to school." The students transcended the naysayers. Dorothy remembered the cynicism of the sister of her employer. "'She's going to school?' the sister would say. 'She'll never be anything.'" Dorothy proved her wrong by becoming a teacher.[23]

"Not Without Aim Do We Depart"

They needed that perseverance, resourcefulness, and work ethic as the real world inched closer with each passing spring day. Their last semester at McDonogh #35 brought eight weeks of practice teaching at Joseph A. Craig School, along with writing lesson plans and observation reports and assuming other duties of an Orleans Parish schoolteacher. For their school flower, the senior Normal class selected a white carnation and asparagus fern. Their class motto declared, "Not Without Aim Do We Depart."[24] In their near future, the Great Depression loomed.

Barely out of their teenage years, the Normal School's Class of 1928 became frontline soldiers in the cause to uplift young minds. They joined the vanguard of what W. E. B. Du Bois described as the "talented tenth." Black enrollment in high school increased six fold between 1918 and 1928, from 143 to 902.[25] The *Louisiana Weekly* described 1928 as one of the best years in New Orleans public-school history: "McDonogh 35 High and Normal leads the city in point of numbers, 110 graduating from the high school and 26 from the normal, making a total of 136. In the high school there are 24 boys and 86 girls finishing, while the normal is unique in that the entire class of 26 is made up of girls."[26]

"We Had Tough Days"

As the Roaring Twenties sobered into the depression years of the 1930s, families faced long periods without paychecks. "How well do I remember," Mrs. Tinson stated. "My daddy was out of a job and I got appointed in 1929. I stepped right in his shoes."[27] There were times spent cooking on furnaces with no stove or electricity. "We had tough days," Dorothy Gardner Clark declared, "but I think we beat them ten to one." She said the sense of family and community at her job made it easier. "The parents were so interested in what their children were doing. There were very few parents who didn't come see about their children."[28]

Two years after graduation, former choral-club member Hazel Owens Miller extracted a pledge from her classmates to meet each year for remembrance and renewal. Her yearbook entry described her as the "last word in everything."[29] She was credited by her classmates with keeping the fire alive.

As the years turned into decades, many of the icons of their youth faded into history. In 1932, the Normal School teaching students moved to Valena C. Jones Elementary School. Eventually, a four-year degree became mandatory to teach. Hurricane Betsy laid waste to the high-school building on South Rampart in 1965. Mrs. Tinson stated, "Despite all of the hardships, I consider those years and those times the best years of my life."[30]

Chapter 7
1929: Fannie C. Williams—a Pioneer in Public Education

> The building of character, the development of ideals, the conscientious effort in promoting the general welfare of the community, is the task of the teacher.
>
> Mercedes Greene Davis[1]

As one of New Orleans' premier educators, Fannie C. Williams steered Valena C. Jones Elementary School through decades of challenge and change. Her civic leadership brought her national recognition and appointments to three presidential commissions. Prominent guests who visited the school included First Lady Eleanor Roosevelt, Harlem Renaissance writer James Weldon Johnson, renowned educator Mary McLeod Bethune, National Association for the Advancement of Colored People leader W. E. B. Du Bois, Tuskegee scientist George Washington Carver, and Carter G. Woodson, who organized black history week in 1926. Olympic gold medalist Jesse Owens visited, as did writer and lecturer Dale Carnegie.

Fannie C. Williams brought primary education to the children of New Orleans. With dogged perseverance, she and a neighborhood group called the Seventh Ward Civic League and the Seventh Ward Educational League spent over two decades lobbying the school board for a decent modern facility. In the Jim Crow era in New Orleans, school-board members and white supremacists were openly hostile to any black educational pursuits. In 1900, the school board adopted a policy of disallowing primary education for black children past the fifth grade.

Born to Educate

Fannie Cornelia Williams was born in Biloxi on March 23, 1882. Her mother was a Methodist Episcopal missionary. During her teens, Miss Williams journeyed to New Orleans and graduated with honors from the College Preparatory and Normal departments of Straight College, on Canal Street. From 1904 to 1908, she taught along the Mississippi Gulf Coast. She returned to New Orleans, where she taught at the Fisk Colored School, across the street from Louis Armstrong's residence in Black Storyville. After teaching in Albion, Michigan, for three years, she returned to New Orleans in 1921, where she became principal at Valena C. Jones Elementary School.

Miss Williams was a "handsome, dark-skinned woman with pressed white hair," recalled Valena C. Jones alumnus and United Nations ambassador Andrew Young. "[She] believed in strict discipline and patrolled the halls of the three-story structure observing classes and saw for herself that everything was in order. Miss Williams went about the task of uplifting the race with great gusto and an almost legendary determination, pacing the halls with her thick ruler ever at the ready."[2]

The Seventh Ward Civic League

Fannie C. Williams' career as a New Orleans educator intersected with ongoing efforts by the Seventh Ward Civic League. This activist group pressed their demands for a quality neighborhood. Their leader was the Reverend Alfred Lawless, founder of the Beecher Memorial Congregational Church and a principal of the Fisk Colored School. In 1905, the League's quest accelerated as supporters organized picnics, fish fries, dances, and raffles to fund the acquisition of six lots for a school. In the meantime, the school board leased a two-story Seventh Ward tenement that had the ominous nickname "Bucket of Blood" because of its bright-red color and reputation for vice and violence.[3] That building was destroyed by a hurricane in 1915. The school board then constructed a one-story, twelve-room building referred to as the "cow stable" because of its linear shape. Despite its modest facilities, the cow stable provided elementary education for neighborhood children. In 1918 the school became known as Valena C. Jones Elementary School. Valena Cecilia McArthur Jones was a native of Bay Saint Louis, Mississippi. After educating children in rural Mississippi, she eventually came to New Orleans, where she was a popular educator. She passed away in 1917 at age forty-four.

After taking time to earn a degree in pedagogy at the Michigan State Normal School, Fannie C. Williams became principal of Valena C. Jones Elementary School in 1921. She held that position for thirty-three years.

A 1930 photograph of the Seventh Ward Civic League pictured Civil Rights attorneys, medical doctors, a chaplain, and Walter L. Cohen, the comptroller of customs under Pres. Warren G. Harding.[4] The officers included legal advisor A. P. Tureaud, Dr. Joseph A. Hardin, the Reverend Joseph Martin, A. J. Chapital, and George McKenna, Sr. Throughout the 1920s, Fannie C. Williams and the Seventh Ward Civic League had lobbied the Orleans Parish School Board for a larger and better equipped building. As the black student population soared, in 1928 they achieved their goal. The school board agreed to finance construction of a building at the corner of Annette and North Miro streets, on the site of the original six lots purchased by the League.[5]

A School Is Born

The school would be located in the heart of the New Orleans Seventh Ward community. The area was primarily residential, with shotgun houses being the predominant housing type. The Beecher Memorial Congregational Church, Church of God in Christ, and Second Mount Olive Baptist Church stood nearby. Even before the new Valena C. Jones School opened in the fall of 1929, the Seventh Ward Civic League raised money to present it with book donations and a $500 gift for its library. At its dedication ceremonies, over two thousand people listened as Dr. Joseph Hardin, and Fannie C. Williams recounted the school's history and spoke optimistically about its future. The *Louisiana Weekly* reported on the uplifting occasion:

> More than two thousand persons witnessed the dedication of the New Valena C. Jones School Tuesday night where they were able to participate in the opening of one of the best equipped school buildings in the country.
>
> From a lowly tenement house, in which the old Miro school was opened some 20 years ago, to the new Valena C. Jones public school which is the supreme achievement . . .
>
> Superintendent of Public Schools Bauer, in his introductory remarks, pointed out the wide difference in the condition of educational facilities for Negros of the city 10 years ago and at the present time. Ten years ago Mr.

The Louisiana Weekly

VOL. V. Price, 5c — NEW ORLEANS, LA., NOVEMBER 2, 1929

DEDICATE THE NEW VALENA C. JONES SCHOOL

MASS MEETING HELD TO RAISE BIG LEGAL FUND

To Fight State Registration Law —Chief Justice Sees Possible Victory

PATRONAGE BAN NOT ON BLACKS ALONE

PORTERS WILL WAGE FIGHT ON PULLMAN PLAN

Randolph Plans Fight To End To Force Pullman Company's Hand

"Y's" FRIEND

MISS ANGENETTA THOMPSON, a junior of New Orleans University, has just returned from Oklahoma City, Oklahoma, after spending a week there with the Regional Y. W. C. A. Conference.

TO CELEBRATE THREE YEARS OF SERVICE

Community Center Sponsored by the Sterns To Have Birthday

WOMAN SHOOTS ASSAILANT

THRONGS SEE MODERN BLDG. IN LOWER CITY

New Building Is Culmination of Long Fight by Several Civic Organizations

To Look After Town's Colored Boys and Girls

Justice Asked at the Hands of Augusta Police

RELATIVES LOSE FIGHT FOR FORTUNE

Storekeeper's Cash Will Be Used To Aid Those Who Are Needy

TWO DEAD FROM GUN SHOT WOUNDS

Work Begun on World's Largest Pumping Station

PARADE COMMITTEE HOLDS ENTHUSIASTIC MEETING

AGED MAN COMMITS SUICIDE

SLASHES THROAT OF WOMAN IN QUARREL

Port of Orleans

> Bauer said, there were 9100 pupils, now there are 21,900 enrolled. Then, the teaching staff numbered 174, now 386; the cost of operating the schools then was $256,000, now it is $670,000.
>
> Twenty years ago the Seventh Ward Educational League was organized with Rev. Alfred Lawless as the leader. E. H. Phillips related the early struggles of the league, and told of the purchase of six lots for a school site, which marked the league's first great success and, of the deeding of the same six lots to the School Board this spring, as part of the site of the present building.[6]

Miss Williams described the school's novel features, such as a radio in the auditorium, an electric refrigerator, and gas ovens for the domestic science department. Jones School had a cafeteria, kitchen, and three stories of spacious classrooms. Miss Williams expressed hope that its state-of-the-art infirmary would curtail the spread of infectious disease in the school community. At the end of the dedication ceremonies, a book containing the names of all the guests was placed in a bank vault, to be opened on the school's silver anniversary. Three weeks later, a proud Valena C. Jones Elementary School community hosted its first parent-teacher banquet in the new building. According to the *Louisiana Weekly*:

> The Parent-Teacher Association of Valena C. Jones School observed Education Week by holding its first annual banquet in the beautiful new building on Tuesday night, November 19. One hundred seventy-five guests sat down to the feast prepared by Miss Philomene Humphrey, Mrs. Lena Richards, cateress, and the girls of the Domestic Science classes. . . . Just before the guests were seated, the Rev. Milton Williams of Beecher Church gave the invocation. . . .
>
> Mr. [Wilfred] Collins as chairman of the library committee gave a very interesting report of the committee's work and announced that 551.00 had been raised. Following the report donations of 10.00 each were received from the Hon. Walter L. Cohen and the People's Insurance Company.[7]

A Neighborhood to Nurture, a Community that Cared

The *American Missionary* magazine wrote about the Jones School: "Rising above the muddy streets and modest dwellings of this section of the city, it is a conspicuous landmark as well as a well-equipped seat of learning. Rarely, if ever, have Negro children been provided with better physical facilities."[8]

The new school became the site of Miss Williams' innovative educational programs. She initiated nursery and kindergarten classes, the first in New Orleans' black schools. Health fairs spotlighted the value of cleanliness and nutritious diets. Dentists examined the children's teeth and taught dental hygiene. She helped establish the city's first black Girl Scout troop, Jones Troop 99. She focused on education as a community matter. When disciplinary problems occurred, Miss Williams often sent for the parents. She formed study groups aimed at improving the parents' reading and math skills. Teachers attended after-hours study groups to learn the latest methodology. Her vibrant Parent-Teacher Association raised money to implement many of her programs.

Miss Williams spent summers traveling and teaching at colleges such as Tuskegee Institute, West Virginia Institute, Alcorn A&M, and Southern University. Popular on the lecture circuit, she conducted workshops at educational institutions across the country. In 1930, Pres. Herbert Hoover appointed her to the Conference on Child Health and Protection. She also sat on a housing conference board during Pres. Franklin D. Roosevelt's administration. Selina Butler Tinson, a retired teacher who studied and taught at Jones, remembered Miss Williams as someone who was well informed and got things done: "When she traveled, she always came back with new ideas in education to present to her faculty. She always kept current. She also relied on her PTA. Even when the school board did not give enough money for supplies, Jones always had what they needed because of the strong PTA."[9]

Many parents considered Jones the most desirable public black elementary school in New Orleans. People from outside its district sought special permits for their children to attend. Fannie Williams gave city children a view of the world beyond their neighborhoods, with field trips to Audubon Park, the Gulf Coast, Baton Rouge, and Tuskegee, Alabama. She also brought the world to Jones. Mrs. Tinson recalled, "People she impressed in her travels would come to Jones to visit her school when they were in the city. She would let the children know they were meeting someone special."[10]

The Valena C. Jones Normal School

Fannie Williams's influence over education in the city expanded a great deal in 1932. That year, the city's Normal School for Colored Teachers moved from McDonogh #35 to Valena C. Jones Elementary School. The Valena C. Jones Normal School provided the two-year certification program required to teach in Louisiana during those times and drew students from Xavier Prep, Saint Mary's Academy, Straight High School, and Gilbert Academy. In 1932, there were ninety-one students in the Normal School and nearly two thousand in the seven elementary grades. Generations of educators learned their skills under Fannie Williams. The Normal School students also provided valuable examples to the elementary students as they interacted with their older classmates.

The Valena C. Jones Normal School students were an expressive and literary lot. They published a booklet titled *The Moving Finger* that fleshed out the world of Valena C. Jones. The 1937 edition contained articles on character building, curriculum revision, and practice teaching in addition to the senior-class prophecies and "last will and testaments." The journal also reported events such as the school's puppet shows, Black History Week activities, and a visit by motivator Dale Carnegie. It contained pictures of the faculty, classes, and clubs. There were photos of Elvera Stewart, who became Miss Valena C. Jones of 1937. Book reviews of *Gone with the Wind* and W. E. B. Du Bois's *Black Reconstruction* also appeared in its pages. The editor in chief was Clyde G. Jones and associate editors were Marguerite Malarcher and Joseph McKelpin.[11] McKelpin became a plaintiff in the case that equalized teacher pay between blacks and whites in Orleans Parish.

In the Normal School, poetry was in the air. Lily Anne Lasalle wrote a poem titled "Dawn":

> The calm,
> Sweet peace that flows
> Into the soul at morn
> Is just the smile of daylight's birth
> At dawn[12]

In 1937, Jones had a fifty-member faculty and 2,700 students. By 1938, Miss Williams had received her master's degree from the University of Michigan at Ann Arbor. Many of her former students made their marks at educational centers across the country.

The Valena C. Jones Normal School was discontinued in 1939 when the state required a four-year degree for teachers. During the forties, Miss

The Jones School faculty, 1930s

Williams continued her extensive involvement in a wide range of civic activities. She spent a great deal of time working with the Claiborne YWCA and was the first African-American to serve on its board of directors. She also sat on the boards of the Red Cross, Flint-Goodridge Hospital, and Family Service Society. A trustee of Dillard University, she had a dormitory named for her in 1946: "Fannie C. Williams, educator, lover of children, builder of character, who by quality of her personality, breadth of mind, and height of ideals, inspired thousands of New Orleans youth to useful lives and achievements, this building dedicated in her honor."[13]

On November 9, 1950, as part of American Education Week, there was a public testimonial in Miss Williams's honor in the Booker T. Washington High School auditorium. Her address was entitled "Opportunity for All." Also in 1950, Pres. Harry Truman appointed her to the Mid-Century Conference.

Fannie Williams retired from Valena C. Jones in 1954. She remained active, tutoring slow learners and traveling. Many of her former students and faculty went on to excel as principals and deans and in other occupations. An active member of the Central Congregational Church, on Bienville Street, she died in 1980 at the age of ninety-eight. Her papers, along with those of teacher Lucille Hutton, are housed at Tulane University's Amistad Research Center.

Chapter 8
1940s: Wright Speaks!

As founder of the People's Defense League, Ernest John Wright became one of New Orleans' preeminent black leaders during the 1940s. With the Central City neighborhood as his base, he organized voter-registration drives, advocated for the rights of working people, and inspired many with speeches, writings, and fearless activism. Established in August 1941, the People's Defense League initiated the strategies and objectives that the Civil Rights Movement of the 1950s and 1960s would utilize. Former member Oliver White told researcher Earl Picard, "The People's Defense League was an organization that I would have said my prayers by."[1] "A voteless people is a hopeless people" became the battle cry of Wright and the People's Defense League as they energized neighborhoods throughout New Orleans with rallies in churches, parks, barbershops, and union halls.[2]

Even before the high tide of his activism, Wright created a special bond with the Central City neighborhood. In 1933, he voiced his optimism for the future:

> Has the depression done anything for the Negro in a constructive way? My answer to this question is an emphatic yes. The common laborer during his free time has been given time to think and see the necessity of Negro controlled activities. Negroes can be seen with push carts, wagons, and old fashioned trucks peddling bread, milk, charcoal, wood, fruits, vegetables, and other commodities that are essential to the life of every human being. Secondly, the Negro is reading and finding out what other groups are doing in regard to industrial education. Recently I visited the Shakespeare Park, which is bounded by La Salle, Third, and Freret Streets, and Washington Avenue, a thickly populated Colored section of the city. I was given a hearty welcome because of my previous visits.[3]

In the 1940s, Ernest Wright emerged as the city's most dynamic and popular Civil Rights figure. He exhorted crowds to action at weekly rallies in Shakespeare Park. As a social worker, he counseled individuals on obtaining goals despite the obstacles of a Jim Crow society. He penned a newspaper column called "I Daresay" in the *Louisiana Weekly*. He documented mistreatment of factory and dockworkers, organized labor unions, and brought intellect and passion to the cause of black progress.

Ernest John Wright was born in New Orleans on July 25, 1909. After graduating from Xavier University Preparatory School in 1929, he earned money working at Freiberg's Clothing Store on Canal Street. His athletic ability in track and field spawned a scholarship to Xavier University, where he received the nickname "Whirlwind Wright."[4] After his father became unemployed during the depression, Xavier University's Sisters of the Blessed Sacrament embraced Wright and helped him complete his education.[5] In 1930, census records placed Wright and brother Earl at 1919 Cleveland Avenue, where they lived with Elizabeth Bennett.[6] Her son Samuel Bennett, Sr., also lived there and drove a taxi. Earl Wright became a sports columnist for the *Louisiana Weekly*. Their neighbors consisted of a candy maker, longshoreman, elevator tender, and seamstress. Wright's family was the only black household on the block.[7]

A Thesis to the Faculty of Xavier University

Wright's college years at Xavier University foretold his future as a labor and political leader. In 1933, he wrote a groundbreaking thesis entitled "Brief Study of Working Conditions of the Colored Citizens in New Orleans, Louisiana," which quantified working and professional classes in black New Orleans during the Great Depression:

> The following report is the result of a study of the Colored worker during the present cataclysm in political and industrial affairs. The present panic has helped the laborer from many angles. It has given him a realization of the value of money and the necessity of sane action in the distribution of it.
>
> The object of making this report is to furnish a thesis to the Faculty of Xavier University and to acquaint the citizens of New Orleans with some authentic information regarding the working conditions of the Colored group. . . .
>
> It is hoped that this information may be used as a starting point in

remedying some of the unemployment difficulties throughout the city, thereby making the worker feel as if he is really earning his wage, and that the government respects his rights as a citizen of this great American Commonwealth. Then, and only then, will the working group cooperate heartily in leading the world to prosperity and happiness.[8]

Wright's thesis examined the "Census of Industry" taken in 1929 by Mr. E. T. Atwell. This study detailed occupations of the black citizenry of New Orleans. It stated that "the largest group of Negroes is found in unskilled and personal service types of labor."[9] The study also noted the burgeoning black professional class, which contained 497 teachers, more than 200 ministers, 60 midwives, 40 doctors, and 23 embalmers. Using this census, Wright reported the black businesses in New Orleans: 18 drugstores, 13 insurance companies, 12 stenographers, 5 automobile concerns, and 8 undertakers.[10]

Sunday Afternoon in Shakespeare Park

After graduating from Xavier University, Wright enrolled in the University of Michigan's master's program before returning to New Orleans. One day, he strolled into Shakespeare Park (now A. L. Davis Park) in Central City. With a bullhorn in hand, he began what became a regular Sunday affair. In the years to come, thousands crowded the park to hear Wright fill the air with electrifying orations. "I just came out into Shakespeare Park, Negroes, 10 or 15 of them, and I just started talking," Wright recalled in an interview with Merle Ramsey. "Then, I'd come out every Sunday afternoon. Then the thing just mushroomed."[11]

A Clear Picture

In early 1939, the *Louisiana Weekly* newspaper initiated the Community Responsibility Program. Ernest Wright became chairman of this program in July. The project aimed to present the city's black population with "a clear picture of the conditions under which they live, also what they might do to improve them."[12] With the closing of the New Deal Works Progress Administration's work-relief program, unemployment rose in a segregated job market. The problems of housing and unemployment endured by blacks in the urban North became exacerbated in the South by massive disenfranchisement. Out of over 430,000 blacks of voting age in Louisiana in 1930, the state contained less than 2,300 black registered voters. In 1940, the voting rolls listed only 886 registered voters out of nearly 475,000 blacks of voting age.[13]

Already a highly respected civic leader, Wright took over the series of forums that served as the cornerstone of the Community Responsibility Program. He became the first black social worker hired by the city of New Orleans and was paid the same as the white caseworkers. He chaired the board of the Sylvanie Williams Community Center, a recreational and social club for uptown youths. Wright also supervised the summer park activities for youths during the 1930s.[14] As the labor movement progressed, he fought for the rights of working people. Zachary Taylor Ramsey described Wright's speaking style as dynamic. "He sermonized with a bit of humor attached to it," Mr. Ramsey told me in 1984. "He was a good speaker with a lot of charisma."[15]

Just shy of thirty, Wright addressed members of the Cotton Compress and Warehouse Union at the Second Baptist Church. He so engaged the crowd at the Congress of Industrial Organizations (C.I.O.) Hall at 2134 Magazine Street that Chairperson Octave Lilly asked him to speak every Tuesday.[16] Wright's talks combined elements of activist philosophies of the times. He possessed the dogged intellect and social outlook of W. E. B. Du Bois. He invoked the "race man" pride of Marcus Garvey along with the pull-yourself-up-by-your-bootstraps teachings of Booker T. Washington. He called for readers of his "I Daresay" column to rise and confront the segregationists' stereotypes of the era. In a 1945 column entitled "Don't Fence Me In," Wright related the tale of a caged elephant who remained in the area even after the fence was removed, and then Wright observed:

> Although the chains of slavery have been moved from our feet; although we have been given the freedom of speech, press, religion, assembly; the right to join labor unions of our choosing; yes, fighting and dying for the preservation of the democratic way of life, many of us are fenced in our minds. Too many of us are mesmerized by the propaganda of the reactionary forces of this country. Too many of us are afraid to launch out into the deep.[17]

Wright's experience in social work contributed to the success of his forums. The *Louisiana Weekly* reported sharp increases in attendance at the forums after he assumed control. Every week in churches, community centers, and labor halls throughout the city, hundreds turned out as Wright spoke on the need to obtain the ballot, reviewed the latest local and national developments, and answered their many questions.

Insurance Strike of 1940

A bitter strike by black insurance workers in New Orleans in 1940 laid the foundation for the rise of the People's Defense League. Author David W. Friedrichs called the group "the oldest Negro voters league in the city and the 'daddy' of all significant post World War II Negro voters leagues to follow."[18] The insurance strike pitted New Orleans' traditional black financial establishments against their agents, who sought more pay and better working conditions. When talks proved futile, the agents contacted Wright, who organized a branch of the United Office and Professional Workers in the C.I.O. It would be one of the first white-collar unions in the South. The owners of the four companies, led by Dr. Rivers Fredericks, stated flatly that they would never negotiate with the C.I.O. The agents struck.

The owners employed sound trucks, leaflets, and newspapers to discredit the strikers, Wright, and the C.I.O. For their part, the agents appeared on Wright's Sunday platform in Shakespeare Park to explain their position. Insurance agent Daniel Byrd produced a copy of a longstanding agreement among the four companies to keep salaries low. Byrd told the rally, "The companies found it necessary to organize, as they put it, for self-protection. How much more necessary is it that the agents organize."[19] Willie Dorsey, the C.I.O.'s first black representative in the city, pledged the support of all the regional workers affiliated with his union. Wright and others canvassed the black community to strengthen grassroots support. Ramsey became the first president of Local 101 of the Insurance Guild. The next year Wright and Ramsey were taken to court on various charges stemming from the strike. Although the men expected to receive probation in exchange for a guilty plea, the judge sentenced them to sixty days in Parish Prison after the insurance companies' executives told the judge that the two were connected to Communism.[20] Upon the pair's release, 5,000 people greeted them, with a massive parade and motorcade leading up Canal Street to a victory rally at Shakespeare Park. If the jail sentence was meant to punish Wright for his organizing efforts, he emerged unrepentant, according to the *Louisiana Weekly*'s account of the rally: "Standing behind the star-spangled blue field of an American flag and beside a sign which carried a line, 'Down with Rivers Fredericks and His Gang of Traitors,' Wright charged that he was the victim of persons with money who paid to have him jailed and a 'lying scandal sheet of a newspaper' which called him a goon. He stated that the 60-day jail sentence was in reality an education, and that now he was willing to fight the battle of the people 'until hell freezes over.'"[21]

The People's Defense League

The 1940 insurance strike ushered in a heightened sense of black power in New Orleans. Wright became the promotional director of a new organization named the People's Defense League (PDL), and Ramsey served as its first president. Ramsey spoke to me about those times, the PDL, and Wright's growing influence:

> The People's Defense League had for its main purpose getting people registered and vote conscious. We instituted marches on the registration offices. Some of us were registered, and some of us were not. We were constantly involved in voter registration, political action from the standpoint of voting, and making our voices heard. The People's Defense League was one of the first black organizations of a civic political nature. . . .
>
> We were in Shakespeare Park at the mass meeting. Our mass meeting ended at the same time that the Communist Party mass meeting began and they linked our meeting, of course, with the Communist Party. Of course, during that time, that was the unspoken thing, being connected with the Communist Party. We knew the significance of communism as an ideology. After that, somebody, during the strike, wrote our names, my name and Wright's name and Rufus Slaughter and Daniel Byrd, and sooner or later gave it to the Committee on Un-American Activities. It was a little hard for us to be considered as

> un-American and all that other bulls--- just to kill black movements. . . .
>
> I remember Wright going to Natchitoches to help Willie Dorsey, who was also organizing workers in this locale. They were almost lynched but for the pleadings of a priest who drove them out of town. Trying to organize some workers up there, they were put in jail. [It was because of] the divine help of God and the assistance of this priest that they let him drive them to the parish line and that they weren't lynched. . . .
>
> The people did listen to [Wright]. His attempts were heard around the country. At that time, there was no Civil Rights Movement except for the NAACP, which was fighting a battle on a legal scale, which was slow. There were very few unions at that time and the unions were segregated. His was a daring move without any local, state, or federal protection. He had the intestinal fortitude to speak out publicly and attack the injustices. . . .
>
> He kept up his activity and as long as he was with the Civil Rights Movement, he had tremendous credibility with the blacks. He should have been as great as Martin Luther King except times were rougher then. No federal marshals or anybody. They would go in Mississippi. There were some terrible politicians—outspoken Negro haters.
>
> He was a household word in every black family. Wright was the first to organize mass demonstrations. During that time when you were talking about voter registration and marching on the registrar's office, there was no city, state, or federal protection. On raw guts, we marched down there.[22]

The People's Defense League served as a grassroots umbrella and information clearinghouse for concerned black New Orleanians. Located at 2506 LaSalle Street, in the heart of Central City, the PDL shared a building with the Federal Funeral Home and the Undertaker Lodge #2. The League meshed with the neighborhood's business community. Wright and his colleagues walked the area's wood-planked streets seeking support. He frequently spoke at church gatherings and cultivated alliances with Central City ministers. Around the corner from the People's Defense League offices, the Reverend A. L. Davis preached at New Zion Baptist Church. In September of 1941, the People's Defense League held its second Victory Mass Meeting at Beulah Baptist Church, where labor leaders endorsed its platforms.[23] In December, the League celebrated Bill of Rights Week at Saint Mark's Baptist Church.[24]

The People's Defense League distributed flyers promoting Wright's speaking engagements. Topics included: "The Negro and the Cross," "The

Negro and Jobs," "Should Negroes Buy War Bonds and Stamps?," "Give Me Liberty or Give Me Death," "Should the Negro Vote in Louisiana? Why?" and "Is America Worth Fighting For?"[25] PDL president Ramsey asserted, "Our organization is fighting for the complete emancipation of the Negro people in this city, state and elsewhere."[26]

Wright continued to organize workers. In September 1941, he joined the regional staff of the C.I.O. His task was to interpret its program to the Negro citizenry and promote interracial goodwill among laborers. That year, Wright enlisted 3,000 laundry workers making nine cents an hour into the Amalgamated Clothing Workers Union.

On December 7, 1941, Japan attacked Pearl Harbor and instigated the United States' entry into World War II. During that period, the PDL wholeheartedly supported the defeat of Hitler's armies, while constantly pointing to the unarguable similarities between the rhetoric of the Third Reich and Southern demagoguery. The People's Defense League chaired a drive to raise $50,000 in war bonds and organized Red Cross donation campaigns. Attacks on blacks at home and on the battlefield intensified, leading to riots in Harlem, Detroit, and other Northern locales. According to the *Louisiana Weekly*, New Orleans citizens expressed outrage when policemen abused a black woman as she hugged her son goodbye at the induction center.[27]

Let's Stand in Our Own Shoe Leather

His admirers called him "the People's Champion." The NAACP appointed him promotional director of its membership drive. During the spring of 1942, police arrested Wright for riding in a sound truck through the Calliope-Rampart shopping area, urging citizens to join the NAACP, fight Jim Crow, and shop only where they were given respect.[28] People referred to Shakespeare Park as "Wright's Auditorium," as he continued to speak there forcibly on labor and political issues.[29] Wright accepted the post of general secretary of the Louisiana Association for the Progress of Negro Citizens, a Civil Rights group headed by the Reverend A. L. Davis. In June of 1943, at a mass meeting at the Fourteenth Ward playground, People's Defense League vice president Wilfred Aubert stated, "It is our intention to bring the objectives of the People's Defense League to every nook and corner of this city. We want every man, woman, and child to know his constitutional rights. . . . .The league will go down in history in this period of bloody warfare, as advocates of true democracy in the fullest extent of the word."[30]

Wright elaborated on his views of freedom's responsibilities:

> The big difference between you and me in this fight for rights, is that I am not afraid to die for a principle, and you are. I am not afraid to go to jail for a principle, and you are. What we need is 10,000 unafraid men as members with their money paid who are unafraid to present themselves to vote, or unafraid to present themselves for jobs to which they are entitled. We can't get anywhere by being afraid. Let's stand in our own shoe leather and quit ye like men.[31]

The PDL emerged as the most outspoken critic of police brutality in the city. At the Sunday rallies in Shakespeare Park, Wright and Chairperson Elizabeth Sanders brought victims of police abuse to the podium. For those who did not live to recount their experiences, the League held memorials and solicited money for their families. The PDL conducted a "Memory Day" for Felton Robinson, who was a mental patient with no history of violence. Precinct policemen shot him three times in his home as his wife begged them not to kill her husband.[32]

"I Daresay"

Wright's "I Daresay" columns transmitted his message of empowerment. He used them to urge people to action. One column called "Let's Stop Shadow Boxing" focused on the primacy of the vote:

> I DARESAY that until the schooled element of the Negro population is willing to lead the way by example and precept, the gaining of full and complete rights for the Negro people will be a long and difficult task. . . . It is about time that the Negroes of this state do some constructive planning and action in the political field. To sidetrack political action; to devote a lot of time to improving the health, housing, education and recreation, is only shadow boxing with these vital issues.[33]

In "We Must Vote," Wright declared, "I DARESAY that the Negro people are their worst enemies. Our freedom is in our hands and it is up to us to release it."[34]

In a 1942 column entitled "The Handwriting Is on the Wall," Wright applauded civil disobedience against the Jim Crow Colored Patrons Only displayed on every bus and streetcar in New Orleans:

> The other day a Negro woman about 50 years of age got on the South Claiborne streetcar. The white passengers occupied all of the available seats except the two rear seats that are always reserved for Negroes. Oodles of Negro passengers, having been taught to keep behind the SCREEN, were huddled together in the rear like sardines in a can. The old lady pushed her way through the crowd and stopped in the aisle about three feet in front of a screen that carried an inscription, "For Colored Only." She beckoned to other women to follow her. They did. The actions of this Negro woman puzzled the white passengers, and as seats became vacant they moved from seat to seat in order that Negro passengers might be seated. I DARESAY that the handwriting is on the wall. The Pharaohs of 1942 must let the Negro people go as they cry out for freedom.[35]

Wright's column "The Green Light Means to Go" encouraged people to move forward with the People's Defense League: "On Sunday afternoon at 4 o'clock in the Shakespeare Park under the banner of the PEOPLE'S DEFENSE LEAGUE, the GREEN light will be turned on for the Negro people to move in the direction of exercising their full and complete rights."[36]

When two fourteen-year-old black boys were lynched in Mississippi, Wright wrote, "I DARESAY" that every lynching of Negroes in Mississippi, or any place else, is a serious blow to national unity, at a time when complete unity is badly needed to win this war."[37]

In a Black History Week column of "I Daresay," Wright stressed the importance of documenting and learning the history of black people:

> Throughout America, Negroes are celebrating "Negro History Week," and rightfully so. The purpose of the celebration is to keep before the American Negro the contributions that race members have made in National and International affairs. The history books in most instances that are used in our schools omit the role the Negro people have played in world affairs. And whenever there is a commentary on the Negro, it portrays weaknesses and not strengths. If it were not for Carter G. Woodson and a few others who have dedicated their lives for the study of the life of the Negro, and his contributions to world culture, perhaps there would be very few scientific studies on the history of the Negro people.
>
> In America . . . the Negro is portrayed as a lover of watermelons, chickens and pork chops. Or a frantic user of the razor; or a dyed-in-the-wool dice player. In other words, the inference is that the majority of the members of the Negro race are strictly the Amos and Andy types. . . .
>
> On Sunday afternoon, the People's Defense League is presenting Rev. Charles Taylor as the main speaker on the Negro History program at the Old Baptist Church located on Third and South Franklin Streets at 3:30 o'clock. Music will be furnished by Gilbert Academy.[38]

A Challenge for Rights

Wright developed a national reputation and addressed labor rallies in places such as South Bend, Indiana, and Detroit, Michigan. He helped organize Mobile, Alabama, shipbuilding workers into the C.I.O. and became vice president of the Louisiana C.I.O.'s Political Action Committee.[39] In a 1944 column, he spoke of the success of organized labor in electing Pres. Franklin D. Roosevelt to a fourth term.[40] Wright had become general secretary of the New Orleans Industrial Union Council C.I.O., representing twenty-eight unions and 35,000 workers.[41]

On the national level, the Civil Rights struggle gained momentum as returning black veterans of World War II rejected second-class citizenship. They sought to make the freedom they fought for overseas available to their children and families in the United States. A young black congressman from Harlem named Adam Clayton Powell introduced a federal Civil Rights bill in 1946. He spoke passionately to a PDL gathering in New Orleans' Booker T. Washington High School auditorium:

> Walk together, children! Stand together, Negroes! We are going to get the things we want. We are moving up. The war is over. The fighting has stopped but the peace has yet to be won. The days are critical. The Negro must arise and make a challenge for his rights.[42]

In February of 1946, the People's Defense League moved into a seven-room house at 2437 Second Street and launched a vigorous voter-registration campaign. Wright formed a coalition with the Reverend A. L. Davis, Raymond Tillman of the Transport Union, and former insurance agent Daniel Byrd, who had become the state president of the NAACP. They sought to coordinate their efforts and place 20,000 blacks on the voting rolls by August 10, 1946.[43]

The People's Defense League evolved into an organized force with ward leaders and precinct captains throughout the city. The League set its sight on a goal of 5,000 members, with annual dues of one dollar.[44] The League offered voter-registration classes in bars, restaurants, barbershops, and churches throughout New Orleans. A women's division emerged, headed by Ida Johnson with Edna Marie Wright, Ernest's wife, as secretary.[45]

The *Louisiana Weekly* posted dispatches from the Civil Rights events:

> Tuesday night, the most enthusiastic show of strength came from the People's Defense League, who called a mass meeting of all their registered voters. The League's auditorium at 2437 Second Street was found to be inadequate for the five hundred and ten persons who arrived with registration certificates. The 1st, 2nd, 7th, 9th, 10th, 11th, 12th, 14th, and 16th wards were represented in this group, which all voted to organize themselves as a permanent body of the People's Defense League. . . .
>
> With August 10th, the date for closing the registration books only a few days away, organizations are mustering their forces for a final attempt

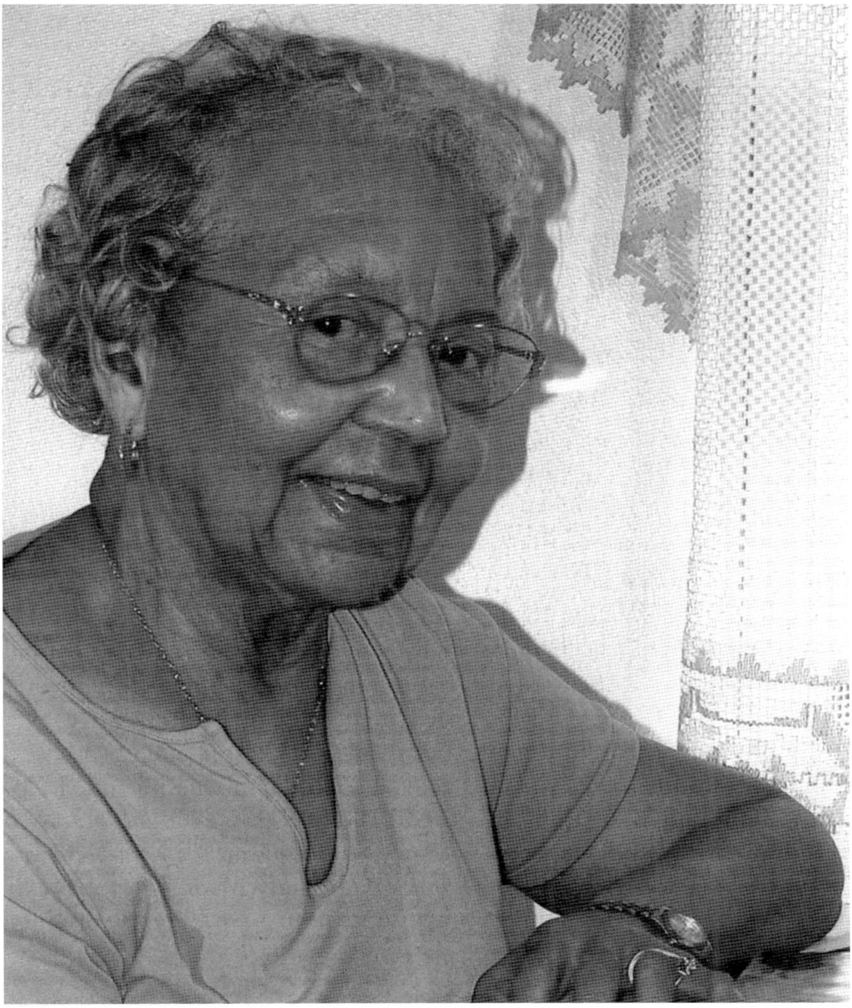

Marie Wright

at the 20,000 voter goal. . . . Walter Augustine, directing the NAACP's Citizens Committee registration campaign, stated at his office, 227 1/2 So. Rampart St., a "hundred percent increase in Negro registration from time of Mayoralty election assured." . . . The committee had 26 schools in operation, which included barber shops, pressing shops, churches and special ward committees. . . .

> Highlights of last campaigning for registration will include sound truck advertising, Friday, Saturday and Sunday and possible radio announcements. The People's Defense League is also organizing a fleet of cars to be made available at different points to take applicants to the registration office.[46]

"Mr. Wright, I Got Nothing but Time"

As the August voter-registration deadline approached, PDL members scoured their neighborhoods in search of potential voters. League president Richard L. Perry summarized the spirit of the times at one of the many voter rallies held in the summer of 1946: "Many barriers have been put in the way of the members of our organization to prohibit them from registering. These barriers are only stepping stones, however, because the Negro people are determined to participate in politics and the devils in hell shall not prevail against them."[47] Displaying this determination, one elderly citizen returned to register daily, telling Wright, "Mr. Wright, I got nothing but time. If they say it [the registration card] is wrong, you will see me tomorrow."[48]

Wright addressed an overflow crowd gathered in the League's auditorium on Second Street. For many, it would be their first ballot:

> From the pulpits to the docks, along the Mississippi River, in the labor union halls, on the street cars, in the corner grocery stores, barrooms and the fraternal halls, the importance of registering to vote in municipal, State, and National elections is spreading like a forest fire. . . . The job of arousing the colored citizens to register and vote in all city and state elections is not completed. There is need for a great deal more education before the majority of eligible voters among us will have accepted this responsibility. But one thing is certain, the New Orleans Negroes are on the march and their political power will continue to manifest itself day after day.[49]

Veteran *Louisiana Weekly* reporter "Scoop" Jones described the final days of the registration campaign:

> Hundreds stood in the heat, on the shady side of the Registrar's office on Lafayette and St. Charles Street Friday afternoon long before the afternoon [two o'clock] opening of the office. Many of these people were still in line

> when 8 p.m. [closing time] came, and were back again the next morning [and final day]. Some of these were lucky to register, while others failed to even get to the registrar's desk.[50]

When the final tally was made public, 4,716 blacks had been accepted, while the registrar's office rejected 6 out of 10 black citizens, claiming they made a mistake on the card.[51] Although their efforts fell short of their goal of 20,000, the PDL became an electoral voice that could no longer be ignored. That year, two candidates for the school board addressed a League meeting and asked for the group's support. A narrow upset victory by a reform candidate over the incumbent mayor displayed the emerging power of the black vote. In November of 1946, citizens organized an Ernest Wright Day and trumpeted his accomplishments. By 1950, the People's Defense League had branches in twenty-six parishes throughout Louisiana. Black registration in New Orleans climbed to 26,000.[52]

Wright established ties with Earl Long's "Old Regular" machine as a means of securing jobs. He hoped to use the alliance to liberalize the voter-registration office so more blacks could be added to the rolls. Wright, then in his midforties and with a growing family, had left the People's Defense League in 1952 to work full time for the Teamsters. The PDL closed its doors in 1954, giving way to a host of other black political organizations aligned with then-mayor deLesseps "Chep" Morrison and the emerging Civil Rights Movement.

In 1957, because of his role in the 1940 insurance strike, Wright became a subject of investigation by the Louisiana Committee on Subversion in Racial Unrest, a legislative body bent on linking the growing Civil Rights Movement with foreign agents and Communism even as that same legislature spent much of its energy suppressing black voting and civil rights.[53]

Race for Lieutenant Governor

In 1960, Wright joined the forefront of a group called Frontiers, Inc., which supported school-integration efforts in New Orleans. In 1963 he ran for lieutenant governor and received nearly forty thousand votes in a campaign based on little more than name recognition. People remembered that it was Wright who pushed back the mountains to plant the seeds of

Ernest J. Wright, Sr., tomb in Saint Roch Cemetery

black political participation. He lived long enough to see New Orleanians elect Ernest Morial as the city's first black mayor in 1979.

Wright had a series of minor strokes beginning in 1976 and had to curtail his many activities. In the early 1980s, his daughter Erness spoke to me of her father and his legacy. Her voice softened as she talked of his final days. "Daddy became saddened after the strokes because his whole life had been one of involvement. People began coming around less and less. After the strokes, he lost some of his reasoning. Quietly sitting home was the most difficult thing in the world for him to do."[54]

Ernest Wright died on the morning of October 25, 1979. His services were subdued. There would be no wake. A short visitation period at Blandin's Funeral Home, on Saint Claude in Treme, was followed by a requiem Mass at Saint Peter Claver Catholic Church. He was buried at Saint Roch Cemetery, in the city's Eighth Ward. The events of that day wrote a quiet closing signature to the life of a man who had spoken so loudly in defense of a voiceless people. Ernest Wright, once called "the indomitable champion of the lowly masses," was laid to his final rest.

Chapter 9

1954: The Life and Times of Lincoln Beach

Located on Lake Pontchartrain in eastern New Orleans, Lincoln Beach emerged as a focal point of recreational life for black people in the city. This backwater area underwent a major renovation in the early 1950s that added amusements, rides, world-class music, and swimming fun. Until it closed in 1964, Lincoln Beach provided the city with a summer-long festival and earned the nickname "the Coney Island of the South." Every week, advertisements beckoned the citizens of hot, humid New Orleans to "Take a Dip Day or Night and Relax in the Cool Summer Breeze on Lake Pontchartrain."[1]

I remembered holiday rides to the renovated beach in my father's Pontiac. We traveled on Elysian Fields Avenue, turned right by Lake Pontchartrain, and proceeded onto a two-lane road with swamps on our right side and fishing camps on our left. To us, the ride was exceedingly long. After walking under a railroad tunnel, we emerged from the midway to swim in the spacious pools. The tilt-a-whirl spun us around. We drove the bumper cars with reckless abandon. An arcade housed a Voice-O-Graph machine that recorded your voice and produced a vinyl record in about a minute. On Fridays, my brother "Big Al" and I reported to the Dryades Street day camp, where Mr. Wynn and Mr. Grady transported us and the other campers on the miles-long excursion to Lincoln Beach.

The Early Years

The lack of a safe and sanitary beach for the city's black youth had been a sore spot for their parents and families for decades. Pontchartrain Beach for whites was built in 1928.[2] The *Louisiana Weekly* pleaded for a safe place to swim and even enlisted the *Times-Picayune* as a partner:

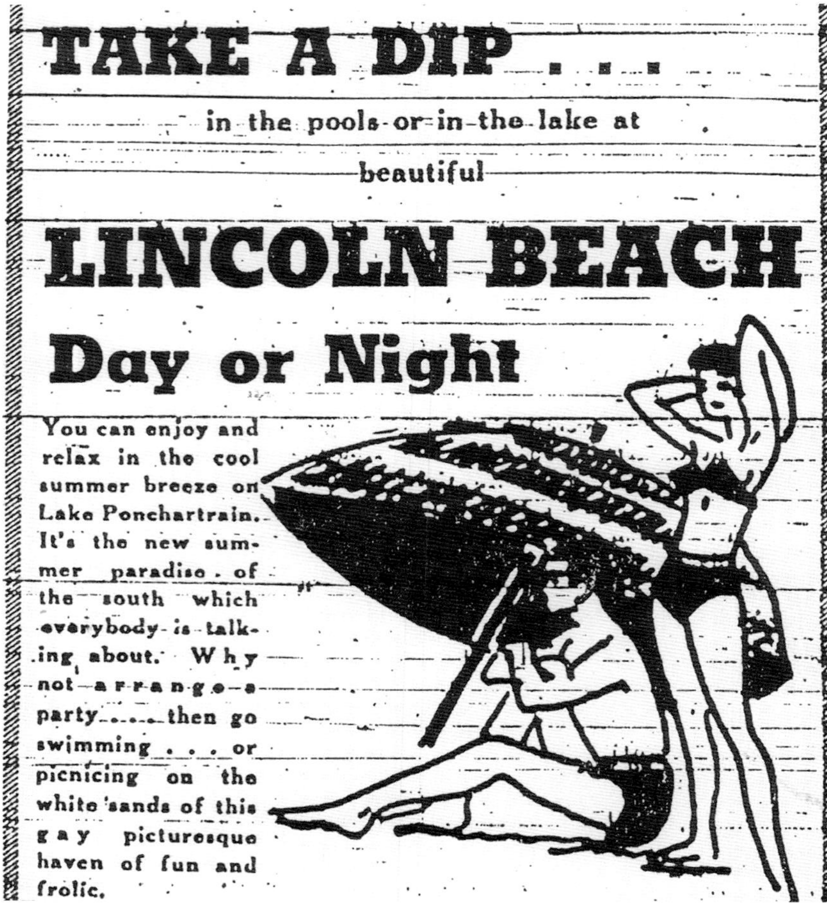

A Louisiana Weekly *ad*

For the past three years we have been waging an almost hopeless battle to secure a site on the lake front for a bathing beach for the Colored citizens of New Orleans. Time after time promises, golden promises were made insuring the Negroes that that they would be cared for. Nothing came from these promises.

Year before last a temporary space was allotted us. Last year we were completely ignored and left to swelter in the semi-tropical atmosphere that we have, while our white brothers sported themselves in the cooling surf of Lake Pontchartrain.

> This year we are proud to note that one white daily—the Times-Picayune—is in accord with us and have put its thoughts into print so that they may go out to the Nordic group. By doing this they are helping us put over a fight for that which is justly ours. Truly our efforts are bearing fruit.[3]

The editor of the *Times-Picayune* supported the cause: "The swimming season again is here and the claim of our Negro citizens to water space for their Race somewhere along the lakefront is still unanswered. There can be no ignoring the right of this demand and the authorities whose duty it is to make the space assignment should not permit another season to go by without action."[4]

Although this plea was made on April 26, 1930, there was minimal progress. The land that became Lincoln Beach typified "Jim Crow" in New Orleans. Acquired by the Orleans Parish Levee Board in 1939, the site's 2.3 acres contrasted sharply with its whites-only counterpart. Pontchartrain Beach provided 50 acres, a $100,000 rollercoaster, and numerous other attractions. The beach for blacks stood twelve miles from the Central Business District, just shy of Rogers Lagoon with spotty public transportation. Sandwiched between fishing camps, the beachfront became victim to erosion. Its polluted water contained raw sewage from nearby camp sites.[5]

The influence of the Civil Rights Movement and successful voter-registration efforts changed things. Black voting strength increased due to United States Supreme Court rulings and renewed activism. In a fluid political climate, the Orleans Parish Levee Board acknowledged the lack of parity between the two areas and awarded a construction contract for expansion and renovation of Lincoln Beach.[6]

Workers equipped barges to transport the sand that extended the beach area 400 feet into Lake Pontchartrain while increasing its width to 1,000 feet.[7] In 1950, the *Times-Picayune* reported:

> The Orleans Levee Board is planning to enlarge Lincoln Beach as a recreation facility for Negroes. The beach is situated between the New Orleans Airport and Little Woods. . . . Negroes have complained of limited swimming space, and Lincoln Beach was considered inadequate. The levee board plans to construct breakwaters to protect the beach and recreation area from erosion. The present beach has been chewed by wave wash."[8]

In 1952, *Dixie Roto Magazine* offered a glimpse into the proposed renovated beach: "With Lincoln Beach serving as the city's major recreational area for Negroes, many felt that facilities were inadequate; they also complain that often the lake was unfit for bathing because of the discharge of waste material from nearby camps. The new pools will furnish suitable swimming facilities at all times, regardless of the conditions of the lake." [9]

As the United States Supreme Court chipped away at unequal facilities, the 1950s bridged a half-century of segregation and a future of equal opportunity. The *Brown v. Board of Education* decision began the dismantling of legal segregation. Lincoln Beach's 1954 dedication occurred within weeks of the Court's ruling against segregated schools. A symbol of separate but equal, Lincoln Beach's grand renovation straddled the realities of changing times in the age of coming equality and integration.

The Dedication Ceremonies

On May 8, 1954, segregated Lincoln Beach was formally dedicated. The invitation-only event caused quite a buzz. Leaders of the black community previewed the million-dollar renovation. They included Dr. Rivers Fredericks, Dillard University president Dr. Albert W. Dent, the *Louisiana Weekly* publisher C. C. Dejoie, People's Defense League representative Richard L. Perry, and attorney Earl J. Amedee. WMRY radio broadcast it live. Ernest Wright, an ally of Levee Board president Louis Roussel, chaired the event. Wright compared the facilities to years past, when water hoses provided the only relief for black children during the summer months. He called the beach "a step forward in the Negroes' fight for first class citizenship."[10]

The dedication ceremonies produced unlikely bedfellows. As a congressman in 1948, Robert F. Kennon led a walkout of the Louisiana delegation from the Democratic National Convention when a favorable Civil Rights measure had been included in the platform. As Louisiana's governor in 1954, he called Lincoln Beach an example of Louisiana's equal treatment of all of its citizens. He promoted it as as a model of how separate can be equal: "When my friend, Louis J. Roussel, . . . said he was going to give the Negroes this grand facility, I was impressed and pleased. . . . It can do much to improve the health of thousands of people, and it will afford a good outlet for the energies of our Negro youth."[11]

Mayor Chep Morrison touted Lincoln Beach as "one of the most modern and well equipped recreational areas for Negroes in the nation."[12] He promised the erection of a trade school for blacks and development of the Pontchartrain Park subdivision. At the ceremonies, Louis Roussel praised the late Capt. Nolan McNeal, a former slave and a champion of black progress. A pool was named in McNeal's honor and a commemorative plaque erected. The ceremonies of the day ended with a swimming and diving exhibition directed by Edward X. Dunn in the newly dedicated McNeal pool. The Booker T. Washington High School band furnished the music.[13]

Fun and Frolic

The Levee Board delayed the grand opening for nearly three weeks because of problems in the water-purification system.[14] Finally, on May 28, 1954, at nine o'clock in the morning, beach manager Walter Wright flung open the gates. Eleven-year-old Paul Vincent Castille of Saint Monica's School purchased the first ticket and led a throng of thousands onto the midway promenade.[15] Lincoln Beach could now move from being a focus of politics to a focus of fun.

The renovated Lincoln Beach held something for everyone. In place of the solitary building of old, the new beach contained a spacious dressing area, amusement rides, the Carver House Restaurant, and extensive landscaping. Picnic shelters and supervised swimming activities made it ideal for family and church outings. Couples dined on the restaurant's outdoor terrace, attended the Friday-night "Dance Under the Stars," or took romantic strolls down the moonlit beach. For music lovers, there were free concerts. Oscar "Papa" Celestin, of the Original Tuxedo Orchestra and the Tuxedo Brass Band, performed from a stage in front of three large pools. As an added attraction, the beach's lifeguard corps conducted swimming and diving exhibitions. The crowds stayed until the 10:00 p.m. closing time.

A generation of New Orleanians honed their aquatic skills at the beach's free Red Cross swimming classes.[16] City youth learned swimming safety and first aid and engaged in competitive meets under the watchful eyes and shrill whistles of the beach's lifeguards. Day campers boarded buses for the long trek, then changed into swim clothes, raced through the icy shower alley, and plunged into the beach's refreshing pools. Lincoln

Beach's extraordinarily skilled divers attracted rapt attention with their crowd-pleasing exhibitions and competitions. Local favorite James "Pump" Chatman entertained spectators with periodic diving exhibitions, including coordinated team diving stunts from the ten-meter board.[17] People knew diver Warren "Whistlin'" Braden as a former Southern University football star. Moilene Jacques swam in a competition as the only woman. An eleven-year-old from Baton Rouge named A. Dalcourt finished third in his first diving competition. Albert Bolton emerged victorious in a Lincoln Beach diving contest. Chatman was expected to win. According to the *Louisiana Weekly*: "The sensational, sturdily built Albert Bolton, finishing second in the low board event, returned with precision diving to become New Orleans' 10 meter board champion. Bolton amassed an almost perfect score with his four 'required dives' and pulled away from Chatman, his nearest rival, by executing a full one and a half somersault lay-out for his 'optional dive.'"[18]

On the Midway, Music Galore

"There will be music galore to make the half-mile strip on the great Midway a most colorful and inviting playland for those who seek relaxation from the hum-drums of a busy life . . . ," the *Louisiana Weekly* reported. "It is the plan of the management to highlight every day of the week from now until the closing day with special attractions, including Rock 'n' Roll nights every Friday night."[19]

Those who performed on Lincoln Beach's midway represented a phenomenal catalog of New Orleans musicians. Fats Domino, Professor Longhair, Dr. John, the Ink Spots, Deacon John, Ernie K-Doe, Irma Thomas, Guitar Slim, Earl King, and the Neville family played, as did luminaries such as Nat King Cole, Ray Charles, Sam Cooke, and Little Richard. The concerts featured the best artists of rock 'n' roll, traditional jazz, and blues. Throughout the summer, Lincoln Beach hosted musical competitions and talent shows. Ernie K-Doe, of "Mother-in-Law" fame, won a talent program there.[20] In an interview with *Offbeat Magazine*, Dr. John recalled his time with Professor Longhair at Lincoln Beach in the 1950s: "He made the new arrangement of 'Mardi Gras in New Orleans' while we was rehearsing. There weren't a whole lot of sessions that I remember who was on the date, but I remember that one."[21]

Trombonist Eddie Hynes recalled his Lincoln Beach gig with Mac Rebennack (Dr. John):

> Mac and I got hired to blow a rock show at Lincoln Beach with a 12 piece group headed up by Wardell. Can you picture 12 black musicians, 2 white musicians and 10,000 Afro-Americans all jumping and grooving together? . . . I was even invited to go up to the Carver House and sit in with the House Band. I think it was Roy Brown.[22]

The Hawkettes performed at Lincoln Beach. Their record "Mardi Gras Mambo" remains a Carnival anthem. "Papa" Celestin, who played at Lincoln Beach in 1954, also performed for Pres. Dwight Eisenhower at the White House. Celestine passed away in December of that year. His second-line funeral parade attracted 4,000 followers.[23]

Did New Orleans Invent Rock 'n' Roll?

In 1947, New Orleanians Roy Brown and Dave Robert "Bob" Ogden made musical history when Ogden and his orchestra recorded Brown's "Good Rockin' Tonight," considered to be the first ever rock 'n' roll recording.

Roy Brown's place in music history is not to be denied. Born in New Orleans in September of 1925, he grew up in Eunice, Louisiana, sang in church, and chopped sugarcane. Brown originated the "crying blues" style of music that laid the groundwork for the New Orleans rhythm and blues sound. His vocals influenced the music of Bobby "Blue" Bland, B. B. King, and Little Richard, to name a few. He went on to record fifteen hits from 1948 to 1951.[24]

Drummer Bob Ogden graduated from McDonogh #35 High School and studied at Xavier University. His life typified the generational continuum of New Orleans musicians. His father, Dave Robert Ogden, Sr., worked as a chauffeur during the day and played the drums with the Maple Leaf Orchestra in the evening. When Bob Ogden and Roy Brown teamed up in Cosimo Matassa's studio in New Orleans, many saw this recording session as a seminal moment in the history of rock 'n' roll. Deejay Vernon Winslow (Dr. Daddy-O) recalled, "If I had to put my finger on an exact moment when rhythm and blues started in New Orleans, I'd have to say it was when Roy Brown came out with *Good Rockin' Tonight*. That really turned things around for music in New Orleans. *Good Rockin' Tonight* was the first instance where New Orleans felt there was such a thing as black music."[25]

Music chronicler Per Oldaeus wrote, "June 1947 saw Roy Brown's original R&B anthem *Good Rockin' Tonight* (DeLuxe 1093) being waxed at Cosimo Matassa's iconic J&M Recording Studio on the corner of Rampart and Dumaine. New Orleans drummer Dave Robert "Bob" Ogden (1914-1991) was the bandleader on that important session. Though little remembered today, Ogden played with quite a few famous acts, including some of the elite of New Orleans musicians."[26]

Music journalist Bill Dahl wrote:

> When you draw up a short list of the R&B pioneers who exerted a primary influence on the development of rock 'n' roll, respectfully place singer Roy Brown's name near its very top. His seminal 1947 DeLuxe Records waxing of *Good Rockin' Tonight* was immediately ridden to the peak of the R&B charts by shouter Wynonie Harris and subsequently covered by Elvis Presley, Ricky Nelson, Jerry Lee Lewis, and many more early rock icons. . . . Clearly, Roy Brown was an innovator and from 1948-1951, an R&B star whose wild output directly presaged rock's rise.[27]

Irish Channel born and raised Earl King played on Thursday nights at Lincoln Beach. The music, rhythms, and blues of New Orleans played on. Larry McKinley, Ernie the Whip, and Sister Bessie Griffin of WMRY radio celebrated the station's fourth anniversary at Lincoln Beach.[28] The Beach sponsored a tribute to legendary New Orleans pianist Walter "Fats" Pichon, who had recently returned from Broadway. In gratitude, Pichon thrilled the audience with favorite musical selections.[29]

In 1958, Lincoln Beach hosted a Negro State Fair, which focused on music, youth, and labor. The fair held a "Music in the Community" program with presentations by soloists, duets, choirs, and groups.[30] At Lincoln Beach, music was always in the air.

Beauty and the Beach

The Beach closed its first year with a monthlong competition for the title of "Miss Lincoln Beach." At times, the contest took on the character of a political campaign, with sponsors taking out ads in the newspaper to promote their candidates. Businesses, political groups, and nightclubs all participated. Miss Geddes-Richards Funeral Home candidate Delores Felton and Miss Struggle Inn's Shirley Champagne were among the many young women who vied for the coveted title.[31] The judging was held on August 29, and the winner was eighteen-year-old June Foster, sponsored by Billboard Esso Service Station. A dramatics student and operetta star at McDonogh #35, Miss Foster was selected over three dozen contestants. She received a fifty-inch, gold-plated cup, a dozen roses, a music scholarship, gifts from music-store owner Phillip Werlein, and a night on the town and was a special guest of Nat King Cole at his New Orleans concert held at the Municipal Auditorium. Yvonne Ganier, sponsored by Monarch Life Insurance Company, won second place; Gloria Davis, sponsored by the NAACP, was the third-place winner.[32]

In the years that followed, Lincoln Beach became a favorite vacation destination for Southern travelers. In 1956, a 3,500-car parking lot was constructed, new rides were added, and the Ink Spots returned by popular demand.[33] When Crash Corrigan and Elaine Dupont entertained, Lincoln

Lincoln Beach sign on Hayne Boulevard today

Beach broke its attendance records with an estimated crowd of fifteen thousand.[34]

With the passage of the Civil Rights Act of 1964, however, Lincoln Beach met the fate of segregated lunch counters and water fountains. Despite its uniqueness in the black South, the Beach was always years behind Pontchartrain Beach. Attendance dropped dramatically in the summer of 1964, and the corporation that managed Lincoln Beach dissolved that autumn. Since its demise, there have been sporadic efforts for a revival, but there has been little activity. On Hayne Boulevard, a crumpled green and orange sign by the parking lot remains. Lincoln Beach's ten years of glory as a summer-long festival for "colored" New Orleans have passed, but the memories and the music live on.

Chapter 10
1950s: A. P. Tureaud and the Martinet Society

Even though we didn't call ourselves a society, we were in fact a learned society, learning from A. P. Tureaud as the "dean" of lawyers in Louisiana. It was he who suggested we have this organization and call it the Louis A. Martinet Society.

Revius O. Ortique, Jr.[1]

Louis André Martinet

The Martinet Society, founded in New Orleans in 1957, was an association of Louisiana Civil Rights attorneys. Its early members were eager lawyers who gathered weekly to review cases, research, and discuss the emerging Civil Rights Movement and its legal implications. As the Society approached its fiftieth anniversary in 2007, the group relied heavily on the examples of its namesake, Louis André Martinet, and founder, Alexander Pierre Tureaud.

Louis A. Martinet was a nineteenth-century New Orleans lawyer, Civil Rights leader, writer, and teacher who rose to prominence for his role in the landmark United States Supreme Court ruling of *Plessy v. Ferguson*. Records at the Amistad Research Center reveal that Martinet was born in Saint Martin Parish on December 28, 1849. Energetic and ambitious, he became a state representative, serving from 1872 to 1875.[2] In 1876, he was in the first graduating class of Straight University Law School and was its first black graduate. He taught French and was appointed to Southern University's Board of Trustees in 1886. Additionally, Martinet served as a deputy United States naval officer, a customs clerk, and a deputy surveyor for the port of New Orleans. Highly visible in Louisiana political circles, he was nominated by the Republican Party for state superintendent of education in the early 1890s. He was instrumental in the formation of the American Equal Rights Association, a national organization aimed at preserving postwar Civil Rights gains.

Martinet faced new and more ominous challenges when Southern states passed laws that discriminated against the region's black citizenry. In 1891, the Louisiana Legislature passed the Separate Car Act, a bill mandating separate railroad coaches for black and white passengers. Black legislators and their allies protested the bill as a violation of the Fourteenth Amendment to the Constitution of the United States of America. For his part, Martinet sent a telegram to Gov. Francis T. Nicholls urging him to veto the measure. When that failed, Martinet joined eighteen influential black New Orleanians to plot a strategy to have the law declared unconstitutional. Calling themselves the *Comité des Citoyens* (Citizens' Committee), they issued an urgent statement calling for "the citizens of New Orleans, of Louisiana, and of the whole Union to give us their moral sanction and financial aid, in our endeavors, to have that oppressive law

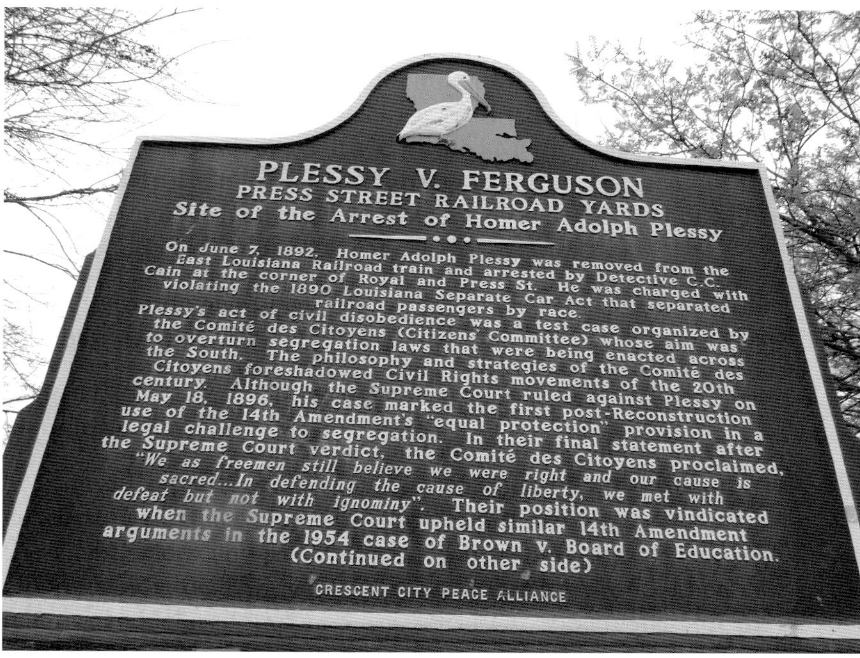

The Plessy v. Ferguson plaque commemorates Homer Adolph Plessy's challenge to segregated railroad trains. He was arrested at the corner of Royal and Press streets.

annulled by the courts,"[3] Martinet served as one of the legal counsels and coordinated the test cases that the Committee hoped to bring before the United Stated Supreme Court.

Martinet also published and edited the *Crusader* newspaper. Along with columnists Paul Trevigne and Rodolphe Desdunes, he wrote commentaries critical of the Separate Car Act and urged readers to boycott the rails. The paper also covered political developments, literature, sports, and social news. In 1894, Martinet published a pamphlet entitled "Violation of a Constitutional Right," which protested the harassment of a Committee member in Slidell.

Their quest to overturn separate-but-equal laws lasted until 1896 when the United States Supreme Court ruled against them in *Plessy v. Ferguson*. By a seven-to-one vote, the Court held that states could segregate the races if equal facilities were provided. This ruling established the color line in the South. Racism became the law of the land. The decision was a defeat for the Committee. In 1897, the group settled its accounts and closed its doors. In their final statement, they said:

> In the name of the people, the Citizens' Committee battled for equal rights, by maintaining the principle that the State was wrong in passing laws which discriminate between its citizens. As freemen we protested against such encroachment on the liberties of the people, by applying to the courts of the country for redress. . . . In defending the cause of liberty, we met with defeat, but not with ignominy."[4]

Shortly thereafter, Martinet ceased publication of the *Crusader*.

In 1898, with the federal government clearly out of the Civil Rights arena, Thomas J. Semmes, chairman of the Committee of the Judiciary for the State of Louisiana, addressed members of the Constitutional Convention, stating, "We met here to establish the supremacy of the white race."[5] What followed were laws that established segregated facilities and effectively removed blacks from state offices, juries, and voter-registration rolls. When Martinet died at his Columbus Street home in 1917, the outlook for blacks was at its lowest point since before the Civil War.

Alexander Pierre Tureaud

Following in Martinet's giant footsteps was Alexander Pierre Tureaud.

Like Martinet, he devoted his legal and leadership talents to defending the mistreated. Tureaud was born in 1899 in New Orleans. In 1925, he received his law degree from Howard University. Shortly thereafter, he returned to New Orleans, where he served as attorney for the local NAACP. He initiated a number of civic and voter leagues and urged blacks to register to vote despite the poll taxes, discriminatory tests, and other barriers enacted following the *Plessy v. Ferguson* decision.

Throughout the thirties and forties, Tureaud's legal talents touched and bettered the lives of many Louisianans. In the 1941 case *McKelpin v. Board of Education*, he forced the Orleans Parish School Board to pay black teachers the same salary as whites. In 1946, he won a voter-registration suit on behalf of Edward Hall and residents of Saint John the Baptist Parish. Also that year, he led an investigation into the lynching of World War II veteran John C. Jones in Minden, Louisiana. He turned over the names of the attackers to the United States government. Taking on a large number of equal-access cases, Tureaud fought for blacks to picnic in City Park, use the Municipal Auditorium, and gain admission to Louisiana State University Medical School.

Tureaud was a scholarly man. In 1935, he coauthored *The Negro in Medicine in Louisiana* with Dr. C. C. Haydel. He also saved things of historical value. His collection contained old *Crusaders*, reports of the Citizens' Committee from the *Plessy v. Ferguson* case, and other touchstones from his extensive experiences. He was familiar with Martinet and his work. Indeed, finishing what Martinet started became Tureaud's mission. In 1949, in *Bush v. Board of Education*, Tureaud initiated legal action that eventually led to the desegregation of New Orleans' public-school system. And in 1954, the United States Supreme Court overturned the *Plessy v. Ferguson* decision, stating that separate institutions were inherently unequal.

The Martinet Society

In 1957, Tureaud founded the Martinet Society. It was composed of a group of young lawyers who gathered in his law office on Orleans Avenue. Over sandwiches, coffee, and soft drinks, they discussed legal cases and politics and availed themselves of Tureaud's extensive library and experiences.

New Orleans native Judge Revius O. Ortique recalled the early days of the Society:

> There were a number of us who came into the practice between 1950 and 1956. Among that number were young lawyers with limited assets. Over the years, A. P. Tureaud gathered a lot of law material. A number of us gathered in his office on evenings and the weekend. He was happy to have us. He was considered our "dean." Before long we began discussing various cases we were having.[6]

Tureaud was elected president of the Martinet Society. The statewide organization was called the Louis A. Martinet Society of Louisiana. Among its stated objectives were the interchange of ideas, legal scholarship, and promoting the administration of justice. Its early members included Ernest Morial, Robert Collins, Lionel Collins, Freddie Warren, and Israel Augustine. Benjamin Johnson was recording secretary and Earl Amedee was treasurer.[7]

The Society provided the young lawyers with access to the community and the golden opportunity to be part of the emerging Civil Rights Movement. Tureaud's national ties gave the members the chance to watch as the Civil Rights Movement unfolded and to meet with the legal minds behind it, such as attorneys Thurgood Marshall and Robert L. Carter. The fifties and sixties were exciting times in Civil Rights, and the Martinet Society members logged long hours making sure favorable court decisions were obtained and implemented. Ernest Morial, the first black graduate of Louisiana State University Law School, worked school-desegregation cases. He stated, "I was inspired by the need for individuals to champion the causes of democracy."[8] Ortique was strong with labor-discrimination cases. The law firm of Nils Douglas, Robert Collins, and Lolis Elie defended Congress of Racial Equality (CORE) members, who were making their mark across the South with sit-ins, freedom rides, and other civil-disobedience campaigns against segregation.

Tureaud stayed active during the sixties. He represented the Reverend A. L. Davis in his suit to integrate the buses, sued for integration of the New Orleans Airport's restaurant, and defended three students arrested in Baton Rouge for sit-ins. He also won a judgment to desegregate Nicholls State College and won school-integration suits throughout Louisiana. In 1965, he represented a white woman who sought admission to Grambling University. In 1969, Tureaud forced the state to provide reading materials

Statue of Tureaud, located at A. P. Tureaud and St. Bernard avenues

Family and friends gather at the home of A. P. Tureaud

on African-American history in *Dana Hubbard v. Fred Tannehill*. He died in 1972 but left behind a wealth of legal talent. His former students rose to the top echelons of their profession.

Revius Ortique became a civil court judge, received four presidential appointments, and became the first black to be elected to the Louisiana Supreme Court. Israel Augustine became the first black post-Reconstruction state judge. Robert Collins was appointed to the federal bench. Ernest Morial became New Orleans' first black mayor. One of his first projects was to change the name of London Avenue to A. P. Tureaud Avenue, in honor of the great Civil Rights lawyer. Tureaud's papers and a bust are housed at the Amistad Research Center on Tulane's campus.

Chapter 11

1960: Two, Four, Six, Eight . . .

> He never considered taking me out [of the school]. We lived in the neighborhood. If there were taxes to be paid, we'd have to pay taxes. So why shouldn't his child have the same opportunities that other kids had? My daddy said if we didn't do it, somebody else may, but somebody else may not.
>
> Tessie Prevost, circa 1985[1]

In November of 1960, Tessie Prevost, six, climbed into the back of a car driven by a federal marshal and was whisked through the streets of New Orleans to her first day at a new school. She made her way down a Saint Claude Avenue sidewalk, finally ascending the eighteen steps that led to the entrance of McDonogh #19 Elementary School.[2] Moments later, two more federal vehicles pulled hurriedly to the curb, carrying first-graders Leona Tate and Gail Etienne. Gail's wide eyes scanned the cluster of people gathered on the walk leading to the large white stucco building.

Across town, Ruby Nell Bridges weaved through a similar scene, clutching her mother's hand as they approached the yellow-brick William Frantz Elementary School. Beneath the feet of those four children lay a serpent that haunted their families for generations. Each tiny step moved a people closer to a dream. A stillness hung in the muggy New Orleans air as the significance of the day's events unfolded. From the Saint Claude Avenue neutral ground, the words of thirty-seven-year-old Emma Phillips would rock legislative halls throughout the Deep South: "We're beginning to win our fight; this is wonderful!"[3]

When Gail, Ruby, Leona, and Tessie entered these two schools on November 14, 1960, it was the result of a long nationwide battle to end legal segregation. Separate but equal had been the law of the land since the waning days of Reconstruction. The United States Supreme Court codified this position in its 1896 *Plessy v. Ferguson* decision. As with other

This historic marker commemorates three six-year-old girls (Tessie Prevost, Gail Etienne, and Leona Tate) who desegregated McDonogh #19 Elementary School on November 14, 1960. On the same day, Ruby Bridges desegregated William Frantz Elementary School.

public entities, the schools were quite separate, but they were never equal. Black pupils and teachers were allocated deteriorating buildings, dingy secondhand books and materials, severe overcrowding, and less than half their fair share of the revenue pie. In New Orleans, for example, some black schools had a pupil-teacher ratio as high as 92:1.[4]

The Fight for Liberty Ensues

Like so many of their counterparts throughout the South, New Orleans

Civil Rights leaders Daniel Byrd and A. P. Tureaud made repeated appeals in an attempt to correct these conditions, to no avail. On September 5, 1952, a National Association for the Advancement of Colored People legal team filed a suit on behalf of Earl Benjamin Bush, calling for an end to the segregated school system in Orleans Parish. Mr. Byrd warned the Orleans Parish School Board, "We are determined to secure absolute equality and nothing less than complete equality is acceptable to our community."[5]

While the decaying buildings and meager facilities caused much concern, segregation was its most hellish with the tender self-concepts of young black children. One example of this was the Orleans Parish School Board's annual McDonogh Day event, where black students would stand for hours in the hot sun with no toilets available. They were allowed to proceed only after all the white children had walked by. In a letter to the school board calling for an end to this practice, civic leaders Iona Berteaux, Veronica Hill, and Ethel Young declared, "For those of our children who understand the significance of this parade, it is a most humiliating experience. For the rest, the parade only serves to condition them before they are old enough to think, to second-class citizenship."[6]

In 1954, when Mayor Morrison vetoed an alternative, more humane plan, a boycott was launched, and only 34 of 32,000 black students were present in Lafayette Square on that McDonogh Day.[7] Elated by the unified showing, Margot C. Farrell of the Walter L. Cohen High School PTA prophesied, "This is just the beginning. It shows that we mean to fight segregation. We are Americans and wish to be treated as all Americans"[8] Less than a week after the boycott, the U.S. Supreme Court handed down a ruling that validated the sentiments of Hill, Berteaux, and Young. The court decreed:

> Separating black children from others solely because of their race generates a feeling of inferiority as to their status in the community that may affect their hearts and minds in a way unlikely ever to be undone. The impact of segregation is greater when it has the sanction of law. A sense of inferiority affects the motivation of a child to learn. Segregation with the sanction of law tends to impede the educational and mental development of black children and deprives them of some of the benefits they would receive in an integrated school system. Whatever may have been the extent of psychological knowledge at the time of Plessy v. Ferguson, this finding is amply supported by modern authority and any language to the contrary in Plessy v. Ferguson is rejected.[9]

The court ruled that schools must be desegregated "with all deliberate speed."[10] That was in the spring of 1954. By 1960, not a single state in the Deep South had complied with the court's judgment for elementary schools. In fact, Southern lawmakers gave top priority to enacting massive amounts of segregation laws. In 1956, Louisiana declared the NAACP an illegal organization for refusing to submit its membership lists. The state passed a law that would dismiss teachers who advocated integration.

The NAACP attorneys continued to walk the Bush suit through the courts. In July of 1959, federal judge J. Skelly Wright ordered the school board to present a plan for desegregating the schools under its jurisdiction. When none was submitted, he devised his own timeline and established the second Monday in November 1960 as the day the barriers would fall. The school board conducted a series of tests for black students who were seeking transfers to white schools. James F. Redmond, then superintendent of Orleans Parish public schools, reported that 135 Negro children had been tested.[11] Leona Tate, Gail Etienne, Tessie Prevost, and Ruby Bridges became the four children who would fulfill the mandate of the court. The integration of New Orleans' public schools rested on the backs of these first graders and their families.

Jimmie Davis had been elected governor in early 1960. At a special session under his command, the legislature rattled off a salvo of laws aimed at thwarting integration efforts. One law called for mandatory jailing of federal marshals and judges who tried to enforce integration.[12] The state should "take the Orleans Parish school board hostage," recommended Rep. Wellborn Jack of Caddo Parish. "Home rule goes out the window when you fight this battle of segregation."[13]

The state lawmakers abolished the Orleans Parish School Board, impounded its funds, and fired the superintendent for refusing to reveal the names of the schools or children chosen for integration. On November 10, a legislative committee led by Risely "Pappy" Triche arrived with an armed police force to take over operation of the schools. The state then declared integration Monday to be a holiday, which Judge Wright promptly canceled. He ordered the legislature not to interfere with the integration process.[14] Governor Davis dispatched plainclothes state troopers to each of the city's white schools to compel observance of the holiday. Earlier that week, large contingents of federal marshals had been flown in to enforce the desegregation order.

Early in the morning on November 14, federal marshals identified by yellow armbands surveyed the situations at Frantz and McDonogh #19 elementary schools. They then dispersed to pick up the four girls. By 9:45 a.m., in the face of incredible odds, two public elementary schools in the Deep South had undergone integration. Cards and letters of congratulations from around the world flooded the local NAACP offices as the national movement for equal rights burst with pride over the courage and dignity displayed by the girls and their parents.

The forces of segregation would not disappear. Arch racist Leander Perez made a direct appeal at a White Citizen's Council rally in the Municipal Auditorium: "Don't wait for your daughter to be raped by these Congolese. Don't wait until the burr-heads are forced into your schools. Do something about it now."[15] The next day, over 2,000 segregationists jammed into the Central Business District, shouting, "Two, four, six, eight, we don't want to integrate!"[16] In their wake lay a trail of stoning victims, stab wounds, and broken ribs. One group tried to shake a sign painter from his scaffold as he desperately clung to life. The next morning a fight involving 200 workers exploded on the Crescent City's docks when it was discovered that the hiring boss was a member of the White Citizen's Council.

Mayor Morrison had spent the previous fourteen years attempting to create a national perception of New Orleans as the model city of a progressive New South. This image quickly dissipated as the town heaved in the reality of the hatred caused by sixty-plus years of legalized racism. With the legal options disappearing, the segregationists embarked on a campaign to intimidate the four girls and any whites who dared bring their children to McDonogh #19 or Frantz elementary schools. White families who attempted to keep their children in those schools were harassed and fired from their jobs.[17] Pulitzer Prize winner and Nobel laureate John Steinbeck described the white women who came to the schools to taunt the children:

> I heard the words, bestial and filthy and degenerate. . . . But there was something far worse here than dirt, a kind of frightening witches' Sabbath. . . . These blowzy women with their little hats and their clippings hungered for attention. They wanted to be admired. . . . These were not mothers, not even women. They were crazy actors playing to a crazy audience.[18]

After tasting this slice of New Orleans not mentioned in travel brochures, Steinbeck lamented, "I could no more have gone to Galatoire's for an omelet and champagne than I could have danced on a grave."[19]

A depiction in the New Orleans Public Library of the first day of school desegregation in New Orleans, painted by Alvena Vajda Seckar (1915-2012)

While Steinbeck was disgusted by the events, the black community bristled with outrage at the abuse the four children suffered and the New Orleans Police Department's refusal to provide adequate protection for whites who chose to send their kids to integrated schools.

The Blackout

Louisiana senator Russell Long urged whites to abandon the school system. Rep. F. Edward Hebert told the nation that blacks in New Orleans preferred segregated facilities. Meanwhile, plans had been carefully mapped for a dramatic "blackout" of the city's heralded Mardi Gras celebration. Anyone who witnessed a Mardi Gras Day on the corner of Orleans and North Claiborne avenues could appreciate how much time and effort went into this day. However, the times were becoming too serious and the stakes too high for the gala balls, parades, and revelry that marked the Carnival season. One by one, New Orleans' famed Carnival clubs announced their support for the "blackout" program, which called for canceling all events and boycotting the city's main shopping area. In addition to the more than one hundred clubs that lined up to express solidarity, students at Xavier University voted to cancel their activities and donated the unspent money to Civil Rights causes.[20] The Saint Augustine High School alumni association gathered names on a petition favoring the action. By December 1960, sales on Canal Street were down as much as 40 percent, and one executive acknowledged that business was worse than during the depression. Tourism was also down, as potential visitors recoiled at the events unfolding on their television screens.

Mayor Morrison was undaunted. He blamed the media for creating the turmoil, declared the city free of racial friction, and urged people to come to New Orleans for a great Mardi Gras celebration. However, Mardi Gras of 1961 was noticeably devoid of black faces. As in the 1954 McDonogh Day boycott, the New Orleans black community united to issue a strong statement against second-class citizenship and in support of the four girls and their families. Spokesman Leonard L. Burns stated, "The objectives of the 'blackout' are to show unity of purpose by Negroes against the forces intent to degrade and deprive them of their human rights and dignity; and secondly, to conduct a selective-buying campaign. . . . In Carnival we had an opportunity to put these objectives into motion and the absence of

Negroes in the usual places on Mardi Gras has caused most of the whites to become aware of the Negro's unity."[21]

The community was no doubt inspired by the tenacity of the six-year-olds who, despite the threats, harassment, and disruption of their lives, finished the school year and paved the way for more peaceful integration efforts throughout the Deep South.

"Days I Will Never Forget"

In 1983, on the twenty-third anniversary of school desegregation in New Orleans, I interviewed the four women who opened the doors to school integration. They reflected on the warmth, and the wounds, that resulted from their unique engagement with history. Gail Etienne recalled the days after McDonogh #19, when in third grade she, Tessie, Leona, and other black children were transferred to another all-white school. This time, however, there were no federal marshals, no national media attention, and no white boycott.

"At Semmes, they [students] used to beat us with ropes, kick us, spit in our eyes for no reason," Gail Etienne recalled. "I would come home crying. We would pile up to try to protect one another. It was terrifying. It stayed like that until we got bigger and decided we better fight somebody back." Gail did not detect a large amount of appreciation from New Orleans for her sacrifices but recognized the significance of her actions. Almost with a sigh she declared, "I guess if I had it do it again, I'd do it again." As for McDonogh #19, "Those are days I will never forget."[22]

During those times at Semmes, Tessie Prevost recalled asking her father, "What was it? What had I done to make people react that way?" She grew to believe that the white children were acting out the bigotry of their parents. "Kids don't really know prejudice. That can only be instilled." Between raising her children and working, Tessie Prevost gained satisfaction from reading the many positive letters she received during the crisis. "Other countries and states appreciated it more than New Orleans. I still have most of the letters and I enjoy just to sit down and read them. These people really appreciated what we did. People who remember me just because of that, people who I never met, told me how proud they were of us, how important it was to the black community."[23]

Leona Tate remembered how one teacher encouraged the students in their hatred. "Miss Dunn was very prejudiced. Whenever we passed her room, she had a habit of holding her nose as if we stunk. After we reported her, she claimed she had a sinus condition."[24]

Ruby Bridges stated of her integration experience:

> I think it's taught me a lot. I don't have any regrets about it and I don't have a complex about it. A lot of times people say they would think I would really have something against white people, but I don't. I think it helped me out. At the time it was going on, I was somebody special.[25]

The volume of hatred had an effect on all four of the girls and they saw psychiatrist Robert Coles periodically during grammar school. If it was taxing for the children, their parents also had much to endure. Ruby's father lost his job within weeks after the schools were integrated. Gail's father went to work at the post office one day to find newspaper pictures of his daughter hung around the workplace. However, the families were convinced of their path and determined not to back down to the segregationists.

A Freedom Ride button

Chapter 12
1961: Lighting Freedom's Torch

> Those on the bus with us were a group of people who had never been in each other's company, bonded by a common goal. Our only weapon was that we were right in what we were doing.
>
> Doris Castle, Freedom Rider from New Orleans[1]

On August 6, 1988, Xavier University in New Orleans hosted the first reunion of former members of the Congress of Racial Equality (CORE). During the early sixties, this Civil Rights group launched "Freedom Rides," sit-ins, voter-registration initiatives, and other campaigns to remove racial barriers. Through CORE, a tight-knit group of young New Orleanians became involved in the struggle for equality.

CORE founder James Leonard Farmer, Jr., attended the reunion, as did past legal counsel and executive director Floyd McKissick. Local CORE activists included Judge Robert Collins, attorney Lolis Elie, Isaac Reynolds, Matt Suarez, Rudy Lombard, Dr. Henry Mitchell, and others. For three days, this group of "Movement" veterans relived the times they changed, remembered fallen comrades, and recorded for posterity their dramatic role in American history.

The Journey of Reconciliation

CORE emerged in Chicago in 1942. It reflected the vision of James Farmer. A graduate of Howard University's Divinity School, he sought to apply the principles of *Satyagraha*, or "soul force," to the American Civil Rights struggle. Popularized by India's Mohandas Gandhi in 1919, *Satyagraha* espoused nonviolent resistance to unjust laws and practices. Since practitioners did not respond in kind to physical and verbal abuse,

Satyagraha required extraordinary amounts of personal commitment, mental discipline, and emotional restraint. They aimed to awaken the world's conscience to the human-rights abuses of unjust systems. By 1944, CORE chapters existed in several Northern cities and Los Angeles.

In 1947, CORE embarked on an interracial bus trip called "The Journey of Reconciliation." Their purpose was to challenge segregated transportation facilities with civil disobedience. Several CORE members served time on chain gangs for violating North Carolina's segregation statutes.

In the 1960s, CORE expanded into the Deep South. The move coincided with a deepening involvement of college students in Civil Rights activities. In February 1960, four students in Greensboro, North Carolina, refused to leave a segregated lunch counter, igniting a sit-in movement across the nation. That spring, police arrested seventeen Southern University students, who were subsequently expelled for conducting demonstrations at segregated facilities in downtown Baton Rouge.

Expelled Southern University student Marvin Robinson became a field director for CORE. He initiated efforts to start a chapter in New Orleans. Dr. Rudy Lombard, one of the reunion's organizers, had been a student at Xavier University when he was approached by Robinson and James McCain in 1960. Like many in his generation, Lombard was moved to action by the Greensboro sit-in. He called it the "lighting of the torch" for those seeking a way to quicken the pace of social change. Lombard recalled:

> I was aware of Marvin. I had followed the activities of Southern in Baton Rouge. He told me CORE was putting together a meeting at the Dryades Street YMCA and asked me to get involved. That's where I met Oretha Castle Haley, Julia Aaron, Jerome Smith, and other students from Southern University. Also present were David Dennis from Dillard, and white students from Tulane including Bill Harrel and Hugh Murray. I asked Lolis Elie to represent us. He agreed to do so, although he knew getting involved with a bunch of crazy students was not the best way to feed a family.[2]

That group became the core of CORE in the city. Lombard became the local chairperson.

In September of 1960, CORE engineered New Orleans' first sit-in of the era. Seven members sat down at Woolworth's "White Only" lunch counter on North Rampart Street and ordered food but were denied service. At 12:30 p.m. the police surrounded, closed, and barricaded the counter. They arrested the CORE members and charged them with "taking temporary possession of a man's business." The arrestees included former Southern students Jerome Smith and Ruth D'aspenza, Tulane students William Harrell and Hugh Murray, Jr., Xavier student Joyce Taylor, Louisiana State University in New Orleans (LSUNO) student William Harper, and Dillard student Archie Allen.[3] Only one had reached his twenty-first birthday. Elements of the black community applauded CORE's actions. On the day following the sit-in, the NAACP Youth Council picketed in their defense. Saint James AME Church donated proceeds from a Fellowship of Prayer offering, while the Studs Social and Pleasure Club solicited donations from its membership. In response to the protests, Mayor Chep Morrison threatened, "No more sit-in demonstrations or picketing of retail stores will be permitted."[4] Despite this rebuke, four days later Lombard, Oretha Castle, Cecil Carter, and Sidney Goldfinch repeated the sit-in tactic at the McCrory's store on Canal Street. Lombard refused bond and issued a statement of CORE's position: "The issue is clear. Segregation is morally wrong. We must oppose it if we are to live with ourselves."[5]

The Actionists

Describing themselves as "actionists," the CORE cadre attended workshops on the philosophy and practice of nonviolent direct action. Despite frequent police harassment and jail terms, New Orleans CORE members sat-in at restaurants, knelt-in at segregated churches, and spent long hours picketing stores on Canal and Dryades streets. Their handouts advised New Orleanians: "Don't Buy Discrimination" and "Register to Vote." They supported efforts to desegregate New Orleans schools. Cultural offshoots of their movement included the New Orleans-based Free Southern Theater.

Attorneys Robert Collins, Nils Douglas, and Lolis Elie defended many CORE activists in the Orleans Parish court system. Elie remembered them as a group of people who transcended traditional Civil Rights organizations. He explained, "What CORE brought were not just people who paid dues and attended meetings; they were more in line with what the Underground Railroad was about. They worked for Civil Rights seven days a week."[6]

The Freedom Rides

Beginning as a demonstration to win enforcement of an Interstate Commerce Commission ruling prohibiting segregation in travel, the Freedom Rides exploded into a defining battle of equality versus racial supremacy. The people who embarked on this harrowing journey fought for a cause higher than themselves.

The Freedom Rides of 1961 replicated the 1947 "Journey of Reconciliation." In May of 1961, James Farmer launched the sequel as a two-week bus ride from Washington, D.C., to New Orleans to test segregated facilities along the way. He called the action a "sit-in on wheels."[7] On May 4, 1961, a contingent of seven blacks and six whites left Washington aboard a Greyhound bus. They intended to reach New Orleans on May 17, with stops in Birmingham, Montgomery, and Jackson. But as the bus dipped deeper into the South, the number and intensity of racial incidents increased. In Charlotte, North Carolina, police arrested twenty-seven-year-old Joe Perkins, who attempted to get a shoeshine at a barbershop in the terminal.[8] In Rock Hill, South Carolina, youths attacked future United States congressman John Lewis and two white CORE members when Lewis refused to leave the white-only waiting area.[9]

On May 12, the group reached Atlanta. After mapping out details for the next phase, they recruited additional riders and boarded a Greyhound and a Continental Trailways bus to Birmingham. The scene turned ugly outside Anniston, Alabama. A mob of 100 segregationists organized by the Ku Klux Klan lay in wait. After repeated unsuccessful tries to board the buses, segregationists flung a firebomb through an open window, injuring twelve passengers. The flames eventually consumed the bus.[10] The second bus brought the remaining passengers to Birmingham. There, a large group of segregationists occupied the terminal, sealing off exits and blocking access to telephones. After a black CORE member defiantly entered the "White Only" reception area, a group of thirty segregationists surrounded him, shoved him backward, and punched him repeatedly in the face. He staggered out into the street and fell to the pavement. A white rider who had intervened ended up on the terminal floor, blood streaming from his face. The mob also attacked newspaper reporters and destroyed their cameras, as no police stepped in.

"A Bunch of Hooligans"

Police protection would not be forthcoming. Alabama governor John Patterson refused to provide bodyguards for what he called "a bunch of hooligans." Alabama congressman George Huddleston declared that the group "got what they deserved." Appeals to Attorney General Robert Kennedy also proved fruitless. While he expressed sympathy for the group's aims, he would not dispatch federal troops to the area. He suggested that the Freedom Riders take a less hazardous coastal route to make their point. Additionally, without the guarantee of a police escort, the bus company could not find any drivers willing to take the risks. After assessing their position the next day, CORE decided to cancel the remainder of the trip. In the course of their short trek, over twenty-five people had been injured, three had been arrested, and a bomb had destroyed a bus. After being rebuffed in their efforts to purchase bus tickets to Montgomery, the Freedom Riders took a flight to New Orleans.[11] For the moment, it seemed that the desegregation of transportation facilities would have to wait.

The Nashville Coordinating Committee

It appeared that the Freedom Rides would become a footnote in Civil Rights history. However, a group called the Nashville Coordinating Committee planned their continuation. Comprised of students from colleges throughout Nashville, Tennessee, the Committee had conducted sit-ins and other demonstrations that resulted in desegregation of lunch counters and movie theaters. These students shared a single-minded quest for equality. The life and death risks did not intimidate them. At age twenty-two, Fisk University student Diane Nash had already been arrested a number of times, including a thirty-day sentence in a Rock

Hill, South Carolina jail. Undaunted, on May 18, 1961, the Nashville Coordinating Committee arrived in Birmingham.

In spite of the previous violence, ten new Freedom Riders arrived at the bus station and demanded tickets to Montgomery. However, a bus driver refused to allow them to board. Though notorious for his racism, Birmingham's sheriff, Eugene "Bull" Connor, had been criticized by some Birmingham businessmen for his handling of the previous Freedom Ride, and he did not desire another confrontation. After four hours, he arrested the students and placed them in protective custody. At midnight of the same day, police awakened the students, brought them to the town of Ardmore, Alabama, near the Tennessee border, and released them. Connor told them, "There is the Tennessee line. Cross it and save this state and yourself a lot of trouble." To that sentiment, twenty-one-year-old Lucretia Collins responded, "We'll be back."

The next day, the Freedom Riders, now twenty-one strong, returned to Birmingham. They took seats in the terminal's white waiting room while policemen held back a crowd of segregationists for eighteen hours. Officials finally relented and allowed the students to leave for Montgomery at six o'clock the next morning. They arrived in the Alabama capital at 10:15 in the morning on May 20.[12] The violence began the moment they left the bus: a baseball bat swung at the head of a black passenger knocked him unconscious. After the students were forced out into the street, a mob of about one thousand awaited them with fists, metal pipes, and clubs. As many as fifteen men pummeled one student as bystanders in the crowd shouted cheers of encouragement and chased away ambulances. Uninvolved blacks also felt the brunt. Nearby, four white youths doused a man with gasoline and set him afire. Police allowed this rampage to continue for nearly two hours before dispersing the mob. At least twenty people suffered serious injury. With national outrage growing and the situation clearly out of control, Attorney General Kennedy dispatched about four hundred federal marshals to Montgomery.

The following night, rioting erupted anew near the First Avenue Baptist Church, where Martin Luther King, Jr., spoke. A mob trying to attack the church engaged federal marshals and National Guardsmen in a series of violent skirmishes. Inside the church, the scent of seeping tear gas meshed with the freedom songs of the 1,500 people penned in the entire night. Dr. King compared the violence to "the tragic days of Hitler's Germany." That night, officials placed Montgomery under martial law. Though

Martin Luther King monument on South Claiborne Avenue near Felicity Street in New Orleans

bruised and bloodied, the Freedom Riders' spirit remained unshaken. Twenty-one-year-old white student James Zwerg, in serious condition from repeated blows to the head, reaffirmed their commitment: "We are not martyrs or publicity seekers. We want only equality and justice, and we will get it. . . . From here we go to Jackson, Mississippi, and then on to New Orleans."[13] Another hospitalized student, William Barbee, declared, "As soon as we're recovered from this, we'll start again."[14] Diane Nash proclaimed, "They beat us and we're stronger than ever. . . . We will not stop. There is only one outcome."[15]

The violence surrounding the Freedom Rides wreaked havoc on Pres. John Kennedy's foreign-policy initiatives. The brutal suppression of the students undermined the administration's attempts to forge alliances with newly independent African nations, as it engaged in fierce competition with the Soviet Union for these ties. While world attention focused on Alabama, President Kennedy felt pressure from foreign governments and newspapers. The *Ethiopian Herald* warned, "Shameful incidents in Alabama can jeopardize the continued friendly relations between the United States and the entire non-white world."[16] In a move to defuse the crisis, Attorney General Kennedy called for a cooling-off period and requested that the riders halt any further activities.

"These Are the Pioneers"

Additional pressure to stop the Freedom Rides came from some Southern white liberals and moderate blacks who characterized the activity as provocative and detrimental to racial progress. Joining Attorney General Kennedy, they urged Dr. King to encourage the students to abandon the unnerving Freedom Rides. Dr. King had built a national reputation and mass movement on the right of people to disobey unjust laws. While fearing for the riders' safety, he acknowledged their effort: "These are the pioneers who are making the way possible for people of all areas to ride buses unmolested by segregation as well as to use the facilities. . . . I can conceive of no great social change or progress without some individuals who are willing to take the blows and who are temporarily misunderstood."[17]

For the historic last leg of the journey, New Orleans CORE members Julia Aaron, Doris Castle, David Dennis, Jean Catherine Thompson, and Jerome Smith arrived in Montgomery to join the ride to Jackson.[18] Ranging in age from eighteen to twenty-two, they committed themselves to being the last generation to endure life under segregationist rule. On Wednesday, May 24, 1961, Dr. King held a prayer breakfast for the riders and wished them well. The Freedom Riders boldly returned to the Montgomery bus terminal, where they boarded buses for Jackson. This time their escort included an armed convoy of forty-two vehicles, two helicopters, and a reconnaissance plane. As the contingent weaved its way through the poverty, oppression, and hope of Alabama's Black Belt, the riders sang songs of freedom: "Hallelujah, I'm traveling; ain't it fine?/ Hallelujah, I'm traveling down freedom's mainline." Just before the Mississippi border, a black woman alongside the road smiled, waved, and reached out to touch the bus. Inspired groups from around the country organized similar rides to the Mississippi capital of Jackson. Doris Castle remembered the journey this way:

> We met the night before in the Montgomery church, where we heard Martin Luther King and other inspirational speeches. The next day we went to the terminal, used the white waiting rooms and water fountains, and was then escorted to the Mississippi line by Alabama guardsmen and state troopers. It's indescribable to think of yourself on a bus in a hostile country and look out and see nothing but white faces armed with machineguns in a combat-readiness position. Those on the bus with us were a group of people who had never been in each other's company, bonded by a common goal. Our only weapon was that we were right in what we were doing.[19]

By focusing national and international attention on the South's violent oppression of blacks, these demonstrations greatly accelerated the removal of racial barriers throughout the country. In addition, the Freedom Rides gave rise to a new generation of college students who faced death, jail, and beatings for the cause of equality.

The twenty-seven Freedom Riders arrived in Jackson that evening. The police arrested them for breaching the peace. When they finally left their jail cells, they explained their actions. Jerome Smith of New Orleans stated how the Freedom Rides showed the world what minorities must suffer. Lucretia Collins simply declared, "I want to be treated like an American citizen."

More New Orleanians would contribute to the Freedom Rides' success as subsequent riders, field directors, attorneys, and supporters. When

Jerome Smith arrived at New Zion Baptist Church, he was greeted with a rousing ovation. Less than a week later, he boarded a bus bound for Jackson.

Isaac Reynolds journeyed with the initial group of riders into Birmingham. Active in the Detroit CORE chapter, he replaced James Farmer on the rides near Sumter, South Carolina, when Farmer left to attend to family matters. Reynolds stated, "We took a very bad beating. We were attacked as soon as the bus arrived. There was obviously an agreement between the Klan and the policemen."[20]

After refusing to be tried in a segregated courtroom, Jerome Smith served four months in the Hinds County jail. Following his release, he led another group of riders to McComb, Mississippi, where a mob beat them.

Doris Castle and Julia Aaron spent four months in the Hinds County jail. Rather than pay fines, many riders spent their summer and autumn serving 120-day sentences there or in Mississippi's dingy Parchman Prison. Isaac Reynolds, Jerome Smith, and Southern University in New Orleans (SUNO) sophomore Sandra Nixon joined them there. Prison life in Mississippi tested their will. Smith only received two linen changes during his four-month sentence. Nixon slept on a concrete floor for four weeks. Officials turned Castle's mother away when she went to visit her daughter. Castle recalled how she and Aaron passed the time adapting popular songs to current events. To the tune of Ray Charles' recording of "Hit the Road, Jack," they sang, "It's your life, Jack; don't be afraid no more."[21]

James Farmer spent forty days in prison. He asserted upon his release, "We have the most dedicated people in America in Mississippi jails. Our imprisonment has brought us new understanding." After their release, the New Orleans contingent returned to the picket lines and lunch counters. In December 1961 they issued a statement underscoring their continuing dedication:

> We feel that we must obey the moral dictates of our conscience, thus, we are impelled to denounce and destroy segregation in all of its sinister forms. . . . We want no praise for our sacrifices. As personalities we are unimportant, but the important factor is that we are trying to create in our country, a way of life that is conducive to the establishment of brotherhood and Americanism.[22]

In addition to focusing international attention on the denial of human rights to Southern blacks, the Freedom Rides greatly increased CORE's stature and membership. Many people heeded the call to descend on Jackson. Freedom workshops at New Zion Baptist Church in New Orleans' Central City trained the rush of volunteers from across the country. By July of 1961, nearly 250 people had been arrested and convicted after five-minute trials in Jackson.

The Freedom Riders' relentless determination put Civil Rights issues at the top of the national agenda. Their bravery profoundly accelerated the removal of racial barriers throughout the country. On May 30, 1961, citing the incidents in Birmingham and Montgomery, the Kennedy administration instructed the Interstate Commerce Commission to formulate clear, enforceable guidelines for the desegregation of the nation's transportation facilities.[23] On June 22, the Greyhound Corporation ordered the removal of White Only and Colored Only signs from all of its depots, including Montgomery. Further, on June 26, in the first action of its kind, the Justice Department filed a suit to end segregation at a New Orleans airport. And in October, the Central, Southern, and L&N railroads agreed to the total integration of their stations.

In addition to the Civil Rights gains, the Freedom Rides sparked an upsurge of student involvement in social causes. This phenomenon dominated the sixties and provided the decade with its character. After the Jackson arrests, CORE expanded their workshops to teach the many volunteers about the risks and rewards of nonviolent resistance. For the rest of 1961, numerous contingents of Freedom Riders crisscrossed the South challenging racial barriers and demanding equality.

Freedom Summer

In 1964, as a member of the Coalition of Federated Organizations, CORE became active in the Mississippi Freedom Summer campaign. The coalition organized the resources of over a thousand volunteers from across the country to establish freedom schools, freedom health and legal clinics, and voter-registration offices. Tragedy shook this endeavor. Someone murdered black Mississippian James Chaney and two white CORE volunteers from New York, Andrew Goodman and Michael Schwerner. A field near Philadelphia, Mississippi, held their remains. Dillard student David Dennis, who headed CORE's Mississippi staff during this period, eulogized Chaney at his funeral.

CORE's continuing full-court press kept Civil Rights at the fore of American politics. They obtained a host of rulings and laws from the Kennedy and Johnson administrations. One by one legal barriers toppled. Congress passed the Civil Rights Bill in 1964, a week after the disappearance of Chaney, Schwerner, and Goodman. The Voting Rights Act came the following year. This legislation transformed the sociopolitical map of the South. The foot soldiers of the Congress of Racial Equality made it happen.

CORE's role in the South declined during the late sixties. Differences over direction and ideology led to Farmer's resignation in 1965. Many members became instrumental in shaping the antiwar and Black Power movements of the sixties and early seventies. Others chose community activism and traditional political pursuits. The Southern CORE chapters eventually dissolved and CORE returned to its Northern bases.

Returning to Remember

In October of 1987, one of New Orleans CORE's most active members during the sixties, Oretha Castle Haley, died of cancer. In March of the following year, her husband, Richard Haley, who directed CORE's Southern office, also passed. According to Amistad Research Center's archivist Florence Borders, the Haleys' deaths prompted the CORE reunion:

> Those at Richard Haley's funeral felt that they should get together and begin a systematic way of recording what their experiences had been to set the record straight. They also felt that most of the times they gathered, there was sadness or grief over the death of an activist. They wanted to meet at a less stressful time so they could relate to each other, reminisce, and record what needs to be left to posterity.[24]

A committee to plan the reunion formed. Isaac Reynolds, one of the original Freedom Riders, compiled a mailing list of former members and made the necessary contacts. Florence Borders arranged for housing and established logistics for conducting interviews. Rudy Lombard secured the use of Xavier University. Xavier held particular significance for CORE. The university housed the original Freedom Riders after segregationists burned their bus in Alabama.

So in August 1988, over twenty-seven years after the first Freedom Rides, the actionists finally arrived in New Orleans. After gathering at Matt Suarez's house for socializing and reminiscing, the group met the next day at the Norman C. Francis Science/Academic Complex at Xavier University. Each related his movement involvement and experiences. Robert Collins had become a federal judge. During the movement years, he and fellow attorney Lolis Elie hid in churches and graveyards on jaunts through the back parishes of Louisiana defending blacks' right to vote. James Farmer told of being tear-gassed by policemen in a church in Louisiana. Reynolds and Benjamin Elton Cox reminisced about integrating hotels in the Carolinas. Cox, one of CORE's great orators, mused how after he threatened to set himself on fire to protest injustice, segregationists mailed him boxes of matches. Richard Haley was "a man, who more than anyone sought no self-gratification or political office," Elie remembered. "He was for the advancement of black people in a very unselfish way."[25] After lunch, the group gathered behind a poster that declared "Freedom Now!" and, in a particularly poignant moment, clasped hands and sang, "We Shall Overcome." The gathering was uplifting.

CORE member Edward Hollander photographed the reunion. David Dennis and Dr. Henry Mitchell, who had walked many a picket line with CORE members, videotaped it. Borders recorded interviews with seven former members, including Farmer, Floyd McKissick, and Dennis.

Later, the group ate dinner at Gallier Hall, where they recognized Virgie Castle. In addition to being the mother of activists Doris Castle and Oretha Castle Haley, she had opened her home for frequent gatherings of many 1960s activists. Lolis Elie recalled, "There were not many people who went on the Freedom Rides who did not spend time at the Castles' home on North Tonti Street. During that time, Virgie Castle mothered everyone." At the banquet, she was proclaimed "Mother of New Orleans' CORE." Lombard commented, "There was a lot of nostalgia in that room and a lot of respect. People who were involved in the Civil Rights struggle were special and exceptional, very courageous, and very political."[26]

Chapter 13

1960s: Mardi Gras through the Ages

La Folie
Donne partout l'heureux signal!
Banissons la mélancolie;
Voici le temps du Carnaval.
(Madness
Sends happy signals everywhere!
Let's banish melancholy;
It's Carnival time.)
Armand Lanusse[1]

During the Carnival season, while most of America wallows in the blue funk between the winter holidays and springtime, New Orleans hosts the biggest, longest-lasting Mardi Gras party in North America. On the last night, as America sleeps after a humdrum, workaday Tuesday, people in New Orleans slosh through the beer cans, the hoops and howls, and the unabashed revelry that closes a season filled with balls, masquerade parties, and three weeks of parades.

In somber moments after the holiday, community leaders suggest that too much time and money is spent on the Carnival season. Others decry the city's "Mardi Gras mentality." However, when the season rolls around again, a fever takes hold. There are coconuts to be painted, Mardi Gras Indian suits to be sewn, tuxedos to rent, and floor-length gowns to be hemmed. Relatives from out of town want the "good gumbo." There are traditions to pass down. Floats need to be packed with doubloons, beads, and trinkets. And New Orleans does not party alone! In Rio de Janeiro and the Caribbean, merrymakers join in this annual winter festival. For all of its frivolity, Mardi Gras is a season that blacks have long observed and represented in unique manifestations. It remains a treasured tradition in black New Orleans.

Mardi Gras History

People of color in New Orleans masked for Mardi Gras as early as the 1700s. *Le Spectacle de la Rue Saint Pierre* (the Saint Peter Street Theater) became the site of nightly masquerade balls during Carnival for free blacks and slaves. Eventually, the Cabildo authorities banned these get-togethers, fearing that blacks were developing a taste for an expensive lifestyle. Complaints also rose that blacks had begun using the cover of their costumes to gain entrance to white social functions—masking for white, as it were. A government report stated, "People of color, both free and slave, are taking advantage of Carnival, going about disguised, mingling with the Carnival throngs in the streets, seeking entrance to the masquerade balls."[2]

According to John Blasingame in *Black New Orleans 1860-1880*, large numbers of black people viewed parades. The 1870s witnessed Carnival processions and balls that lasted until the wee hours of the morning. At one such affair with an international theme, black revelers wore costumes that represented the Scottish queen, a German maid, the Duke of Wellington, and Charles VII.[3]

In 1872, Pinckney Benton Stewart Pinchback, the state's first black governor, signed the bill that established Mardi Gras as a legal holiday in Louisiana.[4] In 1896, newspapers announced the emergence of the Gretna Cyclones, one of the many black marching societies and brass bands that paraded in costume during Carnival:

> Pursuant to annual custom Mardi Gras day, the "Gretna Cyclones," a colored club, paraded in Gretna, McDonoghville and in the vicinity of Harvey's canal. The members were dressed in tailor-made suits and wore the king's colors. Twelve marshals and a brass band preceded them. They made a unique appearance.[5]

Central to preserving the history of black New Orleans, in 1926 the *Louisiana Weekly* newspaper began printing a robust section that published the times, places, and participants of Mardi Gras events. *Louisiana Weekly* reporters E. Belfield Spriggins, Mayme Osby Brown, and others cast a wide net over the social doings of the city. In 1930, the *Weekly*'s social calendar listed seventeen events scheduled between February 7 and March 4. They included debutante receptions, annual Carnival dances, soprano recitals, Whist parties, and a Carnival social given by the Vogue Sewing Club.[6]

Most of those events took place at Piron's Garden of Joy, located atop the Pythian Temple building.

In 1938, after financial issues beset the venerable Pythian Temple, the Mardi Gras balls, dances, and parties moved to other venues such as the Autocrat Club, Bethlehem Temple, Saint Monica Hall, and Xavier University. Clubs that outlasted the Great Depression carried on their traditions and activities. The Young Men's Twenty Club, the Marigolds, the Young Men Illinois, the Rhinestones, the Black Pirates, and the Capetowners Club all held their dances.

In 1940, the popular Jolly Boys and Girls Club presented their seventh consecutive parade, with James Washington as king and Violet Winfrey as queen. The three floats were entitled "King Jolly the Sixth," "Rulers of '39," and "Regal Splendor."[7] The Astoria Restaurant, on South Rampart Street, provided sustenance along the parade route with their Mardi Gras menu. There, one could find a turkey dinner for thirty-five cents, a whole oyster loaf for forty cents, and sandwiches, hard liquor, soft drinks, Creole crab gumbo, and Creole shrimp.[8]

For those in the downtown area, North Claiborne Avenue served as the focal point of Carnival activities. By the 1950s, large oak trees lined the neutral ground from Elysian Fields Avenue to Canal Street. On Mardi Gras Day, North Claiborne came alive with friends and family picnicking, smooching, and strolling. This was the place where many black New Orleanians awaited the Zulus and a chance glimpse of the Mardi Gras Indians. A group called the Skeleton Men sported black thermal underwear painted with bones, loincloths, and large paper-mâché skulls. They rattled bones as they paraded through the crowd. The Million Dollar Baby Dolls and their archrivals, the Gold Diggers, dressed in the skimpiest of skirts for the festivities.

With the upsurge of the Civil Rights Movement, traditional Mardi Gras celebrations in the black community were disrupted. In 1961, a coalition of social-aid and pleasure clubs that organized as the United Clubs, Inc. staged an enormously successful "blackout" of Mardi Gras to protest state and city hostility to the integration of New Orleans public schools. The *New Orleans States-Item* reported:

> Ten Negro clubs have canceled their Carnival activities for 1961 in protest against the Legislature's actions in attempting to block the desegregation of New Orleans public schools.

Baby Dolls today

> Their decision followed an appeal by United Clubs Inc., urging Negro groups to withhold their participation in the Carnival celebration.
>
> Edward Wong, president of the UCI, said the Young Man Twenty-Two Club had canceled its ball and would contribute funds to the National Association for the Advancement of Colored People and the Urban League of Greater New Orleans.
>
> So far, nine other groups have joined the Carnival boycott, UCI's second cancelation since 1957.
>
> They include the Bon Temps, the Townsmen, the T.G.F. Club, the Klassy Kut-Ups Club, the Ad Libitum Club, the Mispas Club, the Young Missus, the Gardenia Stitch and Chat Club and the Bunch Club. Wong said more than 250 clubs have been asked to cancel their Carnival activities.[9]

By Mardi Gras 1961, more than one hundred organizations called off their dances and balls.[10] The money usually spent on costumes and balls was donated to Civil Rights causes. Later in the decade, Zulu came under scrutiny for its depiction of Africans. With the passage of the Civil Rights Bill in 1964, the club toned down its traditional parading attire, but the original blackface and grass skirts returned in 1968. Also in the 1960s, Interstate 10 tore the heart from black New Orleans Mardi Gras festivities; the overpass structure cut through North Claiborne Avenue, destroyed its oak trees and picnic areas, and crippled its businesses.

In the seventies and eighties, the Tambourine and Fan cultural organization, led by former CORE member Jerome Smith, worked to bring the focus of Mardi Gras back to North Claiborne Avenue. It also initiated the "Super Sunday" Mardi Gras Indian parades. This event fell outside of the Carnival calendar and allowed spectators to view the colorful pageant of the Mardi Gras Indian tribes in their splendor. The uptown Super Sunday Mardi Gras Indians processed from A. L. Davis Park in Central City. The downtown Mardi Gras Indians came from Bayou St. John, ending at Hunters Field across the street from the Circle Food Store.

Social and Pleasure

The grand celebration of Mardi Gras in the black community originated at the club level. In a 1938 *Louisiana Weekly*, I saw a picture of my mother as a member of the Ad Libitum Club, which held its dance at the Autocrat Club on Saint Bernard Avenue.[11] Hundreds of New Orleans clubs hosted a wide range of activities during Carnival, from neighborhood parades to elegant formal affairs. They included people from all classes and walks of life. Having the best affair was a source of great pride in the community.

O. C. W. Taylor hosted a show on WNOE radio called *Negro Forum*. He wrote:

> Nowhere in all of the U.S.A. is there a celebration so vast, so universally observed in the city, as the Mardi Gras. The Mardi Gras is not only a celebration. It is an institution. Rich, poor, middle-class, upper-class, Catholic, Protestant, Jew Gentile, white, black, everyone in New Orleans is conscious of and a part of this enormous celebration. . . .
>
> New Orleans is ruled over by kings and queens during the Mardi Gras. Every club dance, more or less, every school, every parade, has its royal family in their regal splendor. Mardi Gras is the most democratic Monarchy ever seen.[12]

How true. Even the Louisiana State Beauty and Barber College fielded a queen with a full court in 1955. In the 1950s, the Laborers' Union Hall was by far the most popular location for dances and balls, with events scheduled almost every night during the Mardi Gras season. The Young Men's Twenty Club, the Vikings, the Original White Swans Social and Pleasure Club, the Bon Temps, and Les Toujour Amis all danced the night away at that venue. Other ball locations included Saint Peter Claver's auditorium, the YWCA, the iconic Autocrat Club on Saint Bernard Avenue, and the old Les Jeunes Amis Hall.[13]

Mardi Gras with Nathan Johnny King, Jr.

One of the great chroniclers of black Mardi Gras clubs in the 1950s was Nathan Johnny King, Jr. He published a series about New Orleans' Carnival that explored the pomp and frivolity of the black Mardi Gras experience. He documented the wonderful photographs, names of officers and members, club origin dates, themes, and commentary associated with the Mardi Gras presentations. He titled the inaugural 1955 edition *SEPIA Mardi Gras in New Orleans*. Subsequent issues were *King's Mardi Gras in New Orleans* (1956, 1963) and *King's Tan Mardi Gras* (1968, 1972).[14]

King's guide gave a peek into a world of New Orleans fantasy, royalty, tradition, and whimsy. His first edition showcased over forty clubs. From his home office at 3226 Second Street in Central City, King gathered information, wrote text, and arranged photographs. His initial staff consisted of himself, James Parker, Roland Wilson, and his brother George King.[15] The traditional colorful balls provided the most captivating aspect of his guide. It also showcased the artistry and craftsmanship involved in presenting the royalty of black Mardi Gras.

In 1955, the Young Men's Illinois Club dressed in tuxedos and tails to honor Queen Ina Claire Watts. With royal crown and scepter, seated upon a velvet throne, Queen Ina presided over their ball themed "Realms of the Maharajas." The Original Illinois Club presented Queen Yvonne Amelie Denison. In a commentary, Nathan King noted that every member of the Original Illinois Club was a "big wheel."[16]

Mardi Gras Costumes

As represented in *SEPIA Mardi Gras in New Orleans*, the many costume balls brought out the inner spacemen, devils, sheiks, and gypsies in the attendees. The Carnation Social and Pleasure Club combined costumes with formality. With the theme of "Penguin Isles," members simulated a penguin look with white shirts and pants and long-tailed black tuxedoes. The 1955 Plantation Revelers wore plantation hats, checkered shirts, starched blue jeans, handkerchiefs around their necks, and stumpy neckties. Dooky Chase and his wife, Leah, dressed in Hawaiian attire for the Vagabonds Ball at the Autocrat Club. Romantic faraway places became the popular theme in 1955. The Blue Birds Sewing Circle presented an "Evening on the Nile." Dunbars' Social and Pleasure Club enjoyed "A Nite in Arabia." The Golden Rod's Social and Pleasure Club recreated "A Carnival in Haiti." The Lords and Ladies' Club danced on "The Isle of Capri."

King's 1956 edition contained more pages, more advertisements, and more social and pleasure clubs posing in their finery. Its cover showed a woman with a pitchfork, tail, and horns at the Bon Temps's "Satan's Inferno" costume ball. That same year, Dorothy Lawless of the Golden Rod's Social and Pleasure Club presented King with a plaque for his energetic civic and community service.

Zulu

> "Walk on pins and needles
> Just to see what they can do.
> Walk on gilded splinters
> With the king of the Zulu."
>
> Dr. John, "I Walk on Gilded Splinters," 1968

The Zulu Social Aid & Pleasure Club has become renowned for its contributions to the New Orleans Mardi Gras experience. It formed after a group of laborers called the "Tramps" attended a play at the Pythian Temple performed by a troupe named the Smart Set. A skit in the production was "There Never Was and Never Will Be a King Like Me."[17] The club's historians documented the rich legacy of the organization: "While the 'group' marched in Mardi Gras as early as 1901, their first appearance as Zulus came in 1909, with William Story as King. The group wore raggedy pants, and had a Jubilee-singing quartet in front of and behind King Story."[18]

The *Louisiana Weekly* documented the parade of 1928:

> CARNIVAL VISITORS ALREADY FILL CITY FOR MARDI GRAS
> ZULU BURLESQUE ON REX TO BE MOST ELABORATE EVER
>
> King Will Arrive Tuesday at 10:30 A.M., at Head of New Basin, on Rampart Street, and Take Usual Route to View Progress of City and Inspect the Thousands of Merrymakers
>
> With thousands of visitors already in the city awaiting the climax of the Carnival season on Mardi Gras, when mirth will hold full sway, His Majesty, the King of the Zulus, will share with Rex the spotlight of attention. The arrival of the King will be awaited with interest and when the royal barge lands at the head of the New Basin canal the royal party will find thousands of loyal subjects ready to greet them. . . . After the parade, the King and Queen will entertain at Celestine's Sans Souci Hall, on Howard Avenue.[19]

In 1931, in the midst of the Great Depression, Zulu king Allen Leon arrived by boat to the streets of New Orleans:

> The new yacht Atlas arrived at 10:30 a.m. with Captain H. S. Weaver in command, bringing the Zulu King with him, while thousands jammed the streets at the head of the New Basin. The king went on his way leading his three floats and his dukes through the magic lantern of dream that

> unwound in its formal ceremony. . . . He took his rolly-polly in and out of the city streets where thousands of black and white subjects wait for the Zulu parade every year . . . the parade moved along with bands of music, passing the Unity office, where it was reviewed. . . . Along the route of the parade coconuts were tossed as souvenirs.[20]

Zulu in 1989

The Zulu Club on Broad Street near Orleans Avenue exuded an atmosphere of tradition, fraternity, and New Orleans culture. Enlarged photographs of past kings and queens covered the walls. Members were greeted with a "Hey, brother." It was Christmastime, and Gene Chandler's "Rainbow '65" played on the jukebox. Above the bar, the winning coconuts in the annual decorating contest were displayed. One was crafted into the character of the "Big Shot of Africa," complete with a fat cigar.

In 1989, I had the opportunity to interview Zulu president James Wright at the Zulu Club. He affirmed that few experiences compared to counting down to Mardi Gras with the Zulus. Pulling off Mardi Gras Day took a lot of intense working and partying. Just before Mardi Gras, the Zulus gathered in hotels, bars, and members' homes referred to as camps. For Wright and his entourage, this Carnival season was a sleepless one: "It's wild! Krewes host parties for the general membership and guests, competing among themselves for the best party and best crowd. A lot of krewes wait until the last hour to have parties to generate enthusiasm."[21]

The final weekend triggered a frenzy of coconut preparation, finishing costumes, and attending parties. On the day before Mardi Gras, Wright's staffers went out to check that the floats were in tiptop shape and the route had been cleared of hanging tree limbs. He stated, "There's no sleep from Monday until you get home about 3:00 p.m. Tuesday. We're out checking details and troubleshooting last-minute problems. About 10:00 p.m. we make sure that Jackson Avenue is clear."[22]

At three o'clock in the morning, Wright, the king and queen of Zulu, and a five-car entourage fully decked out for Mardi Gras left the Broad Street offices with police escorts and sirens blaring. In the camps, with spirits flowing liberally, the 1989 Zulus applied their traditional blackface and put on their traditional costumes as they prepared to rock and roll

King Zulu in all his glory

New Orleans. At dawn, Owens Haynes boarded a boat at the Bienville wharf and rode to Canal Street to arrive as King Zulu of 1989.

Mardi Gras Balls

In 1895, Wiley Knight from Chicago brought formal balls and the social scene of the Windy City into the black Carnival mix. A butler, he founded the Illinois Club. The first Illinois dance in New Orleans was held in the Globe Hall at Saint Peter and Marais streets, where ladies were presented as *Muses* and men as *Othellos*. In the 1920s, there was a split, with the younger members leaving to become the Young Men's Illinois Club. The remaining members called themselves the Original Illinois Club. Invitations to the clubs' popular debutante balls and attendant functions were considered hot properties.

The *Louisiana Weekly* reported on the Young Men's Illinois's 1932 event:

A Zulu rider is depicted on a pillar under the Claiborne Avenue Overpass

> Choosing as their theme, "In Old Japan" the increasingly popular Young Men's Illinois Club staged their sixth annual ball on Tuesday night February 2 in the famous roof garden atop the Pythian Temple. For the occasion the ball had been turned into a lovely Japanese garden with the flaming rays of the summer sun shedding its afterglow. . . . Beginning at nine of the clock Celestin's Original Tuxedo Orchestra played the dreamiest dance music . . . until the signal was given that the Queen and her royal court had arrived. The several hundred guests danced joyfully to the delightful music and gaiety reigned supreme.[23]

The Rhinestone Club's ball also brought beauty and grace to the Pythian Temple:

> One of the most delightful formal affairs of the season, and certainly the most colorful and delightful in the short history of the popular Rhinestone Club, was their annual ball staged Thursday night, February 4 in the Parisian Roof Garden, Piron's Garden of Joy, on top of the famous Pythian Temple.
>
> For this lovely affair, the popular resort had been converted into a beautiful temple where reigned the Gods of Light, the Rhinestone Club members. Using a scheme of dark blue and rhinestones the club made the place more attractive. A fake ceiling of blue hung over head with huge artificial rhinestones scattered about while in the center was an extra sized one that glistened brilliantly as the specially arranged electric lights shed their rays upon it. Imitation posts supported the upper balcony and the stage where McNiel's Sunny South Syncopators dispensed entertaining music, was made to look most beautiful with its curtain of corresponding dark blue with a silvery moon and stars to light it up.[24]

The following year, the Original Illinois Club held their ball:

> The famous Parisian Roof Garden was the brilliant and highly colorful scene of the . . . annual dance given by the historical Original Illinois Club Inc., of which Mr. Wiley Knight is the oldest member, being one of the founders and Mr. Joseph D. Geddes is now president. The entire Temple Building seemed to have taken on a new appearance for the occasion. The main entrance to the building was protected by a canvas canopy of white, while the path to the elevator was made inviting by an avenue of swaying palms, which gracefully nodded their heads as they stood in pots decorated in white paper. The stairway leading up to the roof garden from the sixth floor was resplendent in its trimmings of fresh green smilax from which flew streamers of thin white paper, representing snow.[25]

The Bunch Club Carnival Dance

The Bunch Club began in 1917. In 1989, I interviewed Maurice and Eva Prevost, who attended the club's functions since 1931. Eva always remembered her first Bunch dance. Though the club never presented debutantes, they invited those from other clubs to their dance.

Maurice remembered when former McDonogh #35 teacher George Longe invited him to join: "He brought me into the club. I was happy to go in because it was a group of prominent men and I wanted to be associated with these men. Also, my wife has always been interested in a social life and it was an outlet for her."[26] Maurice joined the Bunch Club in 1939.

The Bunch Club Dance of 1930 was described as a brilliant affair. Strung from the balcony of the Garden of Joy were imitation rose vines crafted by Bunch member E. Belfield Spriggins and a group of McDonogh #35 High School students. On the stage, a white fence was covered with

A Bunch Club hat, medallion, and cape. The 1936 Carnival dance was held at the Pythian Temple.

crepe paper, roses, and Southern smilax. Multicolored twinkling lights accented the effect. Sidney Desvignes's Southern Syncopators provided the music until midnight, when the club members donned crimson plumed hats and capes. Members and their guests followed Spriggins as he led the "Grand March," with twists and turns designed to show off elegant flowing gowns of taffeta, chiffon, georgette, and crepe satin. At one o'clock, a national band, Fate Marable's Cotton Pickers, finished off the evening, playing until three o'clock that morning.[27]

Meetings rotated to different members' houses. Card playing was quite popular at these affairs. In 1939, the dances were held in the Bethlehem Masonic Temple on Dauphine Street in the French Quarter. In 1950, the Bunch Club Dance moved to Xavier University, where it became known for its elaborate themes, invitations, and sets. Utilizing artists, woodworkers, and painters from Xavier's student body and members from the club, Victor Labat coordinated the construction of walls within Xavier's gym to produce a more intimate setting. New props were built each year and always reflected the dance's theme, such as "Gift of the Nile," "An Evening in the Old French Opera House," "Sweethearts on Parade," and "Friday the 13th."[28]

At the 1954 dance, the theme was "Carnival Reflections." The guests

The 1940 Bunch Club Carnival dance was covered in the Louisiana Weekly's *social page*

entered through two large wooden clowns standing by the doorway. In front of the stage were two-foot-high letters on an orange cloth that said: *Bunch Club*. Suspended from the stage was a large mirrored ball. Spotlights from the stage showed off Bunch members and their guests as they danced to the sounds of Herbert Leary and His Music Makers. After dances, members and guests gathered at different homes for breakfast.[29]

In the sixties and seventies, the Bunch Club moved their dance to downtown hotels. They subsequently discontinued elaborate decorations. In the seventies, themes were discontinued and invitations standardized. Instead of monthly meetings at members' homes, the Bunch Club met at Dooky Chase's Restaurant. And the Grand March at the dance was not as long and winding as in the days of E. Belfield Spriggins. Eva Prevost recalled the allure of the Bunch Dance, particularly for the wives:

Guests at the 2013 Bunch Club Carnival dance

The Bunch Club's annual Champagne Sip, photographed at English Turn Country Club by Lloyd Dennis

At the other balls, the debutantes were the center of attention. At the Bunch Dance, the husbands presented and made over you; he comes out and bows to you. It's like you're always making your debut. It's something the ladies always waited for.[30]

Mardi Gras Indians

"Prettiest thing I ever seen,
Mardi Gras Indian down in New Orleans.
He sewed all night and he sewed all day.
Mardi Gras morning he went all the way."

The Wild Tchoupitoulas, "Meet de Boys on the Battlefront"

One of the most fascinating aspects of the black Mardi Gras is the Mardi Gras Indians. Based in black working-class neighborhoods, they employ the call-and-response chants that characterized the music in Congo Square in the 1700s. An exhaustive dissertation by David Draper of Tulane University outlined the customs, rituals, and songs of the city's Indian tribes. According to Draper in 1973, the uptown tribes, or gangs, consisted of the Black Eagles, Wild Magnolias, Cheyenne Hunters, Golden Eagles, Apache Hunters, Golden Arrows, and Iroquois Hunters. The downtown tribes included the White Eagles, Yellow Jackets, Yellow Pocahontas, Cherokee Hunters, and Golden Stars.[31] Their purpose was to "mask Indian" on Mardi Gras Day. In days gone by, the site of the Union Passenger Terminal was a battlefield for settling scores.

The violent confrontations have stopped, but the Mardi Gras Indians have held to the traditions, pride, and artistry of the past. A new suit is created for each Mardi Gras, as mentioned in many songs that have been passed down:

Every year for Carnival time
We make a new suit.
Red, yellow, green, purple, or blue,
We make a new suit.

The Wild Magnolias, "New Suit"

There is nothing quite so photogenic as a Yellow Pocahontas against a clear blue Mardi Gras sky. Function and artistry are integrated at each stage of costume construction. Cuffs, aprons, boots, belts, and crowns are meticulously detailed and lavishly decorated with feathers, rhinestones, pearls, beadwork, and sequins. Downtown tribes generally use a "mummy crown," while uptown tribes employ traditional American Indian headdresses. The latter's costumes contain patches of sequins or stones that depict Indians hunting buffalo or fighting settlers. There are a number of positions in each tribe and they communicate over the several-block span of their parade through a set of signals.

The first figure seen in an Indian parade is the Spy Boy, who is one-half to several blocks ahead of the tribe. He communicates what he sees to the rest of the tribe through signals, expressed by dance or movements with a plywood hatchet. For example, if Spy Boy spots fighting between two tribes, he strikes both curbs with the hatchet. To signal the tribe to stop, he holds his weapon horizontally in front of him. The universal signal for peace among all tribes is stretching hands skyward to make a *U*.

Next seen is the Flag Boy. He travels one-half to several blocks behind Spy Boy. Embedded in his flag is the tribal insignia or name. Flag Boy receives signals from Spy Boy and communicates the messages to the rest of the tribe. Holding the flag horizontally in front at waist level signals the tribe to stop. To indicate a turn, Flag Boy holds the flag high above his head and, after several circular motions with the end of the flag, points it in the new direction.

The signals are communicated from Spy Boy to Flag Boy to the Big Chief, who is responsible for the group and also signals instructions. To stop the parade, Big Chief holds his stick horizontally in front of him. To proceed, he raises the stick above his body and motions forward. Lower-ranked chiefs lead the tribe if something happens to Big Chief. There are also queens, scouts, and the Wild Man, who clears a path through spectators. He is identified by horns on the sides of his headdress. Bodyguards are dressed in civilian clothes and accompany Big Chief. Also, many followers from the neighborhoods travel with the Mardi Gras Indians, chanting with cowbells and tambourines.

Meet a Chief of the Creole Wild West

I interviewed Howard Miller, the Big Chief of the Creole Wild West, the oldest recognized Mardi Gras Indian tribe in New Orleans:

The neighborhood I was born and raised in was Central City. Central City is populated with a lot of Mardi Gras Indians. As a kid, seeing them on the street and early in the morning, I was always fascinated by them. I was in a classroom with a guy that was masking Indian. I had another guy that was living across the neutral ground who was also masking Indian. I started learning how to sew and stuff, and they were teaching me about the Indian, how to be it, and how you're supposed to do it.

Luckily, a Big Chief was living right around the corner from me, and when I transferred to Carter G. Woodson School, a guy says, "You've got to come with us." I started learning to sew and I was able to put my first suit together at the age of thirteen.[32]

Howard's first parade was exciting and life changing:

I was happy to be a part. When I finally made it out that morning I [had been] excited all night. I was with the Apache Hunters when I first started masking. My chief was John Williams, who also sung at the Tick Tock Tavern. When I first masked, I had no idea of the long history and what this culture was about. A lot of times when the Mardi Gras Indians talked, a lot of secrets were kept. A lot of our history was a mystery because we weren't able to document everything and write it down. Everything was given to us by word of mouth and this is why our elders are so important to us. Even today, just like yesterday, they were important to us. They can teach us because they have been there before.

I'm so fortunate and lucky enough to be masking with the Creole Wild West, who had the greatest chief of all. He was born in the 1800s and his name was "Brother" Tillman. "Brother" Tillman was teaching and he taught "Robbe" Lee; 'Robbe' Lee taught Fletcher [Lawrence], who I was fortunate enough to meet him before he died; Fletcher taught Donald Harrison. And it's all come back down to where I am today.[33]

Indian practices were very important in the Mardi Gras Indian culture:

In the beginning, the chief would hold practices in his yard in his backyard, or maybe in his kitchen. Only his tribe would be there, and you may invite other tribes to come over to scrimmage with you. Now during the years, practices became held in public and in bars, and now basically everyone is invited who wants to come to the practices, they can come.

What I try to do in my practices is to teach the young people. These are the next generations of Indians to be coming along, and these are the next ones that are going to lead us. So what I try to do is hold practices, make sure they get the chants down, their dances down, their signals down, and make sure they're able to carry on when we get out there, because we've got to raise the youth to come behind us and we've got to teach them right.[34]

Chapter 14
2000: Sire to Son, Chief to Chief

On Mardi Gras Day 2000, the Yellow Pocahontas donned stunningly beautiful suits, then ran through the throngs on North Villere Street to greet Big Chief Darryl Montana. The Spy Boy, Flag Boy, Wild Man, Queen, Little Braves, Trail Chief, and others followed Big Chief Darryl to Congo Square for a silent, prayerful moment. After that, they began their daylong procession, a Carnival tradition, through the city streets. As Big Chief of the Yellow Pocahontas, Darryl Montana presided over a legacy that has touched his family, neighborhood, and city for generations past and will for generations to come.

The Montana family's role in the Mardi Gras Indian culture dates back to Becate Batiste and the Creole Wild West, believed to be New Orleans' earliest tribe. Darryl's grandmother, Alice, barely remembered her uncle Becate, but his spirit lived with the Montanas for an entire century. Becate was a harbinger of Mardi Gras Indian culture. Alfred Montana was the warrior. Allison "Tootie" Montana, son of Alfred, was the innovator and ambassador. Darryl Montana, son of Tootie, became the tribe's future.

New Orleans provided the backdrop for the Mardi Gras Indian tradition. Its ancestral neighborhoods, unique history, and cultural offerings set the stage for their distinctive pageantry. The Mardi Gras Indians of today walk the same streets, occupy the same homes, and chant the same chants as those long since gone. The Creole Wild West began in the late 1800s in the Seventh Ward neighborhood identified in old New Orleans maps as *la Nouvelle Marigny*, or New Marigny, located roughly between Saint Claude, Saint Bernard, and Elysian Fields avenues. Though not as well publicized as the nearby neighborhoods of Marigny, Treme, and the French Quarter, New Marigny contains a similar mix of nineteenth-century Creole cottages and shotgun houses.

As members of the Creole Wild West relocated around the city, new gangs emerged and took root in other wards. Unlike more fomal Mardi Gras groups, the Mardi Gras Indians had no publicized routes, handbooks, or bylaws. They did not seek parade permits. They did not sip champagne nor schmooze with politicians in front of Gallier Hall on Mardi Gras Day. Yet, their appearances generated more electricity than Rex and Zulu combined. Their breathtaking hand-stitched artistry drew accolades from visitors from around the world. The recognition they sought was not found in the society pages but in the oohs and aahs from the residents in the city's older working-class neighborhoods through which they romped. Each of the approximately sixty-five New Orleans Mardi Gras Indian tribes functioned as a social family fostering unity, sense of purpose, loyalty, and transmission of culture.

Big Chief Alfred Montana

Darryl Montana's grandfather, Alfred Montana, worked as a sign painter and baker. He operated a pie shop on Saint Claude Avenue near Saint Anthony Street. He made violin-shaped wedding cakes complete with strings. Alfred gathered his gang at Indian practice, where they rehearsed the Mardi Gras ritual of chanting and dancing. In his time, members pitched in a quarter or fifty cents to rent apartments for their Indian practice. Alfred practiced around the corner from Darryl's grandmother on Saint Anthony Street. During his early Indian days, he lived at 1015 Dauphine Street, in the French Quarter. On Mardi Gras Day, he put on his hand-sewn suit, went around the corner to Saint Philip Street to get his Second Chief, "Black Benny", and commenced their yearly ritual of masking Indian. Alfred ran with several tribes, including the Eighth Ward Hunters, Wildcats, One-Hundred-One, and Yellow Pocahontas.

He spent time sewing and working on other people's suits, as his two sons, Edward and Allison "Tootie" Montana, watched in fascination. When Tootie was about eight years old, Alfred made a suit for his older brother, Edward. "In those days everything was the big brother," Tootie recalled.[1] But the next year, his father constructed a new red suit for Edward, and Tootie became the proud wearer of the pink suit his brother wore the year before. That suit and the Indian culture created a bond with his father. That bond became dormant after his parents separated. Tootie eventually entered the building trades in New Orleans. He always exhibited a strong work ethic, designing arches for some of the city's most prominent structures.

In modern times, artistry in suit design determines the tribe's stature and character. But in Alfred Montana's day, it was raw guts that got the glory. Tootie Montana recalled, "In those days you didn't get credit for being pretty. You got credit for being bad. It was about fighting and about who pull a gun and run everybody." There was always rivalry between uptown and downtown tribes. In Alfred Montana's time, for the downtown Mardi Gras Indians, crossing the wooden Magnolia Bridge uptown was throwing down the gauntlet. For the uptown Mardi Gras Indians, the same Magnolia Bridge was a line in the sand. Tootie stated, "The further you go over that bridge, the more at stake you were to get into some trouble. My daddy and them would cross that Magnolia Bridge every time."

World War II canceled Mardi Gras until 1946. After the war, Tootie, then in his early twenties, returned home to New Orleans after working in California. The Mardi Gras Indian memories of his boyhood remained with him. In 1947, when he heard that his father was to be chief of an Indian gang in the Eighth Ward, Tootie ventured uptown to his father's house at Saint Andrew near Baronne Street. Mardi Gras Day was only three weeks away. He waited but his father wasn't home. The next Saturday, he waited again. That day, Alfred Montana turned the corner, their eyes met, and a smile broke across both the faces of father and son.

Tootie said, "I heard you pulling that gang in the Eighth Ward."

Chief Alfred Montana responded, "Yeah."

"I want to mask with you. I want to get a suit together," Tootie said.

Alfred was somewhat skeptical. "You don't have but two weeks," he stated.

Tootie was unfazed by the time factor. "Yeah, but I got some help, some people I bum around with." So Alfred welcomed him into the gang. Tootie made what he called "a li'l two-week suit" and prepared to mask Indian.

Big Chief Allison "Tootie" Montana

> Every Carnival, my mother would come out in front my door and pin a scapular on my undershirt, and she wouldn't go to bed until she called my house and found out that boy made it back.
>
> Tootie Montana, 1999

Tootie's mother, Alice, was not keen on his masking. "Aw, boy, you don't want to fool with that," she told him. But in those days, masking Indian was a rite of passage. The Mardi Gras Indians' raw statement of pride affirmed their right to exist. It meant not "bowing down" or "kneeling" before rival gangs. It was a way of life. To be a chief of such men required extra bravado. Tootie stated, "Because being the chief don't mean just saying you're the chief. As far back as you go with Indian and Carnival, to be a chief you had to be something else." Despite his mother's concerns, Tootie joined with Chief Alfred Montana as the Eighth Ward Hunters made their 1947 trek through the city. That was Alfred Montana's last year masking Indian. For Tootie, it was the beginning of an immersion in the Indian culture that lasted his entire life.

In 1948, Robert Guidry led the Eighth Ward Hunters. That year, the tribe counted thirty-seven Indians and was the biggest gang Tootie had ever seen. Tootie went from plain Indian to Second Chief.

The following year, as Tootie stood in the Monogram Bar on Pauger and Marais Street, a man named Wilbur, who playfully walked behind people and pinched their ears to get their attention, tweaked Tootie's ear and the two shared a laugh. Then Wilbur became serious. He told Tootie that he and a man named Joe Simon were interested in starting a new Indian gang. They wanted Tootie to be chief. Wilbur would be Second Chief, and Joe Simon would be Third Chief. Tootie agreed and formed the Monogram Hunters. But at one of their practices, Alfred Montana dropped by to take exception to the name "Monogram Hunters," because of its association with liquor. So after the Yellow Pocahontas stopped masking, Tootie resurrected their name for his tribe.

In 1952, with Tootie as chief, the Monogram Hunters became the Yellow Pocahontas and many of the Eighth Ward Hunters joined them. Tootie recalled the culture's joy and camaraderie: "That Sunday when Carnival's getting closer, we come from practice in a car. We get out that car playing tambourine, doing our number all in the street and thing. I used to love that." Tootie led the gang that Mardi Gras Day and for nearly fifty years thereafter, becoming the foremost Mardi Gras Indian, the Chief of Chiefs. He set a new standard for suit design and decoration.

As the violent aspects of masking Indian dissipated with the times, the suit had become an outlet for competiveness among the tribes. It was inevitable, Tootie remembered, "because they would have to either straighten out, or the jail would be full of Indians on Mardi Gras Day."

Instead of who was the "baddest," it was now who was the "prettiest."

Tootie worked as one of New Orleans' most sought-after wire and metal lathers. He applied construction principles of balance and proportion to suit design. His diligence, competitiveness, and tribal pride staved off fierce challengers who attempted to outdo him.

Tootie told of the 1952 Carnival, when his Second Chief sought out his advice on constructing a double crown and then simply expanded the technique to make a triple crown. When word got back to Tootie that the Second Chief was bragging around the neighborhood how he was going to outdo Big Chief, Tootie bought five more dozens of feathers.

Mardi Gras Day was hot and drizzly that year. Tootie lived above a body and fender shop on Saint Bernard and North Villere Street. He recalled:

> I was in pink and he was in yellow with that triple crown. That Negro wanted to see me so bad. A little bit off in front of my door, they had a post, a fetching post. He hung his crown up there. There were a lot of people around that post looking at that crown. And they said, "You mean to tell me Tootie is going to come out prettier than that?!"
>
> I was taking a little while to come out. That crowd was shoo shooing, the ones that didn't like me and my aunt: "That Negro done looked down there and peep and seen how pretty Second Chief was in that yellow. He's scared to come out now." My aunt said, "Don't worry. He's coming out, and when he comes out, he's got something for y'all to see."
>
> I lived upstairs, li'l narrow stairs. Come up there, that big crown was hanging from the ceiling. When I work, I hang all my crowns from the ceiling. The crown, my uncle John lowered it because he was tall, lowering that crown, setting that big old butterfly crown. The whole apron was a butterfly, front and back. When I move my legs, those circles were doing a number. Came out there, the whole block was black with people. I come out there with all that plush. When that crown came down those steps, that whole block, everybody said, "Awww" at one time. When they said that, it looked like they put life in my body. Aw, man, I was lit up. When finally getting the crown sitting straight on my head, they blinded me, people shooting pictures, taking pictures. Second Chief admitted to me afterwards, "Man, I thought I had you beat."

Tootie Montana pioneered three-dimensional suits, elaborate crowns, and beautiful processions and brought the Mardi Gras Indian culture to the world. He was named a National Endowment for the Arts National Heritage Fellow and was honored by Pres. Ronald Reagan and the

Smithsonian. He was gloriously celebrated at the New Orleans Museum of Art on his fiftieth year of masking. He received a Lifetime Achievement Award from the city of New Orleans for his contributions as an artisan.

Every Mardi Gras, people from the community gathered on North Villere Street to await Tootie's descent of those "li'l narrow stairs." One day, he passed the staff to his son Darryl Montana. How does one get out from under the shadow of Big Chief Tootie Montana?

Big Chief Darryl Montana

> If you're going to come in front of me, come new.
>
> Big Chief Darryl Montana, 2000[2]

Like Chief Tootie, Darryl was imprinted by Mardi Gras Indian culture at an early age. He remembered working on items for his father's suits at age six. His daddy recalled Darryl getting a yellow vinyl school raincoat and cutting it up to make a bird-man suit with wings and a face. Darryl first masked Indian at eleven. He purchased his suit material with money he made washing cars at the body and fender shop. He took pride in always having made his own suit. As a boy, he was the one to fix things, and he thought he would be an electrician. But in later years, the illusions of New Orleans' get-rich-quick streets lured him into a nightmare world of crime, drugs, and finally incarceration.

Darryl reflected on that time:

> I really didn't have an appreciation for my culture, for my history, for my tradition. Not knowing your history is like a ship adrift without an anchor. When I went up before the parole board, they knew me but I didn't know them. They knew me through my father, said I disgraced my family. You're Tootie Montana's son. You have no business in here.

The respect afforded his father also enveloped him. He became drug and alcohol free and used his tale of near-death and redemption to help others. He credited the late Dr. Morris Jeff for putting him on the road to self-awareness: "I found out that my family is known not just in Louisiana. My family is known throughout the world because of my father." For Darryl, Mardi Gras Indian culture became redemption culture. Suit construction became spiritual reconstruction. Family history became salvation history.

Darryl stated, "I'm trying to get guys to know that that is not the life to live. What I try to do on a daily basis is give back to us as a race of people. I'm preserving our culture, our history, and our tradition and making us all understand our ancestors were kings and queens. We're not supposed to be held hostage to anyone or anything, anything meaning drugs."

Like his father, Darryl Montana was a stickler for tradition and honesty in dealing with the Indian culture. Like his father, he created masterful Indian suits and did not water down events and opinions. He did forge his own identity, although getting credit for his suits took a while. People would say, "His daddy did that." But it was Darryl who designed the suits and studded the crowns. His father offered assistance in drawing designs, but Darryl wanted to do it himself. Darryl stated, "That was good knowing that he wanted to share with me. But I think if he had done so, I would not have felt as proud. I'm Tootie Montana's son, but you look at my suit, you don't see Tootie Montana. You see Darryl Montana."

Making a Mardi Gras Indian suit requires Herculean efforts in construction, craft, and artistry. The Yellow Pocahontas pioneered three-dimensional designs in their suits. These take much more effort since their designs protrude from the suit rather than lying flat. Darryl named his suits: "Orange Peacock," "Comeback," "King Tut Revisited," "Determination in Flight."

I visited with Darryl and Sabrina Montana as Mardi Gras 2000 approached. Indian suits on stands looked down at you in a way that overwhelmed with their majesty. During the sewing season, Darryl sat at a glass table in the dining area for hours with scissors, thread, and needles, studding, accenting, and stitching hundreds of designs with stones, pearls, and rice beads. His wife sat on a nearby couch and filled his designs with sequins and beads.

It was an intimate undertaking. His fingertips bore scars and calluses from sewing needles. Like his father, he felt the "fullness," an emotional welling, as the grandeur of the final product transcended the hours, days, and months of monotonous repetition and stitching. That year, he named his millennial suit "Judy's Garden," in honor of fabric artist Judy Darensbourg

Darryl's suits have drawn huge praise for their intricate designs, fabulous three-dimensional depictions, and signature crowns. They have been exhibited at Stella Jones' Gallery, the 1998 Essence Festival, the 1998 American Federation of Teachers Conference, and the New Orleans

A suit of Big Chief Darryl Montana, photographed in his New Orleans East home

Museum of Art. One of his suits was featured in the Louisiana State Museum exhibit entitled "Mardi Gras: It's Carnival Time in Louisiana." His yellow suit was displayed at a museum in California.

New Orleans artist and sculptor John Scott was a fan of Darryl's work. At a meeting at Xavier University, Darryl expressed how honored he was to be in the presence of renowned artisans. "No," Scott replied. "We're honored to be in your presence."

Darryl had spiritual awakenings. As part of an exchange program, he and his gang commiserated with American Indians in Albuquerque, New Mexico. They lived together in tents and offered traditional libations in the Native American manner. It was both a physical journey and spiritual transformation that would sustain him through each Mardi Gras Day:

> I worked from 8:30 to 5:00. I start sewing at 7:00 in the evening, until sometimes 2:00 in the morning, and I have to get up for 6:30. Around Mardi Gras, I get twenty hours of sleep a week. My daddy didn't take the easy way out. I don't take the easy way out. My daddy gave fifty-four years of his life; the love he had he committed himself to the culture. And for a person to make that kind of sacrifice . . . because I know putting that stuff together will kill you.
>
> Basically I'm a quiet person. When I put on my Indian suit Mardi Gras Day, I go through a metamorphosis and turn into this new person. As I get older I go through some of the same stuff my daddy went through. When the house is quiet, and he's sitting up at night by himself, he gets full—he would cry; tears would just start. And even when I talk about it, I get that way.
>
> It's a love. It's a love. It's a respect for your ancestors. And maybe when I put my suit on, I live out my ancestors' dream. The very first year when I became Chief, I felt I had to take them to Congo Square. That's our beginning.
>
> Even beyond the culture, I have truly been blessed. I've been paralyzed once; I've been stabbed in the temple, through the ear, back of the neck, in the back; and I'm still here. And I do know that God has a plan for me.

From Chief to Chief

Sitting around their dining-room table on North Villere Street, Tootie Montana, his wife, Joyce, and son Darryl talked to me about the impact of the Mardi Gras Indian culture on their family and the respect it has brought them. Tootie's first cousin's daughter Gina Montana was the Queen of the Yellow Pocahontas for about five years and became Darryl's

Queen. Tootie's older brother, Edward, also masked with the Yellow Pocahontas. As Tootie's old comrades died off and his body became tired, some of the fun left the arduous process of masking Indian. But during his tenure, Big Chief Tootie developed an appreciation for the community that appreciated him. He stated, "I felt obligated to the public. I wanted to give them as much as I could give them, give y'all something pretty again."

Tootie talked of his abiding respect for the Indian culture, those who carried it in their hearts, the people he had seen, and the stories his daddy and others passed down to him. He remembered "Sonny Boy," the "humbuggish" Big Chief of the Diamond Stars tribe. Then there were the last members of the Yellow Pocahontas before Tootie raised their name again in glory in 1952. He recalled Henri Marigny, a former Chief of the Yellow Pocahontas; Creole; Fletcher; Bit; and a "big tall bright fellow called Eugene." Tootie remembered Charlie Brown, who convinced Alfred

Big Queen Gina Montana

All on a Mardi Gras Day

A program that honored the life of Big Chief Tootie Montana

Montana to head the Eighth Ward Hunters. He told the tale of tall, slim Sidney Pierre, an "old, old man who used to mask with my daddy," running toward his house one freezing Mardi Gras morning, waving his Indian stick. "That was a real Indian," Tootie stated fondly. Then there were Owl; bad "Brother" Tillman; Hoppy, an Eighth Ward Hunter; tall and powerful Danny Lambert; and the Mercadels. He expressed love for the Indian chants, such as "My Indian Red." Tootie recalled:

> We would sometimes sing with church women who also masked Indian. All those women's voices mixed with men's voices. Ooh, boy, it goes through you. I could sing "My Indian Red" and cry. Think about all my family that was living when I first heard that song. And all the people that's dead. Aw, man, it goes through you.

Tootie Montana died on June 27, 2005. While addressing the New Orleans City Council in a strong affirmation for the preservation of the Mardi Gras Indian culture, he suffered a heart attack. He died in the arms of his son Big Chief Darryl Montana, as the other Big Chiefs chanted "My Indian Red."

Chapter 15

New Orleans in the Decade of Change

The following timeline of the 1960s was culled from the pages of the *Louisiana Weekly* newspaper.

1960: Sit-ins and School Integration

January. Segregationist Jimmie Davis was elected governor. . . . A black musician and his white girlfriend were arrested on "miscegenation" charges by the New Orleans Police Department. . . . Madlyn Bridges helped dedicate Mary Dora Coghill Elementary School in Pontchartrain Park with her biography of Mrs. Coghill's life.

February. The student sit-in movement began in Greensboro, North Carolina, when four college students refused to leave a Woolworth's "White Only" counter after being denied service. . . . Milwaukee Braves star Hank Aaron visited the Jax-New Orleans Recreation Department (NORD) championship Conrad Playground team. . . . The Carnival Day Dance at the San Jacinto Club featured Professor Longhair, Jessie Hill, Lil Snook, Benny Spellman, and the Enchanters.

March. With signs proclaiming "Human Rights Are Civil Rights," "We Fought for Freedom Too," and "How Long Must We Wait," 200 Dillard University students marched in front of the Gentilly campus, calling for an end to a segregated society. Later, police arrested four white youths who burned a cross on Dillard's lawn. . . . In downtown Baton Rouge, sixteen Southern University students were jailed for sit-ins at segregated lunch counters.

April. Attorney Thurgood Marshall addressed the Alpha Phi Alpha convention in the Corpus Christi Catholic Church auditorium after being denied permission to use the New Orleans Municipal Auditorium by city administrators. He stated, "There is nothing wrong with being impatient about the lack of freedom in the South, for we know our fight is a righteous one."

July. Managed by Wesley Barrow, the New Orleans Stars baseball team defeated the Birmingham Black Barons to take first place in the American Negro League. Ed Teamer narrated the game on WBOK radio. . . . Art Neville performed at Lincoln Beach on Hayne Boulevard. . . . On screen at New Orleans' "colored" theaters: *Macumba Love* at the Circle, *I Passed for White* at the Clabon, and *Jailhouse Rock* at the Carver.

August. Consumers League spokesman Dr. Raymond Floyd announced a "Fight for Jobs" to protest a lack of black cashiers in the Washington-Claiborne shopping areas. . . . The United Clubs, Inc., a coalition of the city's social-aid and pleasure clubs, issued a statement in support of school integration. . . . Former Valena C. Jones principal Fannie C. Williams retired as a Dillard University trustee. . . . The Congress of Racial Equality (CORE) staged its first New Orleans sit-in at Woolworth's on Canal Street. Refused service and arrested were Jerome Smith, Ruth D'aspenza, Joyce Taylor, William Harper, Archie Allen, and Tulane University students Hugh Murray, Jr., and William M. Harrell. The following week Rudy Lombard, Oretha Castle, Cecil Carter, and Sidney Goldfinch were arrested for a sit-in at McCrory's. . . . Arrested for picketing the Washington-Claiborne shopping area to protest unfair employment practices were the Reverend Avery Alexander, Dr. Henry Mitchell, the Reverend Louis Landrum, Henry Harris, Carlton Roy, and CORE field secretary James McCain.

October. Howard University Medical School dean Dr. Robert Jason spoke at the dedication of a new wing for Dillard University-affiliated Flint-Goodridge Hospital. . . . New Orleanians got involved in the upcoming presidential election. The Reverend A. L. Davis and Clarence "Chink" Henry announced formation of the Kennedy-Johnson Voter's League, as Rose Kennedy visited Xavier University. . . . Dillard University president Dr. Albert Dent and librarian Ernest Wagner broke ground for a new library on campus. . . . New Orleans native Louis Armstrong toured Ghana in Africa.

November. John F. Kennedy was elected president. . . . Drs. Walter Young and Andrew Young, Sr. opened a father-son dental practice on Cleveland Street. . . . Six-year-olds Gail Etienne, Tessie Prevost, Leona Tate, and Ruby Bridges became the first blacks to attend previously white elementary schools in the Deep South since Reconstruction. . . . Longtime Civil Rights attorney A. P. Tureaud was guest of honor at the Louis A. Martinet Society banquet.

December. Dr. Raymond Floyd, president of the United Clubs, Inc., called for a "blackout" of Carnival to protest the lack of a strong response by city officials to violence that occurred in the wake of school integration.

1961: New Orleanians Joined the Freedom Rides

January. Xavier student officers Rudy Lombard, Armand Bertrand, Vincent Roux, and Eugene Staes presented the funds saved from dances canceled during the "blackout" of Carnival. Recipients were the United Negro College Fund, Urban League, National Association for the Advancement of Colored People (NAACP), and CORE.

February. Traditional-jazz clarinetist Alphonse Picou died at age eighty-one. The Eureka Brass Band and Tuxedo Brass Band led the funeral procession and traditional second line, which included fellow musicians, friends, relatives, and beatniks from the French Quarter. Funeral director George Llopis called it the largest jazz funeral he ever witnessed. . . . Jim Sutton, a white resident of the Florida housing project, was fired from his job after sending his child to Frantz School despite a segregationist boycott.

March. The Autocrat Club's Easter dance showcased Snooks Eaglin and the Royal Dukes of Rhythm featuring the Sultans, while WNOE radio sponsored a star-studded concert at the Municipal Auditorium that included Johnny Adams, Aaron Neville, Eddie Bocage, Jimmy Jones, the Five Satins, Slim Harpo, Bobby Mitchell, Lee Dorsey, Chris Kenner, Al "Carnival Time" Johnson, Jessie Hill, Clarence "Frogman" Henry, Earl King, Smiley Lewis, Benny Spellman, and the Tommy Ridgely Band. A ticket was $1.50 in advance, $2.00 at the door. . . . The United States Supreme Court nullified hundreds of segregation laws passed by the Louisiana Legislature in their effort to maintain separate school systems.

April. Constance Bradford, Doris Castle, Julia Aaron, David Dennis, and Jerome Smith were arrested for picketing Woolworth's in New Orleans. Smith remained in jail after refusing to post bail. . . . Walter Orr, a white seaman, was jailed for drinking coffee at a "Colored Only" lunch counter on Canal Street.

May. Dr. Leonard Burns of the United Clubs, Inc., distributed $12,000 to Civil Rights causes. These funds were raised during the Mardi Gras Blackout.

June. Five Louisiana students were arrested after the Freedom Riders arrived in Jackson, Mississippi. Booked with "breaching the peace" and sentenced to 120 days in Mississippi's Parchman Prison were Jerome Smith, Doris Castle, Julia Aaron, Catherine Thompson, and David Dennis. . . . Emmanuel Gregoire, popular principal of Andrew J. Bell Junior High School, died at age fifty. . . . New Orleans councilman-at-large James Comiskey called for the formation of a Human Relations Committee.

July. Departing mayor Chep Morrison named the Reverend A. L. Davis, president of the Interdenominational Ministerial Alliance, as the city's first race relations officer. . . . Roosevelt Taylor, former football star at Joseph S. Clark High School and Grambling University, signed a contract with the Chicago Bears. . . . The Avalons, Royal Dukes of Rhythm, and Lloyd Price performed on the outdoor stage at Lincoln Beach, while James Brown and Chuck Berry entertained at the Municipal Auditorium. . . . Facing a Justice Department lawsuit, the New Orleans airport agreed to serve blacks in its coffeeshop. . . . The Reverend Avery Alexander and Rudy Lombard led a march to the Interstate Commerce Commission's office to protest segregation in interstate travel. . . . Louis Armstrong, Cannonball Adderley, and Gerry Mulligan performed at a benefit concert in New York in support of the Freedom Riders. . . . George Washington Carver High School senior Shirley Thompson returned to New Orleans after being jailed during the Freedom Rides.

August. Morris F. X. Jeff, Sr., announced the winners of the annual skate mobile derby, a contest for black youths sponsored by Sunbeam Bread. Jesse Mimette, George Smith, Frederick Oliver, and Hollis Gordon were awarded bicycles for their efforts. . . . Attorneys Robert Collins and Lolis Elie entered not-guilty pleas for fifteen demonstrators arrested during a sit-in at police headquarters in New Orleans. . . . Civil Rights attorney Jack Nelson filed suit against Tulane University for refusing graduate-school entry to Barbara M. Guillory and Pearlie Hardin Elloie. . . . Mayor Victor Schiro abolished A. L. Davis's job as race relations officer, stating the position was not approved by the City Council. . . . Community leader Daniel Byrd told a Masons convention that New Orleans must overcome its racial problems or become a second-rate Southern city.

October. With support from 125 city organizations, spokesmen Daniel

Thompson and Ernest Wright announced that the Coordinating Council launched a drive to increase voter registration by 25,000 and to raise $10,000. . . . Xavier University broke ground for a new student center. . . . As part of an agreement with the Consumers League, New Orleans Public Service, Inc. (NOPSI), announced that two blacks would be trained as bus drivers. The Reverend Avery Alexander hailed this move forward.

November. New Orleans voter registration stood at 170,676 whites and 35,419 blacks. . . . Of 40 black people who applied to vote this month, only 7 were approved. . . . Louisiana State University in New Orleans (LSUNO) canceled a play entitled *The Queen and the Rebels* after black student Louis Washington was cast in one of the roles.

December. The city denied permission to use the Municipal Auditorium for a rally featuring Dr. Martin Luther King, Jr. The attendees then marched to the Union Bethel A.M.E. Church, where Dr. King presented an award to International Longshoremen Association (ILA) president Clarence "Chink" Henry for the union's voter-registration efforts. In his remarks, Dr. King called on President Kennedy to issue an executive order prohibiting segregation. "You can't stand on the beaches of history and hold back the tide," he said.

1962: Doors Open Slowly

January. Less than a month after denying Dr. Martin Luther King, Jr., the city allowed use of the Municipal Auditorium for a pro-segregation rally sponsored by the White Citizen's Council. . . . The Reverend Percy Simpson presided over the twenty-fifth anniversary celebration of Greater Saint Stephen Baptist Church.

February. Seymour Weiss, president of the Roosevelt Hotel, blamed the Louisiana Legislature's segregation laws for the decline in New Orleans convention business. . . . Chrysler Corporation, a major contractor at the Michoud facility, signed a no-bias pledge in the building of the booster rockets for space flights. . . . Attorneys Ernest Morial, A. M. Trudeau, and A. P. Tureaud filed suit against the slow pace of school desegregation.

March. Victor Schiro won a runoff for mayor over State Senator Adrian Duplantier. . . . While waiting for a bus with her brother, Henderson Dunn Elementary School sixth-grader Ingrid Richardson was killed when a group of white males in a passing automobile hit her in the head with a brick. The previous week, Ingrid reigned as the school's queen. An eyewitness described the scene:

> We were standing there for less than ten minutes when my little girl screamed. Almost at the same time, I heard a thud and turned to see the little Richardson girl falling to the ground. When she fell, the girl remained motionless. Her brother tried to help her, and she stirred and moaned, "Albert, they hit me." Then she lapsed into unconsciousness.

April. In a ruling by Federal Judge J. Skelly Wright, Barbara Guillory and Pearlie Elloie were granted admission to Tulane University Graduate School. . . . Shirley Verret, internationally acclaimed mezzo soprano and New Orleans native, held a free public recital at Dillard University. . . . Charles R. Self of LSUNO won first place in general poetry in a Louisiana College Writers' Society competition. He was the only black participant. . . . Archbishop Joseph Rummel excommunicated Leander Perez, B. J. Guillot, and Jackson Ricau for their continual urging of racial hatred and opposition to the archdiocese's decision to integrate all Catholic schools. . . . White students at Tulane University sat in to protest the expulsion of Edwin Clark for bringing black guests into the school cafeteria. . . . Thirteen-year-old Benjamin Barbee's application to enter the New Orleans Recreation Department (NORD)-sponsored soapbox derby was denied because of his color. He was sponsored by the United Clubs, Inc. . . . The April 14 *Louisiana Weekly* published an editorial that stated, "There are those who are so blind that they cannot accept the fact that the entire world is changing; that darker people of the universe who had been enslaved, oppressed or ignored for centuries are now seeking independence, decent standards of living, and most of all, human dignity."

May. President Kennedy visited New Orleans and addressed integrated crowds. . . . After Judge Wright departed the city, Tulane University sought a new trial to prevent black graduate students from enrolling. . . . Following rousing accolades in Germany and Switzerland, New Orleans mezzo contralto Debria Brown returned to her hometown to do a benefit concert at Xavier University Preparatory High School.

June. Ann Marie Prevost became the first person of color to receive a bachelor's degree in the Louisiana State University system. . . . Jarrold Wilson, a fifteen-year-old McDonogh #35 student, was hit with a rock by a group of white males who ambushed him. . . . The Eureka Brass Band journeyed to Washington, D.C. to represent New Orleans at the

International Jazz Festival. Making the trip were Kid Sheik, Emanuel Paul, Percy Humphrey, Willie Humphrey, Albert Warner, Alcide Pavageau, and "Fats" Houston. . . . Two hundred thirty three blacks registered for first grade at previously all white schools. . . . The NAACP petitioned Mayor Victor Schiro to end segregation at NORD recreational facilities.

August. The Gentilly Warriors baseball team, coached by Eli Penny and Louis Neveu, Sr., won the championship in NORD's thirteen-year-old Negro league. . . . All Catholic schools in New Orleans became desegregated. . . . Forty Central Business District stores desegregated their lunch counters.

October. Fifth-grader Joseph Briley was hospitalized after being hit by a brick thrown by a group of white youths.

December. In its new trial by a different judge, Tulane University once again won the right to refuse admission to black graduate students. However, its board of directors voted to adopt an open-door admissions policy.

1963: *Direct Action Workshops and Voter Crusades*

January. Ernest Morial succeeded Arthur Chapital as president of the local NAACP. . . . Grand Marshals Henry Glass and Alcide Houston led the traditional jazz funeral for clarinetist John Casimir, founder of the Young Tuxedo Brass Band. . . . The Reverend A. L. Davis presided over the Ministerial Alliance's celebration of the 100th anniversary of the Emancipation Proclamation. . . . Writer James Baldwin spoke at several local colleges, including Tulane, Dillard, Loyola, Xavier, and SUNO.

February. New Orleans' voter registration stood at 164,266 whites and 34,814 blacks. . . . Blacks enrolled in Tulane University's graduate school included Barbara Guillory, Pearlie Elloie, Gloria Adams, Charles Hayes, Addison Carey, Willeme Pulliam, George Parker, Purcell Church, and Arthur Leary.

March. The Coordinating Council launched a selective-buying campaign to end discrimination against black workers in Canal Street stores. A handbill read, "Don't Buy Where You Can't Work. We Will Wear Last Year's Easter Outfit with Pride until We Are Employed with Dignity." . . . Dr. Daniel Thompson, who left New Orleans to become dean of Howard University's Sociology Department, returned home to proofread his book *The Negro Leadership Class*.

April. Twenty-six black employees in the cafeteria at LSU Medical Center were fired after they protested the cafeteria management's refusal to serve a black pre-med student. . . . The Coordinating Council selected Irvin S. Daniel to lead its Voter Education and Registration Project. He stated, "When the Negro's voting strength is increased to the point where it is a major election factor, every office holder will be calling at his door." . . . CORE conducted a two-day series of workshops at the Mount Zion Educational Center on Dumaine Street. Topics and presenters included "Techniques of Direct Action," Jean Thompson, Julia Humbles, and Jerome Smith; "Legal Aspects of Civil Rights," Lolis Elie, Robert Collins, and Nils Douglas; and "Political Awareness," by the Reverend A. L. Davis, Leontine Luke, and Robert Valder.

May. The Tulane University student newspaper, the *Hullabaloo*, criticized the school administration for delaying the signing of a contract for the appearance of Metropolitan Opera singer Marian Anderson because she had a white pianist. State law forbade integrated entertainment. . . . Attorney Revius Ortique was elected president of the Louis A. Martinet Society. . . . A small group of segregationists booed and jeered one of the five black women who integrated Saint Joseph's Academy Catholic High School as she and her escort arrived for the school prom. A cross was later burned on the school lawn. . . . The American Legion canceled its New Orleans convention because of segregated hotel facilities. . . . The U.S. Supreme Court overturned the convictions of Rudy Lombard, Cecil Carter, Oretha Castle and Sidney Goldfinch for the 1960 sit-in at McCrory's.

June. As part of the Voter Crusader Corps, over two hundred high-school and college students pledged their summers to a citywide voter-registration drive. New Orleans native Andrew Young, Jr., program director of the Southern Christian Leadership Conference (SCLC), addressed the group: "There are many ways to overthrow a slave system and your very lives are at stake. You have the power in your hands to put 3,000 voters on the registration rolls and you will do it." . . . The first officers of the Youth Department of the Coordinating Council were Joyce Thomas of Booker T. Washington High School, chairman; Walter Collins of LSUNO, vice-chairman; Brenda LaChaux of Booker T. Washington High School, secretary; and Marilyn Thomas of McDonogh #35 High School, secretary. . . . Fifty CORE members were refused admission to the Saenger Theater, where comedian Jerry Lewis was performing. . . . New Orleans police seized all copies of James Baldwin's book *Another Country* and arrested the manager of Doubleday Bookstore on Canal Street on obscenity charges for selling it. However, District Attorney James "Jim" Garrison refused the charges.

July. Clarence "Chink" Henry was elected to a fourth term as ILA president.

August. A three-judge federal panel that consisted of John Minor Wisdom, Herbert Christenberry, and Robert Ainsworth, Jr. ordered the desegregation of all NORD facilities. . . . The March on Washington took place. . . . Sybil Haydel Morial filed suit against a Louisiana law that prohibited schoolteachers from advocating integration. . . . Irvin S. Daniel and Virginia Collins were among ninety persons jailed for picketing the voter-registration office in New Orleans.

October. Chanting, "Freedom," thousands of people marched from Shakespeare Park to City Hall for an interfaith and interracial rally. The Reverend A. L. Davis called the march a beginning. . . . Policemen dragged the Reverend Avery Alexander by his feet from the cafeteria in City Hall and carried activist Sandra Nixon out in a chair after the pair sought service at the segregated facility. Others arrested were Doris Castle, Louis Landrum, and Louis Antoine.

November. Pres. John F. Kennedy was assassinated.

December. Pres. Lyndon Baines Johnson (LBJ) asked for passage of a Civil Rights Bill as a memorial to President Kennedy. . . . In an event sponsored by the Dryades Street YMCA, New Orleans native Mahalia Jackson returned home to give a gospel concert at the Municipal Auditorium.

1964: Civil Rights and Civil Wrongs

January. The U.S. Supreme Court overturned a Louisiana law that required candidates to be identified by race on the ballot. . . . John McKeithen was elected governor.

February. CORE members Doris Castle, Sandra Nixon, and the Reverend Avery Alexander filed a suit to force City Hall to serve blacks in the cafeteria. . . . Dillard University graduate Alvin B. Jones joined Smith, Wiltzer and Peebles, making it the city's first integrated law firm. . . . Virginia Cox Welch, a white teacher at Saint Augustine High School, filed suit to enter SUNO after being denied admission because of state laws. . . . Federal judge Herbert Christenberry deplored the dragging of the Reverend Avery Alexander from the City Hall cafeteria and ordered the cafeteria desegregated. . . . CORE members picketed a White Citizen's Council meeting featuring avid segregationist John Rarick at the Municipal Auditorium.

March. NORD canceled its annual soapbox derby in defiance of a federal order to allow blacks to participate. . . . Sybil Morial presided over the first meeting of the League of Good Government, an integrated women's civic and political organization. . . . CORE opened its local office at 2211 Dryades Street. Richard Haley was appointed director. . . . Larry McKinley presided over the Motown Revue at the Municipal Auditorium featuring Marvin Gaye, Mary Wells, Stevie Wonder, the Temptations, and Martha and the Vandellas.

May. Xavier University Preparatory High School junior Vivian Janet McDonald was chosen to represent the United States at the Sixth International Youth Science Fortnight in London. . . . NORD closed the city's pools rather than integrate them. . . . The Justice Department cited New Orleans on a list of cities that discriminated in voter registration. . . . Former mayor Chep Morrison died in an airplane crash in Mexico.

July. LBJ signed the Civil Rights Act of 1964 into law. Mayor Victor Schiro pledged to uphold the law of the land. For the first time since the nineteenth century, Southern blacks were legally protected to receive service in restaurants, attend theaters, and utilize public accommodations. Arthur Chapital observed, "This event is not the culmination of a year's work or five or ten years but over three hundred years of hard, bitter struggles which included lives, fortunes, and sacred honors, each playing its part.". . . Segregationists burned a cross on the lawn of Xavier University Preparatory High School and harassed blacks who attended previously segregated Pontchartrain Beach. . . . Five white males were arrested in the shooting of eight-year-old Vonelle Jackson at the corner of Boyd and General Meyer in Algiers.

August. Police raided the Quorum, an integrated coffeehouse on Esplanade Avenue that was frequented by the city's beatniks. . . . Twenty-eight-year-old Rivers Frederick II was shot by a white businessman who objected to his presence at the previously segregated Royal Castle hamburger shop at Bell and North Broad. Frederick said, "I saw he had a revolver. He fired two shots through the front windshield of my car. One shot struck me in the face, and I ducked. The other struck the back of my neck." . . . Lincoln Beach announced it would cease operations. . . . According to a study by the Voter Education and Registration Project, only 31 percent of Louisiana's eligible black voters were allowed to register. . . . Led by trombonist Louis Nelson and Kid Sheik of the Storyville Ramblers, the Jolly Boys Social and Pleasure Club held a seven-hour parade through the city streets. . . . Dr. Albert Dent, Norman Francis, Leonard Burns, and Daniel Thompson were named to the board of the local anti-poverty committee as part of LBJ's War on Poverty. . . . A U.S. court ordered the desegregation of SUNO and Delgado. . . . Carver High School graduate Theron Lewis was picked for the Olympic track team. . . . Six white males severely beat fifty-nine-year-old Joseph Hudson as he walked home from church. NAACP leader Arthur Chapital protested the escalating unprovoked attacks by white males on blacks since the passage of the Civil Rights Act.

October. Two white males shot and wounded Alphonse Blunt and Harold Hudson at the corner of Prentiss and Baccich streets. . . . Two white youths were arrested for shooting sixteen-year-old Sylvia Bowman, fifteen-year-old Jacquelyn Wilson, and eleven-year-old Clarence Lewis for no apparent reason. . . . Dillard University student Sherman Copelin was invited to the White House for a meeting with LBJ. . . . The Dixie Cups singing group toured England.

November. An all-white Criminal Court jury acquitted Fred Jackson in the August shooting of Rivers Frederick II. . . . Two white males in an automobile shot Zelma Hebert of Tonti Street as she attempted to cross Freret Street. . . . Dr. Wellington Arnaud filed suit against Arnaud's restaurant under the 1964 Civil Rights Act after he was refused service there.

1965: *The Vote*

January. Police Chief Joseph Giarusso announced the appointment of Sidney Cates as the police force's first black lieutenant. . . . In the face of a suit by Collie Castle, Charity Hospital removed its signs designating separate racial areas. . . . The American Football League moved its scheduled all-star game from Tulane Stadium to Houston after black players were refused taxi service at New Orleans' airport and turned away from French Quarter establishments.

February. The Young Men's Twenty Club celebrated its fiftieth anniversary.

March. Saint Augustine High School senior Vernon Cottles won a first-place prize at the city's first integrated science fair. . . . Carver High School graduate Theron Lewis set a new indoor record in the 440-yard dash, with a time of 47.8 seconds, at the National Collegiate Athletic Association (NCAA) track meet in Detroit.

April. Mardi Gras Indian suits went on display at the New Orleans Public Library. . . . SUNO art professor Jack Jordan's *Crucifixion on Mount Calvary* won first place in sculpture at Atlanta University's National Art Exhibition.

May. Segregationists firebombed the home of fifty-seven-year-old Victoria Johnson, the first black resident of the Saint Thomas housing project. . . . The League of Good Government announced the opening of voter-registration clinics throughout the city. Officers and ward leaders included Delores Hayes, Sedonia Weber, Dorothy Taylor, Marian Wolf, Cora Lee Larks, Odile Deslonde, Marion Roux, and Sybil Morial. . . . Ernest Morial was sworn in as the first black assistant U.S. attorney. . . . A car owned by Samuel Henry, Jr., was firebombed in front of Dooky Chase's Restaurant, the twelfth firebombing of the year.

June. Four white males were given suspended sentences in the 1962 death of eleven-year-old Ingrid Richardson, who was slain with a brick while waiting for a bus. . . . Three white youths stabbed Michael Butler in the neck as he walked along Palm Street. . . . Booker T. Washington High School graduate John Scott joined the Xavier University art faculty after receiving a master of fine arts degree from Michigan State University.

July. Miss Joel Thomas became the year's tenth drowning victim while swimming in the Mississippi River. . . . NORD kept all city pools closed rather than integrate them. . . . The CORE office on Dryades Street was firebombed.

August. LBJ signed the Voting Rights Act. New Orleans voter-registration figures stood at 162,000 whites and 35,794 blacks. The Ministerial Alliance stated, "We recognize that the law within itself is of little value unless citizens register and vote. We also recognize that government is more stable and responsible when an informed citizenry fully participates." Harrison Guy, age 101, stood with thousands of black New Orleanians who sought to register in the days following the Voting Rights Act. Orleans Parish registrar A. P. Gallinghouse filed a suit protesting the law's constitutionality. . . . Gov. John McKeithen appointed twenty-one whites and twenty-one blacks to the Louisiana Commission on Race Relations, including Dr. Albert Dent, who was named vice-president.

October. New Orleans voter registration stood at 158,774 whites and 49,543 blacks. Figures represented a 37 percent increase in black voter registration since the Voting Rights Act. . . . Under the leadership of David Dennis, twenty volunteers from Walter L. Cohen High School and Dillard University steered a drive to repair homes damaged by Hurricane Betsy. . . . Dr. Roy Boggs, Dr. Anthony Hackett, Dr. Wesley Segre, Dr. Richard Timpton, and Dr. George Thomas became the first blacks admitted to the Orleans Parish Medical Society. . . . The Jackie Wilson Show arrived at the Municipal Auditorium, featuring the Impressions, Gene ("Rainbow 65") Chandler, Major Lance, Barbara ("Sad, Sad Girl") Mason, Jerry Butler, Gladys Knight and the Pips, the 3 Ikettes, and Fontella ("Rescue Me") Bass.

November. In town to do a benefit at Loyola University for the New Orleans Jazz Museum, Louis Armstrong was greeted with music from his native city by Paul Babarin and the Onward Brass Band. . . . Victor Schiro defeated Jimmy Fitzmorris in a close mayor's race. The black leadership was split, but Fitzmorris won the majority of the black vote. . . . McDonogh #35 High School graduate Sgt. Levine Banks was killed in Vietnam, as was SP4 Herman Jefferson.

December. Cpl. Willie Francis of Marrero was killed in Vietnam.

1966: *Vietnam Comes Home*

January. Mayor Victor Schiro named A. P. Tureaud as New Orleans' first black assistant city attorney. . . . For the first time, Saint Augustine High School and Xavier University Preparatory High School participated in the Catholic Youth Organization (CYO) basketball tournament at Loyola University. Saint Augustine's Harold Sylvester was named to the All-CYO team. . . . Clarence Jupiter and Millie Charles spoke at Total Community Action's Central City anti-poverty kickoff rally. . . . Harold Perry became the first native-born black American to be consecrated as a Catholic bishop.

February. Pfc. Nathaniel Simmons was reported killed in Vietnam. . . . The Louisiana High School Athletic Association (LHSAA) voted to deny Saint Augustine High School admission to the organization for Catholic high school sporting events.

March. Twenty-three-year-old Richard Perez, a graduate of Corpus Christi Catholic School and Joseph S. Clark High School, and Booker T. Washington High School graduate Isiah Baker were killed in Vietnam. Pfc. Frank Mullen was killed in Vietnam with gunshot wounds to the head and left eye three days after his twenty-third birthday. Herman Penn, eighteen, a former member of the track and basketball teams at Carver High School and the oldest of seven children, was killed near Chau Hai, South Vietnam. Another Carver graduate, Sgt. Lionel Randolph, was killed in Vietnam. In a statement, the Pentagon attributed the disproportionately high number of black deaths in Vietnam to "Negro valor in combat" rather than discrimination in assignments. . . . Six blacks were promoted to the rank of line sergeant in the New Orleans Police Department. They were Lloyd Richards, Lloyd Verret, George Williams, John Raphael, Samuel Reine, and Perry White.

April. Carver graduate Eric Williams and Booker T. Washington graduate Robert Benjamin were killed in Vietnam. . . . Klansman Jack Helm was removed from the Orleans Parish draft board after NAACP president Horace Bynum sent a protest letter. . . . McDonogh Day activities proceeded with schools marching in alphabetical order rather than by racial composition. . . . The Free Southern Theater announced a series of creative-writing workshops at their theater building on Louisa Street and Lausat Place in the Ninth Ward.

June. City Councilman Maurice "Moon" Landrieu sponsored an equal-hiring ordinance for city jobs. . . . Booker T. Washington graduate John Batiste was buried in New Orleans after being killed in Vietnam. New Orleans draftee Adam Weber became one of the first prisoners of conscience in the Vietnam era, after being sentenced to a year in prison for refusing to kill in Vietnam. He offered to serve as a frontline medic but would not accept a rifle. Weber stated, "I don't think anyone has the right to order me to perform an inhuman act."

July. Stokely Carmichael renounced unconditional nonviolence and issued a call for Black Power during a march in Mississippi.

August. Nineteen-year-old Saint Augustine High School graduate Pfc. Chester Simmons was killed in Vietnam. Raymond Duvernay filed suit against the all-white composition of the Orleans Parish draft board. . . . Bethel Lutheran Church on Louisa Street hosted the Free Southern

Theater's performances of *Roots*, by Gilbert Moses, and *I Speak of Africa*, by William Palmer. . . . Only two weeks after recovering from a war wound, Cohen High School graduate Frank August was killed in Vietnam. . . . Educator Lawrence Crocker died from a heart attack. . . . Clarence Barney was named to head the Urban League of New Orleans.

November. Mayor Victor Schiro named Dr. Albert Dent to be the first black on the City Planning Commission. Commissioner George Soule resigned in protest.

December. Ex-Peace Corps worker Vincent Brown was shot by a French Quarter bartender after attempting to use a restroom.

1967: Ernest Nathan "Dutch" Morial Elected to the Louisiana Legislature

January. New Orleans pianist Walter "Fats" Pichon died at the age of sixty.

April. Saint Augustine High School student Harold Sylvester became the first black to receive a Tulane University athletic grant-in-aid.

June. Appointed by the City Council, Norman C. Francis became the first Negro to serve on the City Civil Service Commission.

July. A gang of fifty whites attacked sixteen blacks on the lakefront. The black youths were attending a going-away outing for Reuben Burgess and John Owens, two marine enlistees. . . . Carver graduate Wellington Johnson was killed by a bomb in Vietnam. . . . Saint Augustine High School was accepted into the LHSAA after a court order. . . . William Rouselle, Student Council president at Xavier University, was hired as a correspondent to the New York office of *Time* magazine. . . . For the first time, three blacks participated in the NORD soapbox derby.

August. McDonogh #35 High School graduate and three-time Purple Heart recipient Stanley Ferbos was killed in Vietnam. . . . *Louisiana Weekly* columnist Jim Hall was named as a consultant to the New Orleans Saints football team. . . . A federal court overturned Louisiana's law prohibiting people from marrying those of the opposite race, leaving John Zippert and Carol Prejean free to wed. . . . The New Orleans City Council announced the establishment of a Human Relations Committee.

November. Ernest Morial became the first black elected to the state legislature since Reconstruction. He said, "There are many good-thinking, sensible, and honorable men in the legislature and I am confident they will receive me just as they would any other legislator."

December. Earl Amedee and the Reverend Avery Alexander became the first blacks to be elected to the Orleans Parish Democratic Executive Committee. . . . Nineteen-year-old marine Clarence Jordan was beaten by police after going into a Bourbon Street bar. . . . Lincoln High School graduate Dave Bartholomew was killed in Vietnam.

1968: Black Pride and Black Power

January. Mitchell J. Duncan of North Rocheblave Street, Robert Walls of Abundance Street, Carver graduate Earl London, and Cpl. Murrie Blocker were reported killed in Vietnam.

February. Police arrested representative elect Ernest N. Morial and *Louisiana Weekly* editor Henry Dejoie for "refusing to move on" in front of Morial's domicile at 1242 Magazine Street. . . . Black History Month activities were announced. . . . The First Festival of Afro-American Arts at Dillard University featured John Killens, literature; Tom Dent and Elvard Burt, theater; Vernon Winslow, art; and Edwin B. Hogan, music. Also presented were N. R. Davidson's original play *Malik*, poetry by Sybil Kein, a short story by Joseph S. Clark High School students called "Hands of the Black," and a psychedelic light show by Warren Parker and Raymond Duvernay. David Dennis stated that the festival's purpose was "to discover and appreciate the rich portions of Negro heritage which have long been neglected or overlooked." . . . Free Southern Theater's Creative Writing Workshop celebrated the 100th anniversary of the birth of Dr. W. E. B. Du Bois with a discussion of his *Folkways* recorded autobiography and a narration by Tom Dent.

March. Reuben Burgess, Cohen High Class of 1966, was killed in Vietnam. A gang of white youths attacked his going-away party on the lakefront in July of 1967. Kenneth Moore, McDonogh #35 High Class of 1965, was killed in Vietnam. David L. Smith, nineteen-year-old Lincoln High alumnus, was killed in Vietnam.

April. Dr. Martin Luther King, Jr., was assassinated in Memphis, Tennessee. In his honor, labor leader Clarence Henry ordered a work stoppage at the port of New Orleans as part of a Day of Rededication to the Advancement of Human Dignity. . . . Sidney Cates became the first black captain on the New Orleans Police Department. . . . Blacks appointed to the city's first Human Relations Committee were Israel Augustine, Clothide Bernard, Aline Saint Julien, the Reverend Morris Burrel, Horace Bynum, Henry Hayes, Robert McFarland, Warren McKenna, Alvin Sergeant, Dr. Mack Spears, Ursula Spencer, the Reverend Milton Upton, Daniel Vincent, and Benny Weathers. . . . LBJ signed the Open Housing Act. . . . Former Booker T. Washington High School band member James Richardson was killed in Vietnam.

May. Ernest Morial was sworn in as the first black Louisiana legislator since Reconstruction.

June. Norman Francis became the first black president of Xavier University. . . . Ernest N. Morial boycotted a speech to the legislature by segregationist George Wallace.

July. Cpl. Clayton Johnson, Cohen High School Class of 1965, was killed in Vietnam. . . . Clark graduate Danny Mension became the first Louisiana black admitted to West Point.

August. Israel Augustine, the Reverend A. L. Davis, Ernest Morial, and Henry Dejoie became Louisiana's first black delegates to the Democratic Convention. . . . Booker T. Washington High School graduate Raymond Cobb was killed in Vietnam.

October. Xavier graduate Lavergne Monette became the first black to sing with the New Orleans Opera House Association. . . . Ronnie Pounds and Gordon Butler were killed in Vietnam.

November. New Orleans' voter registration stood at 161,134 whites and 63,165 blacks. . . . Dr. Albert Dent, one of the original organizers of the United Negro College Fund, announced his retirement from Dillard University. . . . Richard M. Nixon was elected president.

December. Dr. Mack Spears was elected the first black member of the Orleans Parish School Board.

1969: *Students Protest and Teachers Strike*

January. New Orleans marked the passing of jazz musicians George Lewis and Adolphe Alexander with a traditional jazz funeral. . . . Attorney Nils Douglas announced the opening of the Southern Organization for Unified Leadership (SOUL) center at 5500 North Johnson Street. . . . Fifty-four students were arrested at Alcee Fortier High School after demanding a black student union, black studies, and fair disciplinary procedures. Dr. Mack Spears voiced his opposition to a black student untion: "I've spent half of my life fighting for human dignity and the oneness of society.". . . Dashiki Theater presented Ted Gilliam's *Hand Is on the Gate* at Saint Frances de Sales Church. The cast included Alfred Dean Irby, Thelma Hinson, Guy West, Jr., Carolyn Sutton, Craig Mitchell, Sara Landrum, N. R. Davidson, and Mattie Stone. . . . In his first year on the varsity team, Harold Sylvester led Tulane University in rebounds.

February. Eleven SUNO students were arrested on campus for protesting a hike in the school's tuition. . . . With the theme "Black Is Beautiful," Zulu paraded on Canal Street for the first time. . . . Mayor Schiro proclaimed February 9 through February 15 as Negro History Week in New Orleans. . . . Fortier High School announced the suspension of eight student protestors. . . . Willie Tee and the Souls played the opening concert at the Jazz Workshop on Decatur Street. . . . A jazz funeral was held for Adolph Paul Barbarin, who died after marching in the Proteus parade with the Onward Brass Band. . . . WDSU-TV's first black reporter, William Rouselle, accepted the position of deputy director of the Human Relations Committee. . . . Xavier University students held a poetry reading and Afro-jazz program as a memorial to Malcolm X. Student president Kenneth Ferdinand stated that the event was an effort "to stimulate awareness and brotherhood through experiences held in common."

April. Eighteen were arrested at school board offices as Orleans Parish teachers began a strike to gain union recognition. . . . A jazz funeral was held for New Orleans trumpeter Joseph "Sunny" Williams. . . . Students at SUNO raised the Flag of Black Liberation. Twenty-seven were arrested and charged with flag desecration, resisting arrest, inciting a felony, and more. One student was severely beaten by police and required twenty-one stitches. Student demands included a black studies program, a noncredit course in black liberation, a new classroom building, a draft counseling center, more books by black authors in the library, a department of education, and revision of the student handbook.

May. Xavier University students blocked the door to the Administration Building, calling for more radical periodicals, more books by black authors, and the elimination of philosophy and theology requirements. . . . Five hundred National Guardsmen were dispatched to SUNO after students seized administrative control. . . . City officials removed the Confederate flag from the City Council chambers.

June. Israel Augustine became the first black Criminal Court judge in Louisiana.

July. Xavier University graduate Wanda Rouzan appeared on ABC-TV's "All-American College Show," singing "It's Not Unusual." . . . Draft resistor Walter Collins was sentenced to five years in prison for refusing induction into the armed forces. He said, "If I am guilty of a crime, it is the crime of thinking."

November. Ethel Mae Williams was chosen as Fortier's first black homecoming queen. . . . SUNO students spearheaded a march against the Vietnam War, from their campus to the Federal Building downtown.

December. With strong black support, Moon Landrieu upset Jimmy Fitzmorris in the runoff for mayor.

Notes

Chapter 1

1. Roulhac B. Toledano and Mary Louise Christovich, *New Orleans Architecture*, vol. 6, *Faubourg Tremé and the Bayou Road* (Gretna, LA: Pelican, 1980), 15.

2. Ibid., 85-88.

3. Ibid., 105.

4. *New Orleans City Directory* (1942): 154.

5. Henry C. Castellanos, *New Orleans as It Was* (Gretna, LA: Pelican, 1990), 334-35.

6. Benjamin Henry Latrobe, *The Journals (Papers) of Benjamin Henry Latrobe, 1799-1820: From Philadelphia to New Orleans*, vol. 3 (New Haven: Yale University Press, 1980), 171.

7. Toledano and Christovich, 15-17.

8. James B. Bennett, *Religion and the Rise of Jim Crow in New Orleans* (Princeton: Princeton University Press, 2005), 144.

9. "Parish in Centennial," *Catholic Action of the South*, March 27, 1941.

10. Ann Masson, "Bearing Witness in Treme: Saint Augustine Church," *Louisiana Cultural Vistas* 13, no. 2 (Summer 2002): 36.

11. Toledano and Christovich, 142.

12. Ibid., 143.

13. "Parish in Centennial."

14. Latrobe, 216.

15. Caryn Cosse Bell, *Revolution, Romanticism, and the Afro-Creole Protest Tradition in Louisiana, 1718-1868* (Baton Rouge: Louisiana State University Press, 1997), 73-74.

16. Charles Barthelemy Rousseve, *The Negro in Louisiana: Aspects of His History and His Literature* (New Orleans: Xavier University Press, 1937; repr., New York: Johnson Reprint Corporation, 1970), 41.

17. *Daily Picayune*, April 15, April 17, May 1, 1846.
18. Ibid., March 28, 1846.
19. Arnold Bertoneau, *Liberator*, April 15, 1864.
20. "The Emancipation Celebration," *Era*, June 12, 1864; "Emancipation Celebration," *Daily True Delta*, June 12, 1864.
21. "Emancipation Celebration, Address of Mr. Joseph A. Craig," *Daily True Delta*, June 12, 1864.
22. "Mass Meeting on Congo Square," *New Orleans Tribune*, April 23, 1865.
23. Ibid.
24. Ibid.
25. *Crusader*, 1891-94.
26. Ibid.
27. Rodolphe Lucien Desdunes, *Nos Hommes et Notre Histoire* (*Our People and Our History*) (1911; repr., Baton Rouge: Louisiana State University Press, 1973), 10, 48.
28. *Soards' City Directory* (1892): 998.
29. Crusader, 1892-94.
30. Esther Barnum Green, interview with author, 2007.
31. Rick Mathieu, interview with author, 2006.

Chapter 2

1. Latrobe, 204.
2. Gwendolyn Midlo Hall, *Africans in Colonial Louisiana* (Baton Rouge: Louisiana State University Press, 1992), 45.
3. Ibid., 127-28.
4. James Andrew Corcoran, Patrick John Ryan, and Edmond Francis Prendergast, "The Church of the Attakapas—1750-1889," *The American Catholic Quarterly Review* 14 (1889): 474.
5. Toledano and Christovich, 65.
6. Christian Schultz, *Travels on an Inland Voyage* (New York: Isaac Riley, 1810), 197.
7. Soi-Daniel W. Brown, "From the Tongues of Africa: A Partial Translation of Oldendorp's Interviews," *Plantation Society* 2, no. 1 (April 1983): 52-53.
8. *The Picayune's Guide to New Orleans* (1904), 43.
9. John Adems Paxton, *The New Orleans Directory and Register* (1822).
10. Castellanos, 159.
11. Ibid., 297.
12. Latrobe, 203.

13. Laura Boulton, *The Music Hunter: The Autobiography of a Career*. (Garden City, NJ: Doubleday, 1969), 136.

14. Faruk von Turk, *The Dance in Place Congo and Creole Slave Songs by George W. Cable Containing Also the Congo Dance* (New Orleans: Turk, 1976), 3.

15. J. H. Kwabena Nketia, *The Music of Africa* (New York: W. W. Norton, 1974), 73-74.

16. Katherine Dunham, *Dances of Haiti* (Los Angeles: University of California, 1983), xxi.

17. Von Turk, 3.

18. Latrobe, 204.

19. Nketia, 38.

20. Ibid., 77.

21. Castellanos, 158.

22. Lafcadio Hearn, *Gombo Zhebes—Little Dictionary of Creole Proverbs* (New Orleans: Turk, 1977), 28, 18, 10, 9, 16.

23. Hall, 212-13.

24. Ibid., 232.

25. Von Turk, 23-24.

26. Ibid., 32.

27. Ibid., 31.

28. Ibid., 20.

29. Jay Robert Nash, *Almanac of World Crime* (New York: Doubleday, 1981), 310; Castellanos, 158, 210-16.

30. Lerone Bennett, Jr., *The Shaping of Black America* (Chicago: Johnson, 1975), 199.

Chapter 3

1. *General Index of All Successions Opened in the Parish of Orleans 1805-1846*, New Orleans Public Library, Louisiana Division; Desdunes, 21; Keith Weldon Medley, "A Legacy of Learning," *New Orleans Tribune*, September 1998.

2. Roulhac Toledano, Sally Evans, and Mary Louise Christovich, *New Orleans Architecture*, vol. 4, *The Creole Faubourgs* (Gretna, LA: Pelican, 1974), xiv.

3. Ibid., 95.

4. Ibid., 28-29.

5. New Orleans Public Library, City Archives, petitions for the emancipation of slaves, 1813-43, VCP320 Louisiana. Parish Court (Orleans Parish).

6. Ibid.

7. Desdunes, 103.

8. New Orleans Public Library, petitions for the emancipation of slaves, 1813-43.

9. Mary Eugenius Gallaher and the Eighth Grade Students, *A History of St. Louis School of Holy Redeemer Parish—A Bicentennial Project* (New Orleans: Holy Redeemer School, 1976), 3.

10. *Louisiana Historical Quarterly* 25 (July): 42.

11. *Harper's New Monthly Magazine* 33 (1866): 248.

12. Desdunes, 103.

13. Bonnye E. Stuart, *It Happened in New Orleans* (Guilford: Morris, 2007), 34.

14. "St. Louis School for Colored Orphans," *Morning Star*, September 1, 1917.

15. Desdunes, 102-6.

16. Ibid., 101-8.

17. Nathan Willey, "Education of the Colored Population of Louisiana," *Harper's New Monthly Magazine* (July 1866): 248.

18. Ibid.

19. Desdunes, 106.

20. Ibid., 107-8.

21. Report by the Board of Directors of the Catholic Indigent Orphan Institute, "Contributions Received November 20, 1915-November 15, 1916."

22. James B. Bennett, 219.

23. Marilyn Medley (Vandergriff), in Gallaher, 7.

24. Desdunes, 107.

Chapter 4

1. Allen T. Woods, *The Woods Directory* (New Orleans: 1912-14), 56.

2. Ibid., 5.

3. Ibid.

4. Arnold S. Rice and John A. Krout, *United States History from 1865* (New York: HarperCollins, 1991), 146.

5. Leonard V. Huber, *New Orleans: A Pictorial History* (New York: American LegacyPress, 1981; repr., Gretna, LA: Pelican, 2014), 108.

6. *Soards' City Directory* (1905): 1017.

7. New Orleans, Louisiana Marriage Records Index, 1831-1925.

8. Woods.

9. *New Orleans Times-Picayune*, August 19, 1909.

10. Lili LeGardeur, "The Knights of Pythias Building at 234 Loyola Avenue," *Louisiana Weekly*, December 6-12, 2004.

11. *New Orleans Times-Picayune*, August 19, 1909.

12. Ibid.

13. Chicago Hotel (New Orleans, Louisiana) Register, 1907-12, New Orleans Public Library, Louisiana Division.

14. Woods.

15. Ibid.

16. Ibid.

17. Chicago Hotel Register.

18. "Fifty Years of Freedom: Negroes of City Celebrate Emancipation Day," *New Orleans Times-Democrat*, January 2, 1913.

19. Ibid.

20. Woods, 11-29.

21. Emmett J. Scott, *The American Negro in the World War* (1919), 313-14.

22. Woods.

Chapter 5

1. Diane Farrell, "Yankee Doodle Dixie," *New Orleans Times-Picayune Dixie Roto Magazine*, February 14, 1954.

2. Louis Armstrong, *Satchmo: My Life in New Orleans* (New York: Da Capo, 1986), 14-15.

3. Ibid., 15.

4. Emily Landau, "Storyville," *KnowLA Encyclopedia of Louisiana*,, January 27, 2011.

5. 1910 United States Federal Census, New Orleans Ward 3.

6. Alecia P. Long, *The Great Southern Babylon: Sex, Race, and Respectability in New Orleans 1865-1920* (Baton Rouge: Louisiana State University Press, 2004), 195.

7. 1910 United States Federal Census.

8. E. C. Wharton, *A History of the Proceedings in the City of New Orleans, On the Occasion of the Funeral Ceremonies in Honor of James Abram Garfield* (New Orleans: A. L. Donnaud, 1881), 249-50.

9. Armstrong, 29.

10. Louis Armstrong, *Louis Armstrong, in His Own Words: Selected Writings*, ed. Thomas Brothers (New York: Oxford University Press, 1999), 79.

11. Flannery Lewis, "Satchmo, Jazz King, Prince Of Trumpet, Louie's Come Home," *New Orleans Item*, April 30, 1948.

12. Latrobe, 215-16.

13. Armstrong, *Satchmo*, 91.

14. Wesley Jackson, "Music Teacher Recalls Satchmo's Early Years," *New Orleans Times-Picayune*, August 22, 1962.

15. "Few Juveniles Arrested," *New Orleans Times-Democrat*, January 2, 1913.

16. Lee Davis, "'Captain' Jones of Milne Retiring," *New Orleans Item*, June 29, 1951.

17. Ibid.

18. Farrell.

19. Jackson.

20. Louis Armstrong; *Satchmo: My Life in New Orleans* (New York: Da Capo Press, Inc., 1986), p. 41.

21. Jackson.

22. "Jazz King Riots S. Rampart Street," *New Orleans Morning Tribune*, June 7, 1931.

23. "Armstrong's Visit Creates a Sensation," *Louisiana Weekly*, June 13, 1931.

24. *Louisiana Weekly*, March 5, 1949.

25. Louis Armstrong, "Me As Zulu! Man, Whatta Surprise," *New Orleans Item*, February 21, 1952.

26. Lewis.

27. Ibid.

28. Davis.

29. Farrell.

30. Edward R. Morrow and CBS, *See It Now: Louis in Accra Opening Welcome* (1956).

31. B. D. Dorkenno, "Country Will Be Asked to Decide," *Daily Graphic*, May 23, 1956.

32. Moses Danquah, "The Magic of Armstrong,"*Daily Graphic*, May 28, 1956.

Chapter 6

1. Donald E. Devore and Joseph Logsdon, *Crescent City Schools: Public Education in New Orleans 1841-1991* (Lafayette: University of Southwestern Louisiana, 1991), 118.

2. 1900 United States Federal Census, New Orleans Ward 7.

3. Scott, 471.

4. Rousseve, 161.

5. Al Kennedy, *Big Chief Harrison and the Mardi Gras Indians* (Gretna, LA: Pelican, 2010), 132.

6. *The Roneagle 1928* (New Orleans: McDonogh #35 High and Normal School, 1928), 130.

7. Ibid., 97.

8. Annabel Egana Nash, interview with author, 1994.

9. Ibid.

10. Ibid.

11. James D. Anderson, *The Education of Blacks in the South, 1860-1935* (Chapel Hill: University of North Carolina Press, 1988), 18.

12. "Miss A. V. Dunn Promoted to Principal," *New Orleans Herald*, September 19, 1925.

13. "Negro Schools Not to Receive New Books for New Course," *New Orleans Herald*, October 3, 1925.

14. "Public Schools Crowded Above Their Capacity," *New Orleans Herald*, September 19, 1925.

15. "Negro Schools Not to Receive New Books for New Course."

16. "Robeson's Voice Singing Spirituals Recorded for Phonograph," *New Orleans Herald*, September 19, 1925.

17. *The Roneagle 1928*, 9.

18. Ibid.; *The Roneagle 1929* (New Orleans: McDonogh #35 High and Normal School, 1929), 9.

19. *The Roneagle 1928*, 106-31.

20. Ibid., 26.

21. Dorothy Gardner Clark, interview with author, 1994.

22. Selina Butler Tinson, interview with author, 1994.

23. Clark.

24. Keith Weldon Medley, "Whatever Happened to the Class of 1928?" *New Orleans Tribune*, November 1994.

25. Devore and Logsdon, 194.

26. "Hundreds to Finish from City Schools," *Louisiana Weekly*, June 9, 1928.

27. Tinson.

28. Clark.

29. *The Roneagle 1928*, 24.

30. Tinson.

Chapter 7

1. *The Moving Finger* (New Orleans: Moret, 1939), 8.
2. Adam Fairclough, *A Class of Their Own: Black Teachers in the Segregated South* (Boston: Harvard University Press, 2007), 279.
3. "A Community Builds a School 1905-1929," http://www.creolegen.org/, accessed January 28, 2014.
4. Arthé A. Anthony, *Picturing Black New Orleans* (Gainesville: University Press of Florida, 2012), 63.
5. "Six Lots Are Donated to School Board," *Louisiana Weekly*, September 8, 1928.
6. "Throngs See Modern Bldg. in Lower City," *Louisiana Weekly*, November 2, 1929.
7. "Jones School Is Host to Its Patrons," *Louisiana Weekly*, November 23, 1929.
8. "An Arresting Personality," *American Missionary* (February 2, 1933): 141.
9. Selina Butler Tinson, interview with author, circa 1988.
10. Ibid.
11. *The Moving Finger* (New Orleans: Moret, 1937), 5.
12. Ibid., 29.
13. *New Orleans Times-Picayune*, June 14, 1980.

Chapter 8

1. Earl Picard, "Blacks in Politics in New Orleans: From Maestri to Morrison" (master's thesis, Atlanta University, 1976), 105.
2. Zachary Taylor Ramsey, interview with author, 1984.
3. Ernest J. Wright, "Brief Study of Working Conditions of the Colored Citizens in New Orleans, Louisiana" (thesis, Xavier University, 1933), 18.
4. "Xavier Powerless Before Team Headed for Grid Title," *Louisiana Weekly*, October 10, 1931.
5. Picard, 100.
6. 1930 United States Federal Census, New Orleans Ward 3.
7. Ibid.
8. Wright, 1.
9. Ibid., 2-4.
10. Ibid.
11. Ernest J. Wright, interview by Merle Ramsey, circa 1970s.
12. "Weekly Community Responsibility Programs Will Be Resumed Under Ernest J. Wright's Supervision," *Louisiana Weekly*, July 1, 1939.

13. Perry H. Howard, *Political Tendencies in Louisiana* (Baton Rouge: Louisiana State University Press, 1971), 422.

14. "Weekly Community Responsibility Programs Will Be Resumed Under Ernest J. Wright's Supervision."

15. Ramsey.

16. "350 Attend Weekly's Fine Community Responsibility Program at St. John B. C.," *Louisiana Weekly*, July 22, 1939.

17. Ernest J. Wright, "I Daresay: Don't Fence Me In," *Louisiana Weekly*, February 10, 1945.

18. Picard, 96.

19. "Executives Maintain They Will Not Bargain with CIO; Agents Sue for Bond Money," *Louisiana Weekly*, September 28, 1940.

20. Ramsey.

21. "Wright, Ramsey Tell It All at Mass Meeting," *Louisiana Weekly*, August 9, 1941.

22. Ramsey.

23. "People's Defense League Holds 2nd Victory Mass Meet," *Louisiana Weekly*, September 13, 1941.

24. "Defense League Set for Bill of Rights Confab," *Louisiana Weekly*, December 13, 1941.

25. *Public Hearings of the State of Louisiana Joint Legislative Committee: Subversion in Racial Unrest Part 1* (1957).

26. "Defense League 'All-Out' for NAACP Support," *Louisiana Weekly*, February 28, 1942.

27. "Civilian Cops' Brutality at Induction Center Starts Near-Riot," *Louisiana Weekly*, August 8, 1942.

28. "Arrest Wright for Urging Negroes to Seek the Ballot," *Louisiana Weekly*, May 9, 1942.

29. Ernest J. Wright, "I Daresay: On Important Matters," *Louisiana Weekly*, June 1, 1946.

30. "Wright Tells 14th Ward Citizens of War Responsibilities," *Louisiana Weekly*, June 26, 1943.

31. Picard, 101.

32. "People's Defense League Make Plans for 'Memory Day,'" *Louisiana Weekly*, August 7, 1945.

33. Ernest Wright, "I Daresay: Let's Stop Shadow Boxing," *Louisiana Weekly*, April 6, 1946.

34. Ernest Wright, "I Daresay: We Must Vote," *Louisiana Weekly*, July 18, 1942.

35. Ernest Wright, "I Daresay: The Handwriting Is on the Wall," *Louisiana Weekly*, August 15, 1942.

36. Ernest J. Wright, "I Daresay: The Green Light Means to Go," *Louisiana Weekly*, June 10, 1944.

37. Ernest J. Wright, "I Daresay: Two Negro Youths Lynched," *Louisiana Weekly*, October 17, 1942.

38. Ernest J. Wright, "I Daresay: On Negro History Celebration," *Louisiana Weekly*, February 17, 1945.

39. "Ernest J. Wright Addresses Mobile Shipyard Workers," *Louisiana Weekly*, February 13, 1943.

40. Ernest J. Wright, "I Daresay: President Roosevelt and Organized Labor," *Louisiana Weekly*, November 18, 1944.

41. "Ernest J. Wright Addresses Mobile Shipyard Workers."

42. "Congressman Powell Urges Orleanians to Come Together for Ballot," *Louisiana Weekly*, March 16, 1946.

43. "Scoop" Jones, "Ballot Drive Falls Short," *Louisiana Weekly*, August 17, 1946.

44. "Scoop" Jones, "Round One of Registration Drive Ends: Leaders and People Learn Many Lessons," *Louisiana Weekly*, August 10, 1946; "Defense League Well on Way to 5,000 Membership," *Louisiana Weekly*, February 23, 1946.

45. "PDL Resumes Operation Registration,'" *Louisiana Weekly*, September 21, 1946.

46. "Scoop" Jones, "A Voteless People Is a Hopeless People," *Louisiana Weekly*, August 3, 1946.

47. "People's Defense League to Complete Registration Plans," *Louisiana Weekly*, July 6, 1946.

48. Wright, interview by Ramsey.

49. Jones, "A Voteless People Is a Hopeless People."

50. Jones, "Ballot Drive Falls Short."

51. Ibid.

52. Keith Weldon Medley, "Remembering Ernest Wright, 'the People's Champion,'" *New Orleans Tribune*, February 1986.

53. *Public Hearings of the State of Louisiana Joint Legislative Committee*.

54. Ernest Wright, interview with author, early 1980s.

Chapter 9

1. *Louisiana Weekly*, July 31, 1954.

2. Catherine Campanella, *Images of America: Lake Pontchartrain* (Charleston: Arcadia, 2007), 65.

3. "Bearing Fruit," *Louisiana Weekly*, April 26, 1930.

4. Ibid.

5. Burk and Associates, Inc., "Lincoln Beach Redevelopment: An Analysis and Design Scheme" (1979), 3.

6. "Board Considers Plans for Beach," *New Orleans Times-Picayune*, September 28, 1948.

7. "Extension Is Aim at Lincoln Beach," *New Orleans Times-Picayune*, February 25, 1950.

8. Ibid.

9. "Lincoln Beach Goes Modern," *New Orleans Times-Picayune Dixie Roto Magazine*, December 21, 1952.

10. "Lincoln Beach Dedication Viewed by Huge Throng," *Louisiana Weekly*, May 15, 1954.

11. "Top Officials to Dedicate Lincoln Beach Saturday," *Louisiana Weekly*, May 8, 1954.

12. Ibid., 7.

13. "Lincoln Beach Dedication Viewed by Huge Throng."

14. "Repairs Halt Lincoln Beach Opening Here," *Louisiana Weekly*, May 22, 1954.

15. *Louisiana Weekly*, June 5, 1954.

16. "Free Swimming Classes Held at Lincoln Beach," *Louisiana Weekly*, June 19, 1954.

17. "Aquatic Show Planned for New Lincoln Beach," *Louisiana Weekly*, July 10, 1954.

18. "2000 Attend Gay Lincoln Beach Fete," *Louisiana Weekly*, August 14, 1954.

19. "Lincoln Beach Slates Formal Opening Sunday," *Louisiana Weekly*, April 28, 1956.

20. Larry Benicewicz, "Remembering Ernie-K-Doe (1936-2001)," http://www.bluesart.at/NeueSeiten/LEKD01.html, accessed January 3, 2012.

21. John Swenson, "Dr. John: A Mac for All Seasons," http://www.offbeat.com/2011/03/01/dr-john-a-mac-for-all-seasons/, accessed January 5, 2014.

22. Eddie Hynes, "Something About Eddie," http://www.bigeasystreetsounds.tripod.com/Id185.html, accessed January 3, 2012.

23. Al Rose and Edmond Souchon, *New Orleans Jazz: A Family Album* (Baton Rouge: Louisiana State University Press, 1978), 26; http://www.the78rpmrecordspins.wordpress.com/tag/papa-celestin/, accessed January 7, 2014.

24. The Blues Foundation, "Past Hall of Fame Inductees: Roy Brown," https://www.blues.org/halloffame/inductees.php?ArtistId=545&YearId=24#ref=halloffame_inductees, accessed January 7, 2014.

25. Jeff Hannusch, *I Hear You Knockin'* (Ville Platte, LA: Swallow, 2005), 71.

26. Per Oldaeus, "Played the Same Thing Every Night for 12 Years," *The Jazz Archivist* 21 (2008): 37.

27. Bill Dahl, "Artist Biography," http://www.allmusic.com/artist/roy-brown-mn0000343396/biography, accessed January 7, 2014.

28. *Louisiana Weekly*, May 29, 1954.

29. "Big Floor Show, Diving Fete at Lincoln Beach," *Louisiana Weekly*, July 24, 1954; "2000 Attend Gay Lincoln Beach Fete."

30. "Negro Fair Set April 24 to 27," *Louisiana Weekly*, April 12, 1958.

31. "Miss Lincoln Beach Contest Set for Sunday," *Louisiana Weekly*, August 28, 1954.

32. "Cute June Foster Cops 'Miss Lincoln Beach' Title," *Louisiana Weekly*, September 4, 1954; "King and Queen," *Louisiana Weekly*, October 2, 1954.

33. "Ink Spots at Lincoln Beach Today," *New Orleans Times-Picayune*, April 15, 1956.

34. "Thousands Jam Lincoln Beach for Fun, Frolic," *Louisiana Weekly*, May 19, 1956.

Chapter 10

1. Revius O. Ortique, Jr., interview with author, circa 1988.

2. Charles Vincent, *Black Legislators in Louisiana During Reconstruction* (Baton Rouge: Louisiana State University Press, 1976), 232, 234.

3. The Citizens' Committee, "An Appeal," September 5, 1891. Amistad Research Center, Tulane University.

4. The Citizens' Committee, "The Annulment of Act No. 111 Commonly Known as the Separate Car Law," 1897.

5. *Official Journal of the Constitutional Convention* (Baton Rouge, 1898), 374.

6. Ortique.

7. Ibid.

8. "Ernest Morial, First Negro LSU Law Graduate Sworn In," *Louisiana Weekly*, February 27, 1954.

Chapter 11

1. Tessie Prevost, interview with author, circa 1985.
2. Dee Shedrick, "A History of McDonogh 19 and Frantz: New Orleans Schools with Legacy," *New Orleans Tribune*, November/December 2010.
3. Walter Goodstein, "1000 Cheer Withdrawal of White Children," *New Orleans Times-Picayune*, November 15, 1960.
4. Mary Lee Muller, "The Orleans Parish School Board and Negro Education, 1940-1960" (master's thesis, University of New Orleans, 1975), 23.
5. Ibid., 25-26.
6. "3 Groups Unite to Protest McDonogh Day Discrimination," *Louisiana Weekly*, February 6, 1954.
7. "Unified Action Marred by Only Two Exceptions," *Louisiana Weekly*, May 15, 1954.
8. Ibid.
9. "Brown v. Board of Education: Case Brief Summary," http://www.lawnix.com/cases/brown-board-education.html, accessed January 10, 2014.
10. "Brown v. Board of Education," in *The Oxford Companion to the Supreme Court of the United States*, ed. Kermit L. Hall (New York: Oxford University Press, 1992), 94.
11. "New Orleans Schools," *Louisiana Weekly*, November 19, 1960.
12. "Arrest of Marshals, Wright; March Announced," *New Orleans Times-Picayune*, November 16, 1960.
13. Liva Baker, *The Second Battle of New Orleans: The Hundred-Year Struggle to Integrate the Schools* (New York: HarperCollins, 1996), 387.
14. Bill Billiter, "No Interference in Schools, Order," *New Orleans Times-Picayune*, November 14, 1960.
15. "Arrest of U.S. Officers Asked," *New Orleans Times-Picayune*, November 16, 1960.
16. "Jeers, Violence Mark March," *New Orleans Times-Picayune*, November 17, 1960.
17. "Two Whites Quit Boycotted School," *The New York Times*," February 2, 1961, p. 17; "New Orleans, 1960: The Vilest Sort of Abuse," *The New Orleans School Crisis*, The Louisiana State Advisory Committee on Civil Rights, 1961, p. 63.

18. John Steinbeck, *Travels With Charley: In Search of America* (New York: Pelican Books, 1962), 257-58.
19. Ibid., 260.
20. "Dance Blackout Nets $2000 for Urban League," *Louisiana Weekly*, April 8, 1961.
21. "'Blackout' Supporters Win Praise of Nation," *Louisiana Weekly*, February 25, 1961.
22. Gail Etienne, interview with author, 1983.
23. Prevost.
24. Leona Tate, interview with author, 1983.
25. Ruby Bridges, interview with author, 1983.

Chapter 12

1. Doris Jean Castle, interview with author, 1986.
2. Rudy Lombard, interview with author, 1987.
3. "Arrest 7," *Louisiana Weekly*, September 17, 1960.
4. "Mayor Morrison Clamps Lid on Demonstrations," *Louisiana Weekly*, September 17, 1960.
5. "4 More CORE Members Arrested in 'Sit-In'," *Louisiana Weekly*, September 24, 1960.
6. Lolis Elie, interview with author, 1987.
7. "Sit-In Backers Start Test Bus Trip to South," *New York Times*, May 5, 1961.
8. "Negro Seized in Test," *New York Times*, May 9, 1961.
9. "Biracial Unit Tells of Beating in South," *New York Times*, May 11, 1961.
10. "Bi-Racial Busses Attacked, Riders Beaten in Alabama," *New York Times*, May 15, 1961.
11. "Bi-Racial Group Cancels Bus Trip," *New York Times*, May 16, 1961.
12. "Freedom Riders Plan to Continue Ride Through South," *Louisiana Weekly*, May 27, 1961.
13. "Bus Segregation Foes Vow to Brave Death," *New York Times*, May 22, 1961.
14. Ibid.
15. David Halberstam, "Negro Girl a Force on Campaign; Encouraged Bus to Keep Rolling," *New York Times*, May 23, 1961.
16. "Ethiopia Is Bitter," *New York Times*, May 24, 1961.

17. Claude Sitton, "Dr. King Refuses to End Bus Test," *New York Times*, May 26, 1961.

18. Emanuel Perlmutter, "Sponsors Are Hoping to Resume Freedom Ride Bus Trips Today," *New York Times*, May 23, 1961.

19. Castle.

20. Isaac Reynolds, interview with author, 1986.

21. Castle.

22. "Freedom Riders Tell of Lurid Experiences in Miss. Jails," *Louisiana Weekly*, December 16, 1961.

23. "Robert Kennedy Asks I.C.C. to End Bus Segregation," *New York Times*, May 30, 1961.

24. Florence Borders, interview with author, 1986.

25. Elie.

26. Lombard.

Chapter 13

1. Armand Lanusse, "Le Carnaval," in *Les Cenelles* (1845); Edward Maceo Coleman, ed., *Creole Voices: Poems in French by Free Men of Color First Published in 1845* (Washington, D.C.: Associated, 1945), 78.

2. Laurence Bergreen, *Louis Armstrong: An Extravagant Life* (New York: Broadway Books, 1997), 29.

3. John W. Blasingame, *Black New Orleans 1860-1880* (Chicago: University of Chicago Press, 1973), 145.

4. An Act Making Shrove Tuesday, or Mardi-Gras, a Legal Holiday (passed Apr. 23, 1872).

5. *Daily Picayune*, February 19, 1896.

6. "Social Calendar," *Louisiana Weekly*, February 8, 1930.

7. "Zulus to 'Hunt Pink Elephants,' Jolly Boys 'Gods of Mirth' in Colorful Carnival Processions," *Louisiana Weekly*, February 3, 1940.

8. "On Mardi Gras Day Eat at Astoria Restaurant," *Louisiana Weekly*, February 3, 1940.

9. "10 Negro Clubs Boycott Carnival," *New Orleans States-Item*, December 7, 1960.

10. "King Zulu and Entourage to Parade Despite Protest," *Louisiana Weekly*, January 28, 1961.

11. "Wouldn't You, Too?" *Louisiana Weekly*, January 15, 1938.

12. O. C. W. Taylor, "Mardi Gras in New Orleans," in *King's Mardi Gras in New Orleans*, ed. Nathan Johnny King, Jr. (1956), 2, 13.

13. Keith Weldon Medley, "Tan Mardi Gras," in *Arthur Hardy's Mardi Gras Guide 2008*, 72.

14. Ibid., 70.

15. Ibid., 71.

16. Nathan J. King, Jr., *SEPIA Mardi Gras in New Orleans* (1955).

17. "Zulu Social Aid and Pleasure Club," http://www.kreweofzulu.com/history/, accessed December 20, 2012.

18. Ibid.

19. "Carnival Visitors Already Fill City for Mardi Gras," *Louisiana Weekly*, February 18, 1928.

20. John Bowers, "The Mighty Monarch Arrives," *Louisiana Weekly*, February 21, 1931.

21. James Wright, interview with author, 1989.

22. Ibid.

23. "Young Men's Illinois in Sixth Annual Ball," *Louisiana Weekly*, February 13, 1932.

24. "Rhinestone Club Revels Midst Joy," *Louisiana Weekly*, February 13, 1932.

25. E. Belfield Spriggins, "Original Illinois Gives Brilliant Affair," *Louisiana Weekly*, March 4, 1933.

26. Maurice and Eva Prevost, interview with author, 1989.

27. "Bunch Affair Brilliant," *Louisiana Weekly*, March 8, 1930.

28. Keith Weldon Medley, "Mardi Gras Mambo," *New Orleans Tribune*, February 1989.

29. "'Carnival Reflections' Theme of Bunch Club," *Louisiana Weekly*, March 13, 1954.

30. Maurice and Eva Prevost.

31. David Elliott Draper, "The Mardi Gras Indians: The Ethnomusicology of Black Associations in New Orleans" (dissertation, Tulane University, 1973), 32.

32. Howard Miller, interview with author, circa 2011.

33. Ibid.

34. Ibid.

Chapter 14

1. Allison "Tootie" Montana, interview with author, 2000.

2. Darryl Montana, interview with author, 2000.

Selected Bibliography

Allured, Janet, and Michael S. Martin. *Louisiana Legacies: Readings in the History of the Pelican State*. New York: John Wiley and Sons, 2013.

Anderson, Beverly Jacques. *Cherished Memories: Snapshots of Life and Lessons from a 1950s New Orleans Creole Village*. Bloomington: iUniverse, 2011.

Anderson, James D. *The Education of Blacks in the South, 1860-1935*. Chapel Hill: University of North Carolina Press, 1988.

Arnold, Rubin. *Marks of Civilization*. Los Angeles: Regents of the University of California, 1988.

Baker, Liva. *The Second Battle of New Orleans*. New York: HarperCollins, 1966.

Bennett, James B. *Religion and the Rise of Jim Crow in New Orleans*. Princeton: Princeton University Press, 2005.

Bennett, Lerone, Jr. *The Shaping of Black America*. Chicago: Johnson, 1975.

Boulton, Laura. *The Music Hunter: The Autobiography of a Career*. Garden City, NY: Doubleday, 1969.

Castellanos, Henry C. *New Orleans As It Was*. Gretna, LA: Pelican, 1990.

Cleman, John. *George Washington Cable Revisited*. New York: Twayne, 1996.

Cobb, Charles E., Jr. *On the Road to Freedom*. New York: Algonquin Books of Chapel Hill, 2008.

Coles, Robert. *Children of Crisis*. Boston: Atlantic Monthly Press, 1967.

Collier, James Lincoln. *Louis Armstrong: An American Genius*. New York: Oxford University Press, 1983.

Conyers, James L., Jr., ed. *African American Consciousness, Past and Present*. New Brunswick, NJ: Transaction, 2012.

Cox, Jim. *Rails Across Dixie*. Jefferson, NC: McFarland, 2009.

Cruise, Boyd. *Index to the Louisiana Historical Quarterly*. Gretna: Pelican, 1998.

Desdunes, Rodolphe Lucien. *Our People and Our History*. Baton Rouge: Louisiana State University Press, 1973.

Devore, Donald E., and Joseph Logsdon. *Crescent City Schools*. New Orleans: Center for Louisiana Studies, 1991.

Din, Gilbert C., and John, E. Harkins. *The New Orleans Cabildo*. Baton Rouge: Louisiana State University Press, 1996.

Dunham, Katherine. *Dances of Haiti*. Los Angeles: Regents of the University of California and Katherine Dunham, 1983.

Emanuel, Rachel L., and Alexander P. Tureaud, Jr. *A More Noble Cause*. Baton Rouge: Louisiana State University Press, 2011.

Evans, Freddi Williams. *Congo Square: African Roots in New Orleans*. Lafayette: University of Louisiana at Lafayette Press, 2011.

Fairclough, Adam. *Race and Democracy: The Civil Rights Struggle in Louisiana 1915-1972*. Athens: University of Georgia Press, 1995.

Gates, Henry Louis, Jr., and Donald Yacovone. *The African Americans*. New York: SmileyBooks, 2013.

Glisson, Susan M., ed. *The Human Tradition in the Civil Rights Movement*. New York: Rowman & Littlefield, 2006.

Haas, Edward F. *DeLesseps S. Morrison*. Baton Rouge: Louisiana State University Press, 1974.

Hall, Gwendolyn Midlo. *Africans in Colonial Louisiana*. Baton Rouge: Louisiana State University Press, 1992.

Hall, Kermit L. *The Oxford Companion to the Supreme Court of the United States*. New York: Oxford University Press, 1992.

Henderson, Michael Nolden, and Anita Rochelle Paul. *Got Proof! My Genealogical Journey Through the Use of Documentation*. Suwanee, GA: Write Image, 2013.

Hogan, Lawrence D. *Shades of Glory: The Negro Leagues and the Story of African-American Baseball*. Cooperstown: National Baseball Hall of Fame and Museum, 2006.

Howard, Perry H. *Political Tendencies in Louisiana*. Baton Rouge: Louisiana State University Press, 1971.

Huber, Leonard V. *Louisiana: A Pictorial History*. New York: Charles Scribner's Sons, 1975.

———. *New Orleans: A Pictorial History*. New York: American Legacy Press, 1981. Reprint, Gretna, LA: Pelican, 2014.

Ingersoll, Thomas N. *Mammon and Manon in Early New Orleans*. Knoxville: University of Tennessee Press, 1999.

Johnson, James Weldon, ed. *The Book of American Negro Spirituals*. New York: Viking Press, 1925.

Kelley, L. M. Blair. *Right to Ride*. Chapel Hill: University of North Carolina Press, 2010.

Kennedy, Al. *Big Chief Harrison and the Mardi Gras Indians*. Gretna, LA: Pelican, 2010.

Benjamin Henry Latrobe. *The Journals (Papers) of Benjamin Henry Latrobe, 1799-1820: From Philadelphia to New Orleans*. Vol. 3. New Haven: Yale University Press, 1980.

Lemmon, Alfred E., John T Magill, and Jason R. Wiese. *Charting Louisiana: Five Hundred Years of Maps*. New Orleans: The Historic New Orleans Collection, 2003.

Lomax, Michael E. *Black Baseball Entrepreneurs, 1860-1901*. Syracuse: Syracuse University Press, 2003.

Long, Alecia P. *The Great Southern Babylon*. Baton Rouge: Louisiana State University Press, 2004.

Nketia, J. H. Kwabena. *The Music of Africa*. New York: W. W. Norton, 1974.

Nkrumah, Kwame. *The Autobiography of Kwame Nkrumah*. New York: Thomas Nelson and Sons, 1957.

Rice, Arnold S., and John A. Krout. *United States History from 1865*. New York: HarperCollins, 1991.

Rousseve, Charles Barthelemy. *The Negro in Louisiana: Aspects of His History and His Literature*. New Orleans: Xavier University Press, 1937.

Sartain, Lee. *Invisible Activists*. Baton Rouge: Louisiana State University Press, 2007.

Schafer, Judith Kelleher. *Becoming Free, Remaining Free*. Baton Rouge: Louisiana State University Press, 2003.

Schwartz, Bernard. *A History of the Supreme Court*. New York: Oxford University Press, 1993.

Scott, Emmett J. *The American Negro in the World War*. 1919.

Smith, Mark M. *How Race Is Made: Slavery, Segregation and the Senses*. Chapel Hill: University of North Carolina Press, 2006.

Stuart, Bonnye E. *It Happened in New Orleans*. Guilford, CT: Morris, 2007.

Sublette, Ned. *The Year Before the Flood*. Chicago: Lawrence Hill Books, 2009.

Thompson, Daniel C. *The Negro Leadership Class*. Englewood Cliffs: Prentice Hall, 1963.

Toledano, Roulhac, Sally Evans, and Mary Louise Christovich. *New Orleans Architecture*. Vol. 4, *The Creole Faubourgs*. Gretna, LA: Pelican, 1974.

Toledano, Roulhac B., and Mary Louise Christovich. *New Orleans Architecture*. Vol. 6, *Faubourg Tremé and the Bayou Road*. Gretna: Pelican, 1980.

Vaz, Kim Marie. *The Baby Dolls: Breaking the Race and Gender Barriers of the New Orleans Mardi Gras Tradition*. Baton Rouge: Louisiana State University Press, 2013.

———. *The Woman with the Artistic Brush*. Armonk, NY: M. E. Sharpe, 1995.

Watts, Lewis, and Eric Porter. *New Orleans Suite: Music and Culture in Transition*. Berkeley: University of California Press, 2013.

Winters, Paul A., ed. *The Civil Rights Movement*. San Diego: Greenhaven Press, 2000.

Work, John W. *American Negro Songs and Spirituals*. New York: Bonanza Books, 1940.

Index

Aaron, Hank, 233
Aaron, Julia, 194, 196, 235-36
Adams, Johnny, 235
Ad Libitum Club, 205
Ainsworth, Robert, Jr., 241
Albert, Josephine, 103
Alcee Fortier High School, 249-51
Alexander, Adolphe, 249
Alexander, Avery, 234, 236-37, 241, 248
Alexis, Lucien Victor, 122, 127, 131
Allen, Archie, 189, 234
Amedee, Earl J., 162, 173, 248
American Anti-Slavery Society, 31
American Equal Rights Association, 36, 170
American Federation of Teachers Conference, 227
American Football League, 243
American Legion, 240
American Missionary, The (magazine), 139
American Negro League, 234
Amistad Research Center, 142, 169, 175
Anderson, Marian, 131, 240
Antoine, Louis, 241
Apache Hunters, 217, 219
Armstrong, Beatrice, 105
Armstrong, Louis, 40, 45, 86, 103, 105-16, 119, 136, 234, 236, 245
Armstrong, Lucille, 103
Armstrong, Mary Ann, 103, 107
Armstrong Park, 43, 55
Armstrong, Willie, 103
Arnaud, Elvina Armstrong, 130
Arnaud, Wellington, 243
Astoria Restaurant, 203
Aubert, Wilfred, 151
August, Frank, 247
Augustine, Israel, 173, 175, 249, 251
Autocrat Club, 203, 205-7, 235

Baby Dolls, 38
Bagneris, Jeanne, 127
Baker, Isiah, 246
Baldwin, James, 239, 240
Bambara, 46-48, 54
bamboula, 43, 49-50, 54
Banks, Levine, 245
Barbee, Benjamin, 238
Barbee, William, 194
Barney, Clarence, 247

Bartholomew, Dave, 248
Batiste, Becate, 221
Batiste, John, 246
Baumann's Drugstore, 99
Bayou St. John, 205
Beaulieu, P. W., 98
Beauregard Square, 55
Bedou, Arthur P., 98
Beecher Memorial Congregational Church, 136-37
Benjamin, Robert, 246
Bennett, Elizabeth, 144
Berry, Chuck, 236
Berteaux, Iona, 179
Bertoneau, Arnold, 31
Bertrand, Armand, 235
Bethlehem Temple, 203, 214
Bethune, Mary McLeod, 135
Big Chief, 218, 219
Bishop Perry Middle School, 66, 76, 78
Black and Tan Lounge, 36
Black Benny, 222
Black Codes, 29, 30, 67
Black Eagles, 217
Black Pirates, 203
Black Storyville, 103, 105-6, 110
Blanc, Antoine, 24
Blocker, Murrie, 248
Blue Birds Sewing Circle, 207
Blunt, Alphonse, 243
Bocage, Eddie, 235
Bocage, O. T., 95
Bolden, Buddy, 82, 106-7
Bon Temps, 205-7
Borders, Florence, 198
Boulton, Laura, 45, 50
Bowman, Sylvia, 243
Boyer and Taylor Company (undertaker), 101
Braden, Warren, 164
Bradford, Constance, 235
Bras Coupé, 54
Bridges, Ruby, 177, 180, 185, 234
Briley, Joseph, 239
Brown, Charlie, 230
Brown, Debria, 238
Brown, James, 236
Brown, Laura, 94
Brown, Mayme Osby, 202
Brown, Roy, 165-66
Brown, Vincent, 247
Bunch Club, 132, 205, 213-15
Burgess, Reuben, 247-48
Burns, Leonard, 183, 236, 243
Bush, Earl Benjamin, 179-80
Bush v. Board of Education, 172
Butler, Gordon, 249
Butler, Michael, 244
Bynum, Horace, 246, 249
Byrd, Daniel, 147, 154, 179, 236

Cable, George Washington, 50-52
Cailloux, André, 31
Cailloux, Felicie, 69
Caledonia, 39
Capetowners Club, 203
Carmichael, Stokely, 246
Carnation Social and Pleasure Club, 207
Carnegie, Dale, 135, 141
Carnival, 201-3, 205-6, 217
Carter, Cecil, 189, 234, 240
Carter, Dennis J. S., 99
Carter, Robert L., 173
Carver, George Washington, 135

Castellanos, Henry C., 20
Castille, Paul Vincent, 163
Castle, Collie, 243
Castle, Doris, 194, 196, 199, 235-36, 241
Castle, Oretha, 189, 234, 240
Castle, Virgie, 199
Cates, Sidney, 243, 248
Catholic Indigent Orphan Institute, 66, 68-69, 75-76
Celestin, Oscar "Papa," 163, 165
Celli, Romeo, 73
Central City, 80-83, 143, 145, 149, 205, 207, 219
Central Congregational Church, 142
Champagne, Shirley, 167
Chaney, James, 197
Chapital, A. J., 137
Chapital, Arthur, 239, 242-43
Charbonnet, Louis, 73, 88
Charity Hospital, 243
Charles, Josephine, 24
Charles, Millie, 245
Chase, Dooky, 207
Chase, Leah, 40, 121
Chatman, James, 164
Cherokee Hunters, 217
Cheyenne Hunters, 217
Chicago Hotel, 95
Choctaws, 47
Christenberry, Herbert, 241-42
Christovich, Mary Louise, 19-20, 24
Church of God in Christ, 137
Circle Food Store, 205
Civil Rights, 197-99
Civil Rights Act of 1964, 168, 241-43
Civil Rights Movement, 169, 173, 203, 205
Claiborne Candy Company, 36
Claiborne YWCA, 142
Clark, Dorothy Gardner, 132, 133
Clark, Edwin, 238
Coalition of Federated Organizations, 197
Cobb, Raymond, 249
Cobette, A. J., 88
Cohen, Walter L., 73, 80, 137
Coles, Robert, 185
Collins, Lionel, 173
Collins, Lucretia, 192, 195
Collins, Robert, 173, 175, 187, 189, 199, 236, 240
Collins, Virginia, 241
Collins, Walter, 251
"Colored Soldier Boys of Uncle Sam, The", 98
Colored Waif's Home Band, 110
Comiskey, James, 236
Comité des Citoyens (Citizens' Committee), 70, 170-72
Community Responsibility Program, 145-46
Congo Square, 31-32, 34, 40, 43, 45-52, 54-55, 217, 221, 229
Congo Square Writer's Workshop, 55
Congregation Hall, 36
Congress of Industrial Organizations (C.I.O.), 146-47, 150, 153
Congress of Racial Equality (CORE), 173, 187-91, 194, 196-99, 205, 234-35, 240-42, 244

Connor, Eugene "Bull," 192
Coordinating Council, 237, 239-40
Copelin, Sherman, 243
Corrigan, Crash, 167
Cottles, Vernon, 244
Coustaut's String Band, 35
Couvent, (Gabriel) Bernard, 63-64, 67
Couvent, Marie C., 63-64, 66-71, 75-76
Cox, Benjamin Elton, 199
Craig, Joseph A., 33
Cray, David, 76
Creole Wild West, 218-19, 221
Crescent Hairdressing College, 93
Crisis magazine, 80, 98
Crockere, Basil, 35, 69-70
Crocker, Lawrence, 247
Crusader newspaper, 35, 171-72
Cuba, 67
Cullen, Countee, 131
Customs House, 80, 83

Daily Spokesman, 98
Damballah, 48
Dana Hubbard v. Fred Tannehill, 175
Daniel, Irvin S., 240-41
Darensbourg, Judy, 227
Dashiki Theater, 250
D'aspenza, Ruth, 189, 234
Davidson, N. R., 248, 250
Davis, A. L., 149, 151, 154, 173, 234, 236, 239, 240-41, 249
Davis, A. L. (Park), 205
Davis, Jimmie, 180, 233
Davis, Peter, 110
Davis Piano Company, 98
Day of Rededication to the Advancement of Human Dignity, 248
Dejan's Orchestra, 132
Dejoie, C. C., 162
Dejoie, Constant C., Sr., 131
Dejoie, Henry, 248-49
Dejoie's Cut-Rate Pharmacy, 83
Dejoie's Hub Shoe Store, 83
Delgado Community College, 243
Delille, Henriette, 22, 24
Denison, Yvonne Amelie, 207
Dennis, David, 194, 197, 199, 235-36, 245
Dent, Albert, 234, 243, 245, 247, 249
Dent, Tom, 55, 248
Desdunes, Rodolphe Lucien, 31, 35, 69, 71, 78, 80, 171
Diamond Stars Mardi Gras Indian tribe, 230
Diaz, Lizadie, 73
Dillard University, 142, 233-34, 238-39, 241, 245, 248-49
Dixie Cups, 243
Dixie Park, 88
Dolliole, Jean-Louis, 66
Domino, Fats, 164
Dooky Chase's Restaurant, 121, 215, 244
Dorsey, Lee, 235
Dorsey, Willie, 147, 149
Doubleday Bookstore, 241
Douglas, Nils, 173, 189, 240, 249
Douglass, Frederick, 129
Draper, David, 217
Dr. Daddy-O, 165

Drexel, Katherine, 71
Dryades Street, 82-83, 93
Du Bois, W. E. B., 135, 141, 146, 248
Dubuclet, C., 94
Duhart, Adolphe, 69
Dunbars' Social and Pleasure Club, 207
Duncan, Mitchell J., 248
Dunham, Katherine, 45, 50
Dunn, Alberta V., 131
Dupont, Elaine, 167
Dutton, Dannon, 78
Duvernay, Raymond, 246

Eagle Saloon, 107
Eaglin, Snooks, 235
Egana, Annabel Nash, 127, 130
Eighth Ward Hunters, 222, 224, 232
Elie, Lolis, 173, 187, 189, 199, 236, 240
Elloie, Pearlie Hardin, 236, 238-39
Emancipation Petitions, 67
Emancipation Proclamation, 31-32, 95, 109, 239
Era (newspaper), 32
Ernie the Whip, 166
Essence Festival, 227
Esteves, Arthur, 70
Etienne, Gail, 177, 180, 184-85, 234
Eureka Brass Band, 238
Excelsior Brass Band and Orchestra, 98

Family Service Society, 142
Fanti, 47
Farmer, James Leonard, Jr., 187, 190, 196, 198-99
Farrell, Margot C., 179
Fate Marable's Cotton Pickers, 214
Fauset, Jessie, 131
Felton, Delores, 167
Ferbos, Stanley, 247
Ferdinand, Kenneth, 250
Ferrouilet, John, 94
First Avenue Baptist Church, 192
First District Emancipation Club, 33
Fisk Colored School, 106, 136
Fitzmorris, Jimmy, 245, 251
Five Satins, 235
Flag Boy, 218, 221
Flag of Black Liberation, 250
Fletcher, Lawrence, 219
Flint-Goodridge Hospital, 142, 234
Flint Medical College, 86
Floyd, George, 83
Floyd, Raymond, 234, 235
Fort Saint Ferdinand, 23, 47-48
Foster, June, 167
Fourth Colored United States Cavalry, 32
Francis, Norman C., 243, 247, 249
Francis, Willie, 245
Francs Amis, 96
Franklin, Dorsey, 95
Frantz Elementary School, 235
Frederick, Rivers, 99
Frederick, Rivers, II, 242-43
Fredericks, Rivers, 147, 162
Freedom Rides, 187, 190,-92, 194-99, 235-36
Free Southern Theater, 189, 246-48

Friedrichs, David W., 147
Friends of Hope Benevolent Hall, 36
Friends of New Orleans Cemeteries, 64, 76, 78
Frontiers, Inc., 157
Funky Butt, 106, 107

Gallinghouse, A. P., 244
Gardner, Dorothy, 127, 131, 134
Garrison, James "Jim," 241
Garroway, Dave, 103
Garth, Mercedes Mayfield, 132
Garvey, Marcus, 146
Gaudin, Juliette, 24
Geddes, Clem, 101
Geddes Funeral Home, 93
Geddes, George, 101
Geddes-Richards Funeral Home, 167
Giarusso, Joseph, 243
Gilliam, Ted, 250
Glee Club of the Dryades Street YMCA, 86
Globe Hall, 36, 210
Gold Diggers, 203
Golden Arrows, 217
Golden Eagles, 217
Golden Rod's Social and Pleasure Club, 207
Golden Stars, 217
Goldfinch, Sidney, 189, 234, 240
Goodman, Andrew, 197
Grambling University, 173, 236
Grand Army of the Republic, 96
Grand Emancipation Programme, 32
Gray, Luther, 55
Great Depression, 133
Greater Saint Stephen Baptist Church, 237
Green, Esther Barnum, 20, 36, 38, 42
Greensboro, North Carolina, 233
Gregoire, Emmanuel, 236
Gretna Cyclones, 202
Greyhound Corporation, 197
Griffin, Sister Bessie, 166
Guidry, Robert, 224
Guillory, Barbara M., 236, 238-39
Guillot, B. J., 238
Guy, Harrison, 244

Haiti, 63-64, 67, 69
Haley, Oretha Castle, 198-99
Haley, Richard, 198-99, 242
Hall, Gwendolyn Midlo, 46
Hall, Jim, 247
Hardin, Joseph A., 137
Harlem Renaissance, 131
Harper, William, 189, 234
Harpo, Slim, 235
Harrell, William M., 189, 234
Harris, Henry, 234
Harrison, Donald, 219
Harris, Wynonie, 166
Hawkettes, 165
Haydel, C. C., 172
Haynes, Owens, 210
Hearn, Lafcadio, 52
Hebert, F. Edward, 183
Hebert, Zelma, 243
Helm, Jack, 246
Henry, Clarence "Chink," 234, 237, 241, 248
Henry, Clarence "Frogman," 235

Henry, Samuel, Jr., 244
Henry, Vance, 130
Herbert Leary and His Music Makers, 215
High Art Café and Restaurant, 95
Hill, Jessie, 233, 235
Hill, Veronica, 179
Hi Smile, 130
Hollander, Edward, 199
Holy Redeemer School, 36, 64, 66, 76
Houma Indians, 22, 47
Huddleston, George, 191
Hudson, Harold, 243
Hudson, Joseph, 243
Hughes, Langston, 131
Human Relations Committee, 236, 247, 249
Humbles, Julia, 240
Humphrey, Percy and Willie, 239
Hunter, Lucille Mouton, 127, 130
Hunters Field, 205
Hurricane Betsy, 134, 245
Hurricane Katrina, 76
hurricane of 1915, 71
Hutton, Lucille, 142
Hynes, Eddie, 165

"I Daresay," 144, 146, 152-53
Ida Club, 35
Illinois Club, 210
Imperial Dental Parlor, 101
Indianapolis Freeman, 86
Ink Spots, 164, 167
Iroquois Hunters, 217

Jackie Wilson Show, 245
Jackson, Fred, 243
Jackson, Mahalia, 241
Jackson, Vonelle, 242
Jackson, W. A., 94
Jack, Wellborn, 180
Jacques, Moilene, 164
Jane Alley, 103, 112
Janssens, Francis, 71
Jeanmard, J. M., 73
Jeanmarie, George, 98
Jefferson, Beatrice, 127
Jefferson, Herman, 245
Jeff, Morris F. X., Sr., 226, 236
Joe Dave's meat market, 20
Johnson, Al "Carnival Time," 235
Johnson, Benjamin, 173
Johnson, Bunk, 107
Johnson, Clayton, 249
Johnson, Ida, 154
Johnson, James Weldon, 135
Johnson, Lyndon Baines, 242-44, 249
Johnson, Victoria, 244
Johnson, Wellington, 247
Jolly Boys and Girls Club, 203
Jolly Boys Social and Pleasure Club, 243
Jones, Alvin B., 241
Jones, Clyde G., 141
Jones, Jimmy, 235
Jones, J. M., 98
Jones, Joseph, 110, 112
Jones, Manuela, 110
Jones Troop 99, 140
Jones, Valena C., 136
Jordan, Clarence, 248
Jordan, Jack, 244
Joseph A. Craig Elementary School, 20, 38, 133

Joseph Moret's String Band, 35
Joseph S. Clark High School, 236, 248
Joubert, L. J., 73
Journey of Reconciliation, 188, 190
Jupiter, Clarence, 245

K-Doe, Ernie, 164
Kein, Sybil, 248
Kennedy, John F., 194, 238
Kennedy-Johnson Voter's League, 234
Kennedy, Robert, 191-92, 194
Kennedy, Rose, 234
Kenner, Chris, 235
Kennon, Robert F., 162
King, Earl, 164, 166, 235
King, Martin Luther, Jr., 192, 194-95, 237, 248
King, Nathan Johnny, Jr., 206-7
Knight, Wiley, 210, 212
Kumbuka Drum and Dance Collective, 55

Labat, Victor, 214
Laborers' Union Hall, 206
Labranche's Drugstore, 99, 132
Ladies of Equal Justice, 96
Ladies of Mercy, 96
Ladies of Morality, 71
Ladies of Providence, 96
Ladies of Silence, 96
Lafon, Thomy, 31, 71
Lala, Pete, 107
Landrieu, Maurice "Moon," 246, 251
Landrum, Louis, 234, 241
Lanusse, Armand, 69, 201
Lasalle, Lily Anne, 141
Latrobe, Benjamin Henry, 22, 24, 43, 45, 49-51, 108
Laveau, Marie, 48
Lawless, Alfred, 96, 136
Lawless, Dorothy, 207
League of Good Government, 242, 244
Lee, "Robbe," 219
Lee, Thomas, 105
Leon, Allen, 208
Les Cenelles, 35, 69
Les Jeunes Amis Hall, 206
Lester, John, 112
Les Toujour Amis, 206
Levere, George W., 34
Lewis, Clarence, 243
Lewis, George, 249
Lewis, John, 190
Lewis, Smiley, 235
Lewis, Theron, 243-44
Lincoln, Abraham, 31, 33-34
Lincoln Beach, 159, 161-68, 234, 236, 243
Lincoln Park, 88
Little Ruby Saloon, 95
Lombard, Rudy, 187-89, 198-99, 234-36, 240
London Avenue, 175
London, Earl, 248
Long, Alecia, 106
Longe, George, 130, 213
Long, Russell, 183
Longshoremen Protective Union, 96
Lords and Ladies' Club, 207
Louisiana Commission on Race Relations, 245

Louisiana High School Athletic Association (LHSAA), 245, 247
Louisiana Orchestra, 98
Louisiana Purchase, 22
Louisiana State Beauty and Barber College, 206
Louisiana State Museum, 229
Louisiana State University, 238
Louisiana State University in New Orleans (LSUNO), 237
Louisiana State University Medical Center, 240
Louisiana Weekly, 131, 133, 138-39, 144-45, 147-48, 151, 154, 156, 162, 164, 202, 205, 208, 210, 248
Loyola University, 239
Luke, Leontine, 240
L'Union, 31

madras, 45
Maenhaut, Constantine, 67, 71
Magnolia Bridge, 223
Mahogany Hall, 107
Malarcher, Marguerite, 141
Malcolm X, 250
Mandinkas, 47
Manetta, Manuel, 86
March on Washington, 241
Mardi Gras, 201-3, 205-9, 217, 221
Mardi Gras Blackout, 183, 203, 235-36
Mardi Gras Indians, 38, 107, 203, 205, 217-19, 221-27, 229-30, 232, 244
Marigny, Faubourg, 22, 64, 66-68, 75
Marigny, Henri, 230
Marigolds, 203
Marshall, Thurgood, 173, 233
Martinet, Louis A., 70, 169-72
Martinet Society, 169, 172-73, 235, 240
Martin, Joseph, 137
Mary, Aristide, 31, 40, 71
Masson, Ann, 24
Mathieu, Agnes, 19
Mathieu, Rick, 42
Maurice, Margaret, 98
Mayfield, Mercedes, 129
McCain, James, 188, 234
McCarty School, 131
McCrory Store, 234, 240
McDonald, Vivian Janet, 242
McDonogh #19 Elementary School, 177, 181, 184
McDonogh #35 High and Normal School, 121-22, 127, 129-34, 213
McDonogh Day, 179, 183, 246
McKay, D. W., 88
McKeithen, John, 245
McKelpin, Joseph, 141
McKelpin v. Board of Education, 172
McKenna, George, Sr., 137
McKinley High School, Baton Rouge, 127
McKinley, Larry, 166
McKissick, Floyd, 187, 199
McNamara, Bernadette, 76
Medley, Marilyn, 75
Mension, Danny, 249
Meunier, Gotton, 19
Miller, Howard, 218-19

Million Dollar Baby Dolls, 107, 203
Mississippi Freedom Summer, 197
Mitchell, Bobby, 235
Mitchell, Henry, 187, 199, 234
Monette, Lavergne, 249
Monogram Hunters, 224
Montana, Alfred, 221-24, 232
Montana, Allison "Tootie," 22-26, 229-30, 232
Montana, Darryl, 221-22, 226-27, 229, 232
Montana, Edward, 222, 230
Montana, Gina, 229
Montana, Joyce, 229
Montana, Sabrina, 227
Montegut, Joseph, 98
Moore, Kenneth, 248
Morial, Ernest N., 173, 175, 237, 239, 244, 247-49
Morial, Sybil Haydel, 241-42, 244
Morrison, deLesseps S. "Chep," 157, 163, 179, 181, 183, 189, 236, 242
Morris, William, 83
Morton, Jelly Roll, 82
Moses, Gilbert, 247
Moss, Arnold, 101
Mount Zion Baptist Church, 106
Moving Finger, The, 141
Mullen, Frank, 246
Municipal Auditorium, 181, 233, 235-37, 241-42, 245
Murray, Hugh, Jr., 189, 234
music, 34

Narcisse, Raymond, 73
Nash, Diane, 191, 194
Nashville Coordinating Committee, 191
National Association for the Advancement of Colored People (NAACP), 80, 83, 98, 135, 151, 154-55, 172, 179-81, 235, 239, 243, 246
National Association for the Advancement of Colored People (NAACP) Youth Council, 189
National Endowment for the Arts, 225
National Jazz Foundation, 112
National Youth Administration, 36
Negro History Week in New Orleans, 250
Nelson, Jack, 236
Nelson, Ricky, 166
Neville, Aaron, 235
Neville, Art, 234
New Marigny, 221
New Orleans Black Republican, 129
New Orleans Herald, 130-31
New Orleans Museum of Art, 226, 229
New Orleans Opera House Association, 249
New Orleans Police Department, 183, 246
New Orleans Public Library, 79
New Orleans Public Service, Inc. (NOPSI), 237
New Orleans Recreation Department (NORD), 233, 238-39, 241-42, 244, 247

New Orleans Saints football team, 247
New Orleans Tribune, 31
Newton, Marita, 81
New Zion Baptist Church, 196, 197
Nicholls, Francis T., 170
Nicholls State College, 173
Nichols, Thomas L., 27
Nickerson School of Music, 98
Nixon, Richard M., 249
Nixon, Sandra, 196, 241
Nketia, J. H. Kwabena, 45, 50-51
Noble, Jordan, 32, 82
North Claiborne Avenue, 205

Odd Fellows, 107
Ogden, Bob, 165
Ogden, Dave Robert, Sr., 165
Oldendorp, Christian, 48
Old Regular political organization, 157
Oleander Park, 88
Oliver, Joe, 107
One-Hundred-One Mardi Gras Indian tribe, 222
Onward Brass Band, 245, 250
Open Housing Act, 249
Original Illinois Club, 207, 210, 212
Original White Swans Social and Pleasure Club, 206
Orleans Ice Cream Works, 83
Orleans Parish Democratic Executive Committee, 248
Orleans Parish Levee Board, 161
Orleans Parish Medical Society, 245
Orleans Parish School Board, 172, 179-80
Orr, Walter, 235
Ortique, Revius O., 173, 175, 240
Ory, Kid, 82
Owens, Hazel, 127, 134
Owens, Jesse, 135
Owens, John, 247

Paddio, Willard, 132
Palmer, William, 247
Parks, Rosa, 95
Patterson, John, 191
Penn, Herman, 246
People's Defense League, 143, 147-51, 153-54, 156-57, 162
People's Industrial Life Insurance Company, 36
Perez, Leander, 181, 238
Perez, Manuel, 86
Perez, Richard, 246
Perkins, Joe, 190
Perry, Harold, 245
Perry, Richard L., 156, 162
Phillips, Emma, 177
Picard, Earl, 143
Pichon, Walter "Fats," 166, 247
Picou, Alphonse, 235
Pierre, Sidney, 232
Pinchback, P. B. S., 202
Piron, A. J., 132
Place Congo, 46
Plantation Revelers, 207
Plessy, Homer, 31, 36, 40
Plessy v. Ferguson, 121, 169, 171-72, 177
Pontchartrain Beach, 242
Pontchartrain Park, 163, 233

Porter's Tailoring Company, 83
Pouilly, Jacques de, 24
Pounds, Ronnie, 249
Powell, Adam Clayton, 154
Prejean, Carol, 247
Presley, Elvis, 166
Prevost, Ann Marie, 238
Prevost, Eva, 215
Prevost, Maurice and Eva, 213
Prevost, Tessie, 177, 180, 184, 234
Price, Lloyd, 236
Professor Longhair, 164, 233
Pythian Temple, 83, 86-87, 96, 98, 203, 208

Quorum Coffee House, 242

Ramsey, Merle, 145
Ramsey, Zachary Taylor, 146-48
Randolph, Lionel, 246
raquette, 47, 54
Rarick, John, 242
Raymond, Roma J., 98
Rebennack, Mac (Dr. John), 164-65
Rebirth Brass Band, 40
Redmond, James F., 180
Reynolds, Isaac, 187, 196, 198-99
Rhinestones, 203, 212
Ricard, F. P., 83, 98
Ricau, Jackson, 238
Richardson, Ernestine, 129, 132
Richardson, Ingrid, 237, 244
Richardson, James, 249
Robeson, Paul, 131
Robichaux Orchestra and Brass Band, 98
Robinson, Felton, 151
Robinson, Katie, 83
Robinson, Marvin, 188
Rochon, Rosette, 66
Roosevelt, Eleanor, 135
Ross, J. S., 95
Roudanez, Louis Charles, 31
Rouselle, William, 247, 250
Roussel, Louis J., 162-63
Rousseve, Charles Barthelemy, 27, 130
Roux, Vincent, 235
Rouzan, Wanda, 251
Royal Castle hamburger shop, 242
Royal Dukes of Rhythm, 235-36
Roy, Carlton, 234
Rummel, Joseph, 238

Saenger Theater, 240
Saint Augustine Catholic Church, 20, 23-24, 27, 29, 38
Saint Augustine High School, 183, 241, 244-47
Saint Bernard Circle, 95
Saint Gerard Majella Alternative School, 66, 76
Saint James AME Choir, 86
Saint James AME Church, 189
Saint Joseph's Academy Catholic High School, 240
Saint Louis Cathedral, 24, 43, 49, 67-68
Saint Louis Cemetery #2, 64, 68-69, 76, 78
Saint Louis School of Holy Redeemer Parish, 74
Saint Malo, Jean, 52-53
Saint Mary, Faubourg, 22
Saint Mary's Academy, 38

Saint Monica Hall, 203
Saint Peter Claver, 206
Saint Pierre, Michel, 35
Sanders, Elizabeth, 151
San Jacinto Club, 233
Sarah Goodridge (school), 86
Satyagraha, 187
scarification, 48
Schiro, Victor, 236-37, 242, 245, 247, 250
Schultz, Christian, 45, 48
Schwerner, Michael, 197
Scott, John, 229, 244
Second Mount Olive Baptist Church, 137
Select Restaurant, 94
Self, Charles R., 238
Semmes, Thomas J., 171
Senegal, 47
Senegambia, 46
separate-but-equal laws, 171
Separate Car Act, 170-71
Seventh Ward Civic League and Seventh Ward Educational League, 135-37
Seventh Ward Educational League, 96
Shakespeare Park, 143-45, 147-48, 151, 153, 241
Sidney Desvignes's Southern Syncopators, 214
Simmons, Chester, 246
Simmons, Nathaniel, 245
Simms, T. A., 95
Simon, Joe, 224
Sisters of the Holy Family, 24
Skeleton Men, 203
slavery, 52
Smith, Alfred O., 95
Smith, David L., 248
Smith, Henry W., 98
Smith, Jerome, 189, 195-96, 205, 234-36, 240
Smith, Wiltzer, and Peebles, 241
Société des Jeunes Amis, 71, 96
Sonny Boy, 230
Soule, George, 247
Southern Christian Leadership Conference (SCLC), 240
Southern Organization for Unified Leadership (SOUL), 249
Southern University in New Orleans (SUNO), 86, 196, 239, 241, 243-44, 250-51
Southern University of Louisiana, 233
Southwestern Christian Advocate, 98
Spears, Mack, 249-50
Spellman, Benny, 233, 235
Spotts, M. J., 93
Spriggins, E. Belfield, 202, 213, 215
Spy Boy, 218, 221
Staes, Eugene, 235
Steinbeck, John, 181, 183
Stella Jones' Gallery, 227
Stevens, George, 132
Stevens, Myrtle Watts, 131-32
Stewart, Elvera, 141
Story, William, 208
Straight College, 136
Straight University Law School, 169
Studs Social and Pleasure Club, 189
Suarez, Matt, 187, 199

Sutton, Carolyn, 250
Sylvanie Williams Community Center, 146
Sylvester, Harold, 245, 247, 250

Tambourine and Fan, 205
Tammany's Social and Pleasure Club, 107
Tate, Leona, 177, 180, 184, 234
Taylor, Dorothy, 244
Taylor, Joyce, 189, 234
Taylor, O. C. W., 206
Taylor, Roosevelt, 236
Teamer, Ed, 234
The Negro in Medicine in Louisiana, 172
Third Ward, 110
Thomas, Joel, 244
Thompson, Catherine, 236
Thompson, Daniel, 237, 239, 243
Thompson, Jean, 240
Thompson, Jean Catherine, 194
Thompson, Shirley, 236
Tillman, "Brother," 219
Tillman, Raymond, 154
Tinson, Selina Butler, 121-22, 130, 132-34, 140
Tio and Doublet Orchestra, 35
Tissoneau, Rose, 19
Toca, Albert, 95
Toledano, Roulhac B., 19-20, 24
Tommy Ridgely Band, 235
Toomer, Jean, 131
Total Community Action, 245
Touchard, Joseph, 94
Tremé, Claude, 20
Treme, Faubourg, 17, 19-20, 22-23, 27, 30-31, 33-36, 38-40, 48, 67, 121
Trevigne, Paul, 171
Trudeau, A. M., 237
Tubman, Harriet, 95
Tulane Music Publishing Co., 98
Tulane University, 79, 234, 236, 238-40, 247, 250
Tureaud, A. P., 137, 169, 17-73, 175, 179, 235, 237, 245
Tureaud, A. P. (Avenue), 175
Twine the Taylor, 95

Underground Railroad, 31
United Clubs, Inc., 203, 234-36, 238
United Negro College Fund, 235, 249
United Office and Professional Workers, 147
United Sons of Honor Hall, 106
United States Supreme Court, 169, 171-72, 177, 179-80, 235, 240-41
Unity Industrial Insurance Company, 130
University of New Orleans, 79
Urban League, 80, 235, 247

Vagabonds Ball, 207
Valder, Robert, 240
Valena C. Jones Elementary School, 134-37, 139-42, 234
Valena C. Jones Normal School, 141
Vance, J. Madison, 86
Vautier, Father, 73

Verret, Shirley, 238
Victor Dubois' Great Southern Hotel and Restaurant, 83
Victor Talking Machine Company, 131
Vietnam War, 245-49, 251
Vignes-Wilson, Cora, 93
Vikings, 206
Violation of a Constitutional Right, 36
Vogue Sewing Club, 202
Voodoo, 45, 48
Voter Crusader Corps, 240
Voter Education and Registration Project, 240, 243
Voting Rights Act, 198, 244-45

Wagner, Ernest, 234
Wallace, George, 249
Walls, Robert, 248
Walter L. Cohen High School, 245
War on Poverty, 243
Warren, Freddie, 173
Washington, Booker T., 79, 146
Washington, James, 203
Washington, Louis, 237
Watson, Jason, 78
Watts, Ina Claire, 207
Watts, Myrtle, 129
Weber, Adam, 246
Welch, Virginia Cox, 241
Werlein, Phillip, 167
White Citizen's Council, 181, 237, 242
White Eagles, 217
White, Oliver, 143
White, Walter, 131
Wildcats Mardi Gras Indian tribe, 222
Wild Magnolias, 217
Wild Man, 218, 221
Wild Tchoupitoulas, 217
William Frantz Elementary School, 177, 181
Williams and Stevens Stock Company, 86, 95
Williams, Eric, 246
Williams, Ethel Mae, 251
Williams, Fannie C., 135-37, 139-42, 234
Williams, John, 219
Williams, Joseph "Sunny," 250
Willie Tee and the Souls, 250
Wilson, Jacquelyn, 243
Wilson, Jarrold, 238
Wilson, Woodrow, 95
Winfrey, Violet, 203
Wisdom, John Minor, 241
WMRY radio, 162
Woods, Allen T., 79-83, 86, 88, 96, 98, 101
Woods, Dennis, 80
Woods, Eliza, 94
Woods Famous Creole Kitchen, 130
Woods, Florence Johnson, 80
Woodson, Carter G., 135
Woolworth's Five & Dime, 132, 189
World War II, 147, 150, 154
Wright, Edna Marie, 154
Wright, Ernest John, 143, 144-54, 156-58, 162, 237
Wright, James, 209
Wright, J. Skelly, 180, 238

Wright, Walter, 163

Xavier High School, 127
Xavier University of Louisiana, 132, 144-45, 183, 187-88, 198-99, 203, 214, 234, 237, 239, 244, 249-50
Xavier University Preparatory High School, 242, 245

Yellow Jackets, 217
Yellow Pocahontas, 217, 221-22, 224, 227, 229-30
Yorubans, 47
Young, Andrew, 136, 240
Young, Andrew, Sr., 234
Young, Ethel, 179
Young Men Illinois, 203
Young Men's Christian Association, 83
Young Men's Illinois Club, 207, 210
Young Men's Twenty Club, 203, 206, 244
Young Tuxedo Brass Band, 239
Young, Walter, 234
Young Women's Christian Association, 206

Zippert, John, 247
Zulu Social Aid & Pleasure Club, 107, 203, 205, 208-9, 250
Zwerg, James, 194